THE REVOLUTION ON THE UPPER
OHIO, 1775-1777

DRAPER SERIES, VOLUME II

THE REVOLUTION

ON THE

Upper Ohio, 1775-1777

Compiled from the Draper Manuscripts in the
Library of the Wisconsin Historical Society
and published at the charge of the Wisconsin
Society of the Sons of the American Revolution

EDITED BY

REUBEN GOLD THWAITES, LL. D.
Secretary of the Society

AND

LOUISE PHELPS KELLOGG, PH. D.
Editorial Assistant on the Society's Staff

JANAWAY PUBLISHING, INC.
Santa Maria, California

Notice

In many older books, foxing (or discoloration) occurs and, in some instances, print lightens with wear and age. Reprinted books, such as this, often duplicate these flaws, notwithstanding efforts to reduce or eliminate them. The pages of this reprint have been digitally enhanced and, where possible, the flaws eliminated in order to provide clarity of content and a pleasant reading experience.

Copyright © 1908
State Historical Society of Wisconsin

Originally published
Madison, Wisconsin:
1908

Reprinted by:

Janaway Publishing, Inc.
732 Kelsey Ct.
Santa Maria, California 93454
(805) 925-1038
www.janawaygenealogy.com

2013

ISBN: 978-1-59641-302-3

Made in the United States of America

CONTENTS

	Page
INTRODUCTION. *The Editors*	ix
EXPLANATION	xx

Documents

	Page
Movement to Kentucky; Frontier Forts	1
Letter for Cornstalk	7
Orders for the Militia	8
Virginia hears of Lexington and Concord	10
Garrison at Point Pleasant	12
Affairs at Fort Pitt	17
Virginia arms	21
Treaty at Pittsburgh, 1775	25
British Report of Treaty	127
Connolly's Plot	136
The Frontiers, early in 1776	143
A Captain's Commission	145
Information regarding Detroit	147
Indians visit Niagara	151
Alarm in Kentucky	153
Protection for the Frontier	155
Garrison for Point Pleasant; Indian Affairs	158
Conference at Fort Pitt	159
Report from Niagara; neutrality to be maintained	171
Frontiers of Virginia	172
News from Fort Randolph	185
Indian depredations	188, 205, 209, 249
Threatened hostilities	190, 218, 245

CONTENTS

	Page
Forts on the Ohio	195
Reinforcements ordered	196
Disposition of the Indian Tribes	199
Fort Randolph re-inforced	204, 209, 239
News from Williamsburgh	214
Treaty of 1776	216
Situation at Grave Creek	224
Supplies from New Orleans	226
Militia arrangements	229
Pluggy's Town Expedition ordered	236
Situation at Wheeling	242
Allies to be protected	244
Pluggy's Town Expedition abandoned	247
Return of Military Stores at Fort Pitt	258
INDEX	259

ILLUSTRATIONS

Page

Map from Crèvecœur's *Lettres d'un Cultivateur Americain* (Paris, 1787), consisting of sketch-maps of the Muskingum, Scioto, and Big Beaver rivers	*Frontispiece*
Portrait of George Morgan (silhouette)	30
Portrait of Peyton Randolph	66
Portrait of Lewis Morris	76
Portrait of James Wilson	90
Portrait of Gov. Henry Hamilton	128
Portrait of Governor Blacksnake, Seneca chief	160
Portrait of Gyantwahchia (or John Abeel, John the Cornplanter), Shawnee chief	162
Portrait of Red Jacket, Seneca chief	164
Portrait of Gov. Patrick Henry	232

INTRODUCTION

In May, 1905, the Society published from the Draper Manuscript Collection in its possession, a *Documentary History of Dunmore's War, 1774*. While the material was selected, annotated, and put through the press by the present Editors, the bill for printing was generously met by the Wisconsin Society of the Sons of the American Revolution. The latter organization kindly offered to pay for the printing of a second Draper volume, edited at the cost of the Society, to be in due course succeeded, the hope was expressed, by a third and possibly others. This proposition being accepted it was determined to follow *Dunmore's War* with two volumes, both bearing upon the conduct of the Revolutionary War on the Upper Ohio River. The present is the first of these.

We were led to this selection from the Wisconsin Historical Society's abundant store of manuscript sources, by considerations of logical sequence. The events herein chronicled immediately succeeded and in considerable degree were the direct outgrowth of Dunmore's War. In a sense the district involved was much the same as that affected by his lordship's operations; the military leaders were in many cases those who had served in the expedition of 1774; the rank and file was composed of the like race of fearless, independent frontiersmen, who fretted at martial discipline and democratized the militia which had been organized for the defense of their homes against the aborigines.

The documents chosen for publication herein do not afford a continuous history of any one campaign or group of men. They do, however, shed light upon the principal incidents and the prominent characters of the long frontier stretching from the Greenbrier region in southwestern Virginia to the post at Kittanning on the Upper Allegheny. The time is the first two years of the Revolutionary struggle—March, 1775, to May, 1777, inclusive—and deals with the defense of the border while still in the hands of the militia of the Western counties. The coming to Fort Pitt, June 1, 1777, of an officer of Continental rank, sent by Congress to take command of the West, marked an epoch in the military history of the region. It is with the advent of General Hand that our initial volume closes. This earlier history of the Revolution in the trans-Alleghany region has been but little known or understood. Comparatively few documents concerning it have thus far been published; secondary accounts in general dismiss the subject with a hasty paragraph. It is hoped that the present publication of contemporary material will lead to a more considerate treatment of what we believe to be an interesting and significant period.

It will be remembered by readers of the preceding volume, that when Lord Dunmore left the frontier in the autumn of 1774, bearing with him the Shawnee hostages, he embodied a small garrison at Fort Dunmore, and another at Fort Blair near the mouth of the Kanawha. They were the only fortifications upon the frontier at the beginning of 1775. When the governor found himself involved in quarrels with the colonists, one of his last executive acts was to order the evacuation of these posts. The colonists thereupon quickly seized the first, which reverted to its earlier name of Pitt; Fort Blair was actually evacuated, and its buildings burned by lurking Indians during the summer of 1775.

The attitude of the Indians towards the colonial cause was of vital importance to the Western borderers. Lord Dunmore's treaty of the previous autumn had been but provisional. The Shawnee hostages were still in his hands; the Mingo prisoners were in confinement at Fort Pitt; his lordship had promised the Indians to come to Fort Pitt in the spring and arrange a permanent peace. Meanwhile his agent upon the frontier, Dr. John Connolly, was a professed Loyalist. Connolly dismissed the imprisoned Mingo to their homes, with messages urging their people to rely upon the English king, their father, and to come to Fort Pitt to treat with him as the representative of the governor. In his *Narrative,* Connolly asserts that it was his "first work to convene the Indians to a treaty, restore the prisoners, and endeavour to incline them to espouse the royal cause."[1]

Meanwhile the people of West Augusta district had formed a committee of safety. This met at Pittsburgh early in May, and drafted a petition to Con-

---

[1] *Pennsylvania Magazine of History and Biography,* xii, p. 314.

gress setting forth their fear of a rupture with the
Indians on account of Lord Dunmore's conduct.[2] The
matter was referred to the delegates from Virginia
and Pennsylvania, the former of whom took cogniz-
ance thereof in their state assembly, which appointed
commissioners to meet the tribesmen and endeavor
to complete the peace in favor of the colonies. Later,
Congress appointed a like commission, and the two
met jointly at Pittsburgh in September.

Rumors of the Revolutionary conflict had by early
summer reached the Indian towns, resulting in much
confusion and misunderstanding among the aborigines.
Upon one occasion Lord Dunmore had employed the
Shawnee hostages with him as a personal guard
against colonial violence. They not unnaturally,
therefore, fancied themselves likewise hated by the
"Long Knives," and destined to fall victims to the
enmity of the latter. Similar suspicions were excited
in the Indian villages by Loyalist traders, and the
king's Indian agents were already gathering the
Northern tribes to resist the proposed American invasion of Canada.

Whether British or Americans were first to enroll
the tribesmen in their armies is even now a mooted
question. There were differences in the situation.
The slight aid that the Americans might receive from
Indian warriors enlisted in their interest, was far out-
weighed by the danger of retaliatory attacks to which
they thereby exposed their long and weak frontier.
Obviously, their safest policy was to secure native

---

[2] *Journals of Continental Congress* (new ed.), ii, p. 76

neutrality. To the British, on the other hand, the employment of barbarian allies had long been customary in colonial wars. Their incursions would create a needed diversion upon the frontier. As early as 1775, secret orders were received from the ministry, not only to enlist the sympathies of the tribesmen, but actually to enroll them in the royal armies.[3]

On the Western border, the Americans were prompt. Connolly's earlier treaty had had the effect somewhat to allay the fears of the warriors. The influence of a Frenchman in the British interest, sent from Detroit to the Indian villages with belts of wampum, was quickly counteracted by that of the Virginia envoy, Capt. James Wood. In September, 1775, there gathered at Pittsburgh the largest Indian delegation ever seen at this frontier fort—Ottawa and Wyandot from the neighborhood of Detroit; Mingo, Shawnee, and Delawares from the Ohio valley; Seneca from the Upper Allegheny. All united in a pledge of peace, friendship, and neutrality with the new American nation.

The importance of these early negotiations can hardly be overestimated. Not only was thereby set free from both the Pennsylvania and Virginia frontiers, a body of competent riflemen who hastened eastward to swell the Continental army; but the way was opened for Kentucky settlement, which involved the general occupation of Western territory, and ultimately the settlement of the Western boundary at the Treaty of Paris. Had the Pittsburgh treaty proved

---

[3] *Amer. Archives*, 4th series, iii, p. 6; New York Historical Society *Proceedings*, 1845, p. 167.

unsuccessful, the entire trans-Alleghany region must surely have been evacuated, George Rogers Clark's expeditions against Kaskaskia and Vincennes could hardly have occurred, and the West might easily have reverted to aboriginal occupation, and become a reserve for the British fur-trade.

Another secret danger averted by the vigilance of the colonial authorities, was that known as "Connolly's Plot." This was a scheme not entirely impracticable; with the aid of troops from Canada and the contingents already stationed at Niagara, Detroit, and the Illinois, it would not have been difficult to capture the militia garrison at Fort Pitt and force a passage into the heart of Virginia, before an invasion from that quarter was suspected. The arrest of Connolly and his agents, in the autumn of 1775, not only checked this enterprise, but led to the evacuation of the Illinois by British military forces, and their concentration at Detroit.

Aside from the machinations of both Indians and Royalists, the American commandant at Pittsburgh had reason to fear an invasion from the British fort at Niagara. Here the attitude of the Allegheny Seneca stood the colonists in good stead. While not averse to negotiating with their British father at Niagara, they announced to both contestants that the passage of an army from either side through their territory would be regarded as an act of war, to be stoutly opposed by the confederated Iroquois. This no doubt saved Fort Pitt from a siege similar to that sustained by Fort Stanwix in 1777.

The frontier has ever been a region of daring adventure and picturesque achievement. One exploit worthy of a place among the hero tales of American history, had its origin on the Upper Ohio during the early Revolutionary years. The chief need of the rebellious colonists was gunpowder. The English commandant at Niagara told the Indian tribesmen that the colonists would soon be beaten, since they had no powder and could no longer secure any from the mother country. Urged by this necessity, young Capt. George Gibson of the Virginia line, who had formerly been a trader on the lower reaches of the Ohio, conceived the project of securing a supply from the Spanish authorities at New Orleans, and transporting it up the Mississippi and Ohio rivers to Fort .Pitt. The Virginia authorities sanctioned the scheme. Choosing as his co-operator another noted frontier officer, Lieut. William Linn, the two set forth in a skiff, under the guise of Indian traders, and after a perilous journey arrived at their destination. At New Orleans, fresh difficulties awaited them. Governor Galvez, although favorable to the Americans, was disinclined to break with the British consul, who suspected the strangers, and inveighed against their presence. By a private undestanding, therefore, Gibson was thrown into prison, and at once all British suspicions were lulled.

Meanwhile Oliver Pollock, an American sympathizer residing at New Orleans, aided Linn to secure the coveted powder from the Spanish authorities. With forty-three men in several barges the latter left New Orleans September 22nd, with a cargo of ninety-eight barrels (over 9,000 pounds) of the precious explosive.

After severe hardships, and much suffering from illness and lack of provisions, the expedition reached Arkansas Post on the twenty-sixth of November, being received with marked kindness and courtesy by the Spanish commandant.[4] There the adventurers passed the winter hunting, and curing meat for the spring advance.

Gibson, now released from confinement, returned to Virginia by sea, carrying news of his successful undertaking. Orders were sent out by the Virginia authorities to hasten a detachment to the aid of Linn, but that officer was beforehand with his plans. By the third of March he had reached the mouth of the Ohio, where an American from Kaskaskia met him with provisions. The Spanish at St. Louis, not so friendly as their colleagues farther south, sent a band of Indians to intercept the party at the Falls of the Ohio (Louisville); but before the arrival of the savages the little company had already passed, and by the first of May safely landed the valuable cargo at Wheeling. For brilliancy of conception, cool daring, and successful accomplishment, this exploit deserves high rank among the minor achievements of that heroic time.

During the year 1776 the rigorous work of defense went forward. The line of forts was extended, the militia enrolled and drilled, and scouting parties mainrained both in the interior and along the Ohio boundary. In the autumn, while Congressional commis-

---

[4] Letter of Linn to Pollock, dated "Arkansaws, Novr. 30, 1776," Draper MSS., 60J277.

sioners were conducting negotiations at Pittsburgh, a general alarm was sounded. A number of men were killed and scalped along the border, families hastily moved in from outlying settlements, or "forted" in their neighborhood, and consternation prevailed. In Kentucky, a party carrying gunpowder to the forts was attacked, several killed, and the rest scattered, and all but three of the posts in that district were abandoned.

Most of these breaches of the treaty signed by the Indians in 1775 were the work of a small body of irreconcilables, known as Pluggy's Band. An expedition to invade their territory and burn the village was called out by Congress, and only abandoned through fear of thereby inciting a general Indian war. The winter of 1776–77 was an anxious one, and with the opening of the season of 1777 advices made it certain that the border would be harried by tribesmen under British influence. A call was thereupon made for a unified national defense, and Gen. Edward Hand, an experienced Continental officer, sent to Fort Pitt to take command. The period of partial peace was over, that of active warfare at hand.

The prompt ability with which the backwoodsmen managed their own affairs during the early years of the Revolution in the West, is worthy of notice. They performed a double duty with energy and loyalty. Organizing temporary governments with the militia company as a unit, and engaged in vigorously defending their own homes from savage neighbors, they nevertheless loyally supported the newly-constituted, but far-distant, state authorities both with men and equipment. The Eastern armies were to a considerable degree recruited from the frontiersmen; Western riflemen formed a valuable adjunct of the Continental forces. The first contingent from beyond New England to join Washington at Cambridge, was Daniel Morgan's battalion of sharpshooters from the upland border of Virginia.

But if loyalty was characteristic of the frontier, there also lurked treachery and treason. The best and the worst of the race gather upon the borders of civilization. As usual, there were those not averse to an Indian war for the sake of the spoils and the excitement. To keep faith with the Indians, on the part of the authorities, proved often exceedingly difficult. At the beginning of the Treaty of Pittsburgh the White Mingo, one of the chiefs most friendly to the American cause, narrowly escaped assassination. Indian envoys not infrequently suffered harsh treatment from fanatical and enfuriated militiamen. The horrors of Indian warfare were not entirely due to British incitement. In many cases, American frontiersmen but reaped the bitter harvest of their own rash deeds.

It should not be overlooked, however, that during these fateful years armed encounters with British and Indians were but incidents in the main purpose of the pioneer, who sought to occupy and subdue the wild land, to make it fruitful and blossom, and fill it with American homes. Kentucky was first permanently settled during the early years of the Revolution. The frontier of Virginia, while restrained within the limits of the territory south of the Ohio, was fast being strewn by farms and small communities. The importance of Pittsburgh and Wheeling as Western ports of entry was being recognized. The West was becoming homogeneous, self-conscious, nationalistic.

We are under obligations to the Rev. Joseph H. Bausman, of Rochester, Pa., for permission to copy the silhouette of Col. George Morgan, given in his *History of Beaver County, Pennsylvania.* Dr. William Cabell Rives of Washington, D. C., has enabled us to add greatly to the value of the volume by furnishing therefor a careful transcript of the official report of the treaty held at Pittsburgh in September and October, 1775, the original manuscript of which he inherited from his ancestor, Dr. Thomas Walker, one of the treaty commissioners. Valuable assistance in the reading of the proof of the entire volume has been rendered by Miss Annie A. Nunns of the Society's staff.

R. G. T.
L. P. K.

EXPLANATORY

Following the names of the writer and recipient of each document is given its press-mark in the Draper Manuscript Collection, by which the original can readily be identified if its further consultation is desired. The capital letter or letters refer to the series to which the document belongs; the volume number precedes the series letter, the folio or page number follows. E. g., the press-mark 4QQ7 means Vol. 4 of the Preston Papers, p. 7; the press-mark 45J101 is equivalent to Vol. 45 of the George Rogers Clark Papers, p. 101.

Immediately after the press-mark, the nature of the document is indicated by the descriptive initials customarily employed in describing manuscripts:

- A. L. — autograph letter unsigned (usually a draft in the author's handwriting).
- A. L. S. — autograph letter signed.
- L. S. — letter signed (text being in another's handwriting).
- D. S. — document signed.

THE REVOLUTION ON THE UPPER OHIO, 1775-1777

MOVEMENT TO KENTUCKY; FRONTIER FORTS

[Col. William Preston to Lord Dunmore.[1] 4QQ7—A. L., draft in Preston's handwriting.]

FINCASTLE, March 10th. 1775

My Lord—Herewith your Lordship will receive two Letters from Capt Russell[2] & Col^o Henderson's Proposals for Settling the Lands on the Ohio under the Company's Purchase; as one of the Letters relate chiefly to that Transaction I shall only observe that between five hundred and a Thousand Cherokees came in & that the whole Business was to be concluded this Week, as the Indians had no Objections to the Sale.[3]

---

[1] For biographical sketches of Lord Dunmore and Col. William Preston, see *Documentary History of Dunmore's War* (Madison, Wis., 1905), pp. 425-431.—ED.

[2] A sketch of William Russell will be found in *Ibid.*, p. 6, note 9.—ED.

[3] Richard Henderson, a prominent North Carolinian, conceived the plan of settling a large tract of land between the Kentucky and Cumberland rivers, to be purchased from the Cherokee Indians. For the carrying out of his scheme, he organized the Transylvania Company, purchased goods to the value of £10,000 sterling, and invited the Cherokee to hold a treaty at Sycamore Shoals, on the Watauga River. Early in March, 1775, the Indians began arriving, and about twelve hundred in all collected. After some opposition on the part of

That a great Number of Hands are employed in cutting a Waggon Road⁴ through Mockeson & Cumberland Gaps⁵ to the Kentucky which they expect to compleat before Planting time; & that at least 500 People are preparing to go out this Spring from Carolina beside great Numbers from Virg[a] to Settle there & that the Company intends to have a Treaty with

---

Dragging Canoe and his band, the purchase was consummated on March 17, the treaty being signed by Oconastota, Little Carpenter, and many prominent chiefs. The Transylvania Company settled Boonesborough, opened a land-office, and held one legislative session in Kentucky. But their claim was protested by North Carolina, Virginia, and the Kentucky settlers already on the ground. In 1778 the Virginia legislature granted the Transylvania Company 200,000 acres of land on Green River as indemnity for their expense in settling Kentucky.

Henderson went out with the first group of settlers, his journal on that trip being among the Draper MSS., 1CC. In 1779 he was commissioner from his state for extending westward the boundary line between it and Virginia, and visited Boonesborough in the spring of 1780. After serving in one session of the North Carolina Assembly, Henderson died at his home in Granville County, Jan. 30, 1785. The above account is abridged from a sketch by Dr. Lyman C. Draper in Draper MSS., 3B341-345, 5B83.—ED.

⁴ Before the conclusion of the treaty at Watauga, Henderson dispatched Daniel Boone with a company of experienced woodsmen to open a road to the Kentucky River, a distance of some two hundred miles. This was the origin of the well-known Wilderness Road, later traversed by thousands of emigrants into the new West. It was a wagon-road only as far as Powell's Valley; after that, until 1792, but a pack-horse trail. See Thomas Speed, "Wilderness Road," in Filson Club *Publications* (Louisville, 1886), No. 2. For the list of Boone's co-workers see R. G. Thwaites, *Daniel Boone* (New York, 1902), p. 117.—ED.

⁵ For reference to Moccasin Gap see *Dunmore's War*, p. 60, note 2. Cumberland Gap was first discovered by Dr. Thomas Walker, April 13, 1750, and named in honor of the English duke of that title. See J. Stoddard Johnston, "First Explorations of Kentucky," Filson Club *Publications*, No. 13.—ED.

the Wobaush Indians[8] & give them a considerable present to Permit the Settlement on those Lands. The Cherokees I hear says that Col⁰ Donelson promised them £500 for the Lands above the Kentucky which has not been paid & therefore they believe themselves at liberty to sell them a second Time;[7] & the Company it is said have furnished themselves with the Journals of our house of Burgesses & other Authentick Papers to make it Appear that Virginia looked upon those Lands to be the property of the Cherokees.

It is generally believed that had the Commissioners been there from this Government, & met the Indians before they Saw the Goods that the Sale might have been prevented; however that be the matter is now become Serious & demands the Attention of Govern-

---

[8] The Wabash Indians were not a distinct tribe; this was a collective term for the tribes residing on or near Wabash River, comprising the various divisions of the Miami, with the Mascoutin and the Kickapoo. They frequently raided the territory below Kentucky River. There seems to have been no attempt, however, on the part of the Transylvania proprietors to communicate with the Wabash Indians.—ED.

[7] For the Indian purchase here referred to, see *Dunmore's War*, p. 5, note 8, also p. 20. Col. John Donelson was born in Maryland about 1726; but he early removed to Pittsylvania County, Va., where he owned iron-mills and was a man of importance, representing his county in the Virginia house of burgesses. In 1771 he was employed to survey the Cherokee boundary line. Becoming interested in Western lands, he moved his family (1779-80) to central Tennessee. Descending Tennessee River with a fleet of flat-boats, he joined James Robertson at Nashville, and laid the foundation of that settlement. In 1781 he removed to Kentucky, returning to the Cumberland settlement in 1785. This latter year he visited Virginia, and was employed by Georgia to lay out a town at the Tennessee bend, being killed in the wilderness in the spring of 1786. His daughter Rachel became the wife of President Andrew Jackson.—ED.

ment otherwise it is too likely that valuable & extensive Territory will be forever lost to Virginia.

It has been said here that your Lordship intended to have those Lands Surveyed and Sold for the Crown at a reasonable Price. If, so, I can think of no step so effectual to settle that Country, as the Virginians at least, & perhaps many of the Carolinians would rather Purchase even at a higher Price from the Crown & be assured of a good Title than run any Risque under the Carolina Company. But as that Company has declared that they will not suffer any Land to be Surveyed below the Kentucky, I am apprehensive this step could not be taken unless the Business could be Supported by an armed force; & how that could be effected, either by the removal of the Garrison or a large part of it from point Pleasant[8] to the Falls or by raising a Company for that Purpose your Lordship can best determine.

Should y^r Lordship incline to dispose of the Land in this or any other Manner & order it to be laid off in Lotts, I will cheerfully wait for my Fees until money can be raised out of the Sales, & should any unforeseen accident prevent the Sales thereof I am willing to run the Risque without having any charge against your Lordship or the Govern^t. for that service.

Tho' there are yet Lands to Survey for Officers & Soldiers[9] I was affraid to Send out any Surveyors this

---

[8] For the garrison at Point Pleasant, left there at the close of the campaign of 1774, see *Ibid.*, pp. 309, 310.—ED.

[9] Preston here refers to the bounty lands granted by Gov. Robert Dinwiddie to the officers and soldiers from Virginia who took part in the French and Indian War (1754-63). After the king's proclamation of 1763, these lands could not

Spring untill I first acquainted your Lordship therewith & untill I would receive further Instructions, & the rather as I have been informed by Col° Christian[10] and others that your Lordship intended to send me Instructions how to proceed in this important Business.

The bearer Capt. Floyd who was out last year as a Surveyor[11] can inform your Lordship fully of the Probability of settling that Country as above proposed, & of the Numbers who have already removed, & are about to remove there this Spring in order to plant Corn let the Consequences be what it will.

Upon the whole my Lord it appears to me that the Country will very shortly be inhabited by Numbers of Industrious People who can not be prevented from going there; & it now remains with your Lordship to take such immediate Steps as you may Judge most expedient to encourage those People, to dispose of the Land for the Crown, & to secure to the purchasers proper Titles for the Same

By the last returns Capt Russell had from the Point he informed me that the Flour & Indian Corn there would not last longer than the middle of this Month, upon which Report I conveened several Officers who advised to have some Corn purchased on Clinch &

---

be surveyed on Ohio waters until after the treaty of Fort Stanwix (1768). Washington was much interested in these claims, and in 1770 visited the upper Ohio on their behalf, employing William Crawford as surveyor. The surveyors from Fincastle County who were down the Ohio in the spring of 1774, were laying out these patents. See *Ibid.*, pp. 1, 7, 22-25, 110-133.—ED.

[10] For a brief biography of Col. William Christian, see *Ibid.*, pp. 429, 430.—ED.

[11] For John Floyd, and a letter written while surveying in the West, see *Ibid.*, pp. 7-9; consult also pp. 42, 143, 144.—ED.

Send it on Horse back to Sandy Creek & from thence to the Fort by Water,[12] for an immediate Supply; but as this will be attended with considerable Expense to the Country I could not venture to advise Capt Russell to purchase more than 75 or 100 Bushells untill I would inform your Lordship thereof, which I was about to do by Express had I not prevailed on M^r. Floyd to go down, for which reason your Lordship will perhaps think proper to Order his Expenses to be repaid.

Capt Russell is of opinion that Col^o. Stephen would order Some Flour by the way of Fort Dunmore on an application from your Lordship.[13] It will be necessary either to send a Supply of Flour down, or have the Company discharged and the stores disposed of; which last would discourage the settling of that Country; but could part, even fifty men be Sent to the Falls it would certainly answer a good purpose on the present occasion.

Should your Lordship Honour me with any Instructions relative to ordering a Supply of Flour to the Point, or to the Surveying of the Lands on the Ohio I shall take the utmost Pleasure in Obeying them with the greatest Punctuality.

I am Your Lordships most Ob^t. & very hbl^e Sevt

W. P.

---

[12] Clinch River is an upper tributary of the Tennessee, on which a considerable settlement was beginning to spring up. It was contiguous to the headwaters of Sandy River, that affluent of the Ohio River which now forms the boundary line between Kentucky and West Virginia. Sandy was more easily navigated than the Great Kanawha, hence this suggestion with regard to provisioning the fort at Point Pleasant.—Ed.

[13] For Col. Adam Stephen and Fort Dunmore, see *Dunmore's War*, p. 191, note 35, and p. 35, note 60.—Ed.

LETTER FOR CORNSTALK

[Edmund Winston to Col. William Preston. 4QQ8—A. L. S.]

BEDFORD March 20th, 1775

Dear Sir—I received only last Week the Favour of your Letter of January the 9th. I happened to get early Information of Capt. Russell's coming in, & procured the Governor's Letter to the Corn Stalk,[14] which Col^o. Christian has before this I suppose delivered to Captn. Russell. The Letter from his Lordship was not so full as I could have wished, for I think it contained not more than twenty Words, however it was all could be got. I wrote to Captn. Russell in Jan'y last recommending my Affair to him, & now send another Letter of which I must trouble you to procure a Conveyance. After all perhaps it will be necessary that I should go out, and I shall be glad of a Line from you advising what it is proper to do on my Part. I am D^r. Sir

Your affectionate

E. WINSTON[15]

To Col^o. William Preston of Smithfield

---

[14] Russell's absence from Fort Blair, at the mouth of the Great Kanawha, was but temporary. Visitors to Kentucky called on him at his garrison in the early summer. See letter of June 12, *post*, and Draper MSS., 1CC 89. For Cornstalk, the Shawnee chief, see sketch in *Dunmore's War*, pp. 432, 433.—ED.

[15] Edmund Winston was a son of William, maternal uncle of Patrick Henry. Born in Hanover County about 1745, he inherited a considerable property, and for many years was judge in the Virginia courts. He married first Alice Winston, second Dorothea Dandridge (widow of Patrick Henry), and died upon his estate in Bedford in 1818. His father had investments in Western lands, to which, doubtless, Winston refers in this letter.—ED.

ORDERS FOR THE MILITIA

[Col. William Preston to Col. William Christian. 4QQ14—
A. L., draft in Preston's handwriting.]

Sir—As the Militia Law of 1757 has expired & the Invasion & Insurrection Laws of the same Date will expire in June, Probably before the Assembly can meet to revise those Laws therefor the Militia must now be regulated and Diciplined by the only Law in force for that Purpose I mean that of 1738.[16] And as the safety of the Frontier Inhabitants in a great measure depends on a well regulated Militia, It is the Duty of every Officer in Fincastle[17] to use his Authority and Influence for that Purpose, by making themselves acquainted with the only Militia Law in Force & as frequently as may be convenient for the People to call private Musters of the Respective Company's and by duely exercising the Soldiers under their Com-

---

[16] The Virginia Assembly, or House of Burgesses, met at Williamsburgh, May 24, 1774. Two days later it was prorogued by the governor for passing resolutions of sympathy with the oppressions of Massachusetts. By various prorogations, the meeting was postponed until June 1, 1775, when, after a stormy session, the house adjourned never to reassemble—the authority passing to the convention assembled by the people of the state. The organization of the militia under act of 1738 was recommended by the Virginia convention which met at Richmond, March 20-27, and it was doubtless in obedience to this request that Preston issued these orders. See also Force, *American Archives*, 4th series, ii, p. 169.—ED.

[17] Fincastle County, embracing all southwestern Virginia and Kentucky, had but a brief existence. Formed out of Botetourt in 1772, it was in 1776 superseded by the three counties of Montgomery, Washington, and Kentucky. While it existed, Col. William Preston was county-lieutenant, and Col. William Christian colonel of its militia regiment.—ED.

mand, as also to see that they are provided with Arms & Ammunition as that Law directs; or as nearly so as they Possibly can. Should any Officers have neglected to Quallify into their Commissions it is necessary they should take the first Opportunity to do so.

And as a general Muster will be held some time in Sepr. or Octr. next of which Notice will be given. The Officers are to keep Just Returns of the Delinquent in their Companies, that they may be enabled to make a due report thereof on Oath to the Court Martial, that such Delinquents may be fined according to the S^d. Law.

I would request you to give Instructions to all the Captains in this County agreeable to the above & earnestly Exhort them to a punctual Discharge of their Duty, especially as the Savages have lately committed some Murders on the People about to Settle to the Westward[18] & we don't know how soon they may fall upon the Inhabitants. I am Sir y^r hble Servt.

W. P.

May 1st. 1775

29th Ap 1775

To Col. Christian

---

[18] This refers to the attack upon Boone's men, who were cutting a road to Kentucky; see note 4, *ante*. Early on the morning of March 25, 1775, a party of Indians crept up to their camp, fired upon the sleeping men, and killed Capt. William Twitty and his negro, besides wounding Felix Walker. Two days later, the same band killed in the near neighborhood two men from the party of Samuel Tate. See Draper MSS., 3B.—ED.

VIRGINIA HEARS OF LEXINGTON AND CONCORD

[Rev. John Brown [19] to Col. William Preston. 4QQ15—
A. L. S.]

Dr Sr—I look upon myself indespenciblly obligated to return you thanks for your two Epistles & have no other way to demonstrate it but by as speedy an Answer as I possibly can, therefore I sit down to tell first the proceedings of the Pres{bry} relative to the semenary for the Education of youth.[20]

* * * * * * * * [21]

What a Buzzel is amongst People about Kentuck? to hear people speak of it one Would think it was a new found Paradise; & I doubt not if it is such a place as represented but ministers will have thin congregations, but why need I fear that? Ministers are moveable goods as well as others & stand in need of good land as any do, for they are bad Farmers.

* * * * * * * * [22]

---

[19] For a sketch of Rev. John Brown see *Dunmore's War*, p. 27, note 42.—ED.

[20] This was first called Augusta Academy, which was opened for students in May, 1776. Three years later it was removed to Lexington, and rechristened Liberty Hall. In 1782 the institution was incorporated. Its work drew the attention of Washington, who in 1796 gave a considerable donation to this Western seminary, whereupon the trustees changed the name to Washington Academy. Later, it became Washington University, and upon the death (1871) of Robert E. Lee, who had served as its president, received the present name of Washington and Lee University. A subscription paper for starting this academy is found in Draper MSS., 7ZZ7.—ED.

[21] The omitted portion gives the names of those appointed to solicit subscriptions, and the prospects of success, of which latter Brown was not very sanguine.—ED.

[22] Here the original deals with family affairs, and the desire of Rev. James Waddell to acquire by purchase the estate of Springhill.—ED.

This very moment Boston's News Struck my Ears & affects my Heart, tho' it is but what I expected we live in a terrible world (terrible indeed) when men of the same Nation make a merit of sheding one anothers Blood. I have not seen the express; but as I am informed that the Kings army in a Town some distance from Boston killed 6 of the inhabitants & wounded severals, for which reason the N. England men rose to the number of 4^{000} & surrounded 1200 upon a hill & killed 150 at the expense of 50 of their men perhaps you have the account more perfect than I.[23] 3 ships of the line with 4 Companies of marines are come to V:rginia to keep us in Order. it is said they have taken the magazine in W:burg[24] I think it is time for the Continent to do something for the deffense of Life and Liberty. I am no polotition yet I can see that we are in no posture for deffense, were we independent of England & laws military and civil,

---

[23] The news of the battle of Lexington and Concord reached Virginia the last of April, and was published in the *Virginia Gazette* of the twenty-ninth of that month. It is interesting to note that in less than six days it had crossed the Blue Ridge and was known to the dwellers in the Shenandoah Valley, and that it was thought to have spread as far as Preston's home at Draper's Meadows, near Blacksburg, in present Montgomery County, on waters draining into the Ohio.—Ed.

[24] April 20, Governor Dunmore ordered the captain of the "Magdalen," lying at anchor in the James, to carry off twenty kegs of powder from the public magazine in Williamsburgh, and place it on board the vessel. This alarmed the Virginia patriots, and at the time Brown was writing this letter, Patrick Henry at the head of the Hanover County militia was advancing upon the capital. An armed collision at this time was prevented, and the king's officers prevailed upon to pay the value of the powder to the patriot leaders. During his alarm over this affair, Dunmore armed the Indian hostages who had the previous autumn been brought in from the Shawnee town.—Ed.

money struck to support an army, it wou'd not (I am apprehensive, be easy to subdue us or Make us Slaves as is intended. As far as I am acquainted I find the spirit of resentment increased among the people, but what can they do? They are like sheep in the Wilderness without a head. May the Good Lord who can bring order out of confusion order all things for his own Glory & protect his Church & people in america from all ill designing men is the earnest Prayer of D[r]. Brother your's

JOHN BROWN

May 5th 1775

P. S. Wou'd not £50 p[r] 100 [acres] be sufficient price for Spring Hill Plantation which I am apprehensive M[r]. Waddell[25] woud be willing to give.

Col[o]. William Preston in Smithfield, Fincastle County.

GARRISON AT POINT PLEASANT

[Capt. William Russell to Col. William Fleming.[26] 4QQ19 A. L.]

FORT BLAIR June 12th 1775

Dear Maj[r].—I Rec[d]. your welcome Letter by Thomas Tays; which, be assure'd, in this remote De-

---

[25] Rev. James Waddell, afterwards famous as the "blind preacher," and described by William Wirt, in *Letters of the British Spy* (N. Y., 1832), pp. 195-205, was born in 1739 either in Ireland or on the sea. Educated under Dr. Samuel Finley, he was licensed to preach in 1761. First residing in Lancaster County, Virginia, he removed to the upper country about the date of this letter. He served the Tinkling Spring congregation until 1783, when he removed to Louisa County, where he died in 1805. The estate of Springhill, of which he purchased 1300 acres for £1,000, was part of the original estate of Col. James Patton, for whom Preston was executor.—ED.

[26] For Fleming, see *Dunmore's War*, pp. 428, 429.—ED.

partment, contributed more than a little to my Satisfaction.

I had some Days before the Receipt of yours, been favour'd with the shocking Acc^t. of three Battles being fought near the City of Boston, between the Brittish Troops, and Americans; tho', must acknowledge my great joy, in our victories obtained over the Enemies Tyranic Pride.

The unheard of Acts of Barbarity, committed by the Brittish Troops, will doubtless stir up every lover of his Country, to be Zealous, and forward in it's defence, to support our Liberty; tho', I doubt not, but many sychophants to Brittains Interest, will now appear Patriots;— as long as our Arms prove Victorious; but, should ever our present success change, and in ever so small a manner, be Sully'd, you'l find Traytors enough prick up their Ears, and in a Profetic language, display their presuggested knoledge of Events. I have, as long as in my power, procrastinated our departure from this Garison, expecting that ere now, we should Receive some Orders from the Convention, that might countermand the Governors Letter to me,[27] but as none such have yet come to hand, I am this Morning preparing to start off our Cattle up Sandy, and expect, that Comm^d. will leave this Wensday, or thursday at farthest, and shall Decamp

---

[27] The Virginia convention which met at Richmond, March 20-27, 1775, provided for embodying the militia of the state (see Preston's orders, *ante*, pp. 8, 9), but not the garrisons of the frontier forts. By one of his last executive acts, the governor ordered the garrisons at Fort Dunmore (Pitt), Fort Fincastle (Wheeling), and Fort Blair (Point Pleasant) disbanded, and the stockades evacuated. See *Amer. Archives*, 4th series, ii, p. 1189.—Ed.

myselfe with a Convoy to the other stores next Monday, and expect to overtake the Stock, at the big painted Lick[28] about sixty Miles up Sandy.

I expect you have hear'd of Col°. Preston's Orders, to Maj`r`. Engles[29] to take possession of the Cattle, and Horses in my care at this Garison; but, as I found not a word, in his Lordship's Orders to me, Similar to the Colonels pretended authority, I took the oppinion of my officers, who judged it most to the Interest of the Country, that I should keep together the Stock and Stores, and Convoy them into the Settlement, and dispose of them myselfe, unless contra Orders come to me from the Convention. I am in a singular manner obliged to you, for your Advice in the disposal of the Beves, and horses, I have on hand of the Country's; and as your oppinion corroberates with our Resolutions, I trust all things will go right, and will I hope, at least open the Eyes of the designing Col°. to see his folly, in aiming to make use of me as a Tool, in any one [Ms torn] his unfair Intentions. The Garison we intend to let remain, as I think the distruction of it at this time might prove Injurious to the Country.

The Corn Stalk left me, last thursday; and in the space of four Days [conve]rsation, I discovered that it is the Intention of the Pick Tribe of Indians [to be tr]oublesome to our new Settlements whenever they

---

[28] Probably where Paintsville, Johnson County, Ky., now stands, at the junction of Paint Creek with the Levisa fork of Sandy River.—ED.

[29] For a brief sketch of Col. William Ingles, who acted in Dunmore's War as commissary, with the rank of major, see *Dunmore's War*, p. 101, note 46.—ED.

AT POINT PLEASANT

can; and he further assured me, that the Mingoes[80] behave in a very unbecoming manner Frequently upbraiding the Shawanees, in cowardly making the Peace; & call them big knife People; that the Corn Stalk can't well account for their Intentions. if this be true, and a rupture between England and America has really commenced, we shall certainly Receive Trouble at the hands of those People in a short Time, as they got the news of the Battles in the Shawanee Towns, eight, or ten days before the Corn Stalk came here; Tho' I am confident, the Shawanees will always be our Friends. The Corn Stalk brought me two of the Horses taken by that party of Cherrokees; who, murdered the People on Kentucke in March. The Shawanese took the Rascal, who had them; but, he made his escape from them, it is supposed he is return'd to the Cherokee Nation. It appears to have

---

[80] The Pick tribe were a division of the Shawnee, who lived in the neighborhood of the modern Piqua, Ohio. The name is doubtless taken from Pickawillany, where a branch of the Miami, led by La Demoiselle (or Old Britain), settled in 1748 in order to make a treaty with the English. Gist and Croghan visited this town in 1750, finding there a number of British Indian traders. Two years later a force of French and Indians, under the command of Charles Langlade of Wisconsin, fell upon this village, destroyed it, and burned its chief. After the French and Indian War, the Miami withdrew to the Northwest, being succeeded by the Shawnee. Their chief town, known as Piqua, was two and a half miles north of the present Piqua, on the west bank of the Great Miami, south of the entrance of Loramie's Creek. This and adjacent villages (collectively called Piqua) were especially hostile to the whites during the Revolution, being twice raided by George Rogers Clark, in 1780 and again in 1782.

For the Mingo see *Dunmore's War*, p. 28, note 47. They were irreconcilables in the war of 1774, and refused to make peace with Dunmore until he sent a force to raid their town. See *Ibid.*, p. 303, note 17.—ED.

been the Pics, that fired on Boones Camp when the two Men were kill'd, out of his Party.[81] I had resolved when I left home to go from this Place to Kentucke; and especially since I Rec^d. my other Warrant; but hearing of the troublesome Times, in the Country, I am greatly purplex'd in mind, to hear more certain acc^t. how affairs are likely to go in Virginia; nor can I fall upon any method, to save the Stores so effectual, from the danger of the Indians, as to bring them into the Settlements; and after seeing Col^o. Christian and your selfe, I hope to be satisfy'd in the present Times.

I have wrote several Letters to Col^o. Henderson, since I returnd to this Post, and have had it in my power, to calm the Minds of several Comp^{ys}. who, have gone down this River, so that I hope, the new Country about Kentucke will Settle quickly: I have also Wrote Maj^r. Connelly,[82] so that I wood fain hope, our wishes, and endeavours may prove effectual, to the speedy Settling that Country.

I have heard the Convention is to meet some Time this Month; and have wrote to Inform Col^o. Christian,[83] respecting the present Temper, of the neighboring Tribes of Indians, to the Shawanees; which, I think is really necessary, the Convention should be made acquainted with, that they may judge accord-

---

[81] See *ante*, p. 9, note 18.—ED.

[82] For Dr. John Connolly see *Dunmore's War*, p. 42, note 77. Evidently Russell was not yet informed of Connolly's plans to side with the English and attack the American frontier—see *post*.—ED.

[83] The convention met again July 17, Col. William Christian representing Fincastle County.—ED.

ingly; and as your Letter to me got brook open on new River, his may also, and probably miscarry; therefore, I think it best to send off Henry Boyer,[84] and Geo. Oxen as an express, one with this Letter to you, and the other is to let my Family know of my coming, and withall to have some Horses taken out to Sandy, to carry in the Stores upon. If Col°. Christian should be down the Country, and any opportunity offers, pre [MS torn] to dispatch my Letter, sent to him, by M^r. Engles last Week [MS. torn] this may find you, and Lady, and little Son in Health;[85] and that the Almighty may comfort, and protect you in the present troubles, is the harty wish of yours most Affectionately.

[WILLIAM RUSSELL]

[To Col. William Fleming]

AFFAIRS AT FORT PITT

[Summary of printed documents concerning movements at Fort Pitt and vicinity, during the spring and summer of 1775.]

Upon the retirement of Lord Dunmore (November, 1774), from his military expedition into the Indian country, he left a garrison of seventy-five men in Fort

---

[84] Although then but a youth, Henry Bowyer took part in Dunmore's War, and was wounded at the Battle of Point Pleasant. He afterwards enlisted in the Revolutionary cavalry under Col. William Washington. Becoming a prominent citizen of Botetourt County, he was clerk of its courts, 1791–1831, and died in 1833.—ED.

[85] Mrs. Fleming was a sister of Col. William Christian; for their son see *Dunmore's War*, p. 182, note 27.—ED.

Dunmore, under the command of Maj. John Connolly, promising to return in the spring and complete the treaty with the Indians, that had been begun at Camp Charlotte.[86] Twelve Mingo prisoners were left in confinement in the fort, while the Shawnee hostages accompanied the governor to Williamsburgh. But by the spring of 1775 the American Revolutionary movement had gained such force in Virginia that the governor was unable to revisit the frontiers, or treat further with the Indian tribes.

Meanwhile the boundary difficulty between Virginia and Pennsylvania reached an acute stage, each colony claimed jurisdiction of the forks of the Ohio, and reprisals were alternately made upon the magistrates of each colony. Affairs reached such a state of confusion that in July the delegates of both colonies, assembled in Continental Congress at Philadelphia, addressed a friendly letter to the inhabitants west of Laurel Hill, advising them to lay aside their unhappy differences and co-operate for the defense of American liberties.[87]

West Augusta, Virginia, organized at Pittsburgh, May 16, a committee of correspondence to keep in touch with a standing committee of seven members to care for American interests in that part of the country, and sent delegates to the two Virginia conventions in March and July. The same day Westmoreland County, Pennsylvania, organized at Hannastown, and

---

[86] *Ibid.*, pp. 301–306, 386.—ED.
[87] This letter is found in *Amer. Archives*, 4th series, ii, p. 1723.—ED.

subscribed to the Association.[38] Although the boundary difference was not settled until 1780, the patriots of both colonies seem to have suspended their animosities in the common struggle for liberty.

Although American born, Major Connolly adhered to the Royalist side. In February he visited Williamsburgh[39] and had a conference with Dunmore, who instructed him to secure the Indians for the king, and induce them to espouse His Majesty's cause. On his return to Fort Pitt, Connolly sent runners to the Delaware towns, inviting the chiefs to come in and receive the prisoners and such messages as might be sent them by the royal governor. Sometime in June the Delaware chiefs and a few of the Mingo visited Pittsburgh. According to Connolly's own report they gave assurances that they would support the king, and in comfirmation thereof received presents and a belt of wampum. Connolly intimates that he outwitted the patriot faction, who were led to approve his negotiations with the Indians without understanding their purport.[40] To a neighboring magistrate he admitted that, to secure a confirmation of his lands,[41] he was planning to take White Eyes, the Delaware chief, to England.

---

[38] *Ibid.*, pp. 613–615.—Ed.

[39] See his letter to Washington, dated "Winchester, Feb^r. 9th, 1775," in S. M. Hamilton, *Letters to Washington* (Boston, 1902), v, p. 101.—Ed.

[40] "A Narrative of the Transactions, Imprisonment and Sufferings of John Connolly, an American Loyalist and Lieutenant Colonel in His Majesty's Service," in *Pennsylvania Magazine of History and Biography*, xii, pp. 315, 316. See the report at the Treaty of Pittsburgh, *post.*—Ed.

[41] Letter of Arthur St. Clair, July 12, 1775, in *Pennsylvania Archives*, iv, p. 637.—Ed.

In July Connolly, still acting on the governor's orders, disbanded the garrison at Pittsburgh, and accompanied by three Indian chiefs made his way toward Williamsburgh, and joined Dunmore, then on board of a British man-of-war off York.

The final session of the Virginia House of Burgesses took into consideration the necessity of quieting the Indians on the frontier,[42] and appointed Thomas Walker, James Wood, Andrew Lewis, John Walker, and Adam Stephen[43] commissioners to ratify a peace with the tribesmen. James Wood was chosen to visit the Indian towns and give notice of a conference to be held at Pittsburgh in September.[44]

---

[42] *Amer. Archives,* 4th series, ii, p. 1209.—ED.

[43] For sketches of these Virginians see *Dunmore's War,* pp. 191, 242, 426-428. Col. John Walker was a son of Dr. Thomas Walker. Born in Albemarle in 1744, he served in the Revolution, was captured by the British, and later served as United States senator from Virginia by appointment (May-December, 1790). He died in 1809.—ED.

[44] James Wood was the son of a colonel of the same name, who served with Washington in the French and Indian War, and founded the Virginia town of Winchester. Born in 1750, James the younger served as captain in Dunmore's division in 1774; the following year, after the suspension of the House of Burgesses, of which he was a member from Frederick County, he made a hazardous journey to the Indian towns. See his journal, *post.* In 1776 he became colonel of the 8th Virginia regiment, and serving through the war, retired with the rank of brigadier-general. In 1789, he was one of the presidential electors, and from 1796-99 was governor of his state. Noted for his philanthropy and anti-slavery principles, he died at his home in Winchester in 1813.—ED.

VIRGINIA ARMS

[Thomas Lewis to Col. William Preston. 4QQ29 — A. L. S.]

Rich^D. Augt. 19th 1775.

Dear Si^r—Tho I wrote to you two Days Since least miscarriage should Happen I have now Set Down to write you or rather to repeat the Same thing to you that I mentioned before —— — yours of the 8th & thirteen July Came to hand, but the last too late to be before hand with the Fincastle Petition however they were both presented on the Same Day.[45] A Committee was appointed to Consider the matter, their report was not made till ye 15th of the present month & is as Followeth ——— "The Committee to whom the Petitions of the Committee & Surveyor, of Fincastle, & a proclamation of L^d. Dunmore Dated the 8th May 1775, were refered have had the Same under their Consideration & Came to ye Following Resolutions

Resolved that untill the Committee appointed by the Convention in March last, to Enquire whether the King may of Right advance the terms of Granting Lands in this Colony, Shall have made their report, the recommendation then made, that all persons should forbear to purchase or Accept Grants of Land under the late Instructions from the Govr. be observed & that in the mean time, all Surveyors be & they are hereby Directed to make no Surveys under the Said Instructions, nor pay any regard to the Said proclamation."

---

[45] For these petitions see *Amer. Archives*, 4th series, iii, p. 367.—Ed.

I Showed your Exculpatory Letter to ye Leading members, no blame was laid or attempted to be Charged on you. The Committee of last march being otherwise Engaged, had not reported, & could not do it now for want of Some Original papers & Charters that Could not be obtained at present, but it is to be hoped they will attend to this matter Soon as to what passes here it is difficult to Say with Certainty not an Ordinance is yet Compleated. a variety of opinions retards this Buissiness. 1000 regulars are voted to be, Divided into two Regiments, the Commander Col^o. Henry of the first Wm Woodford of the other, W^m. Christian (of whose military powers much have been Said here) is first L. Col^o. & one Scott ye Second, one Eps & Spotswood majors ——— 8000 minuit men in 16 Batalions are to trained & paid for the time of training 425 for posts on the Frontiers viz 200 at Pitsburg[46] 25 at Wheeling, 100 at y^e

---

[46] August 7, the convention resolved that "John Neavill be directed to march with his Company of one hundred men, and take possession of *Fort Pitt,* and that the said Company be in the pay of this Colony from the time of their marching."

Capt. John Neville was born in Virginia in 1731. He served with Washington on Braddock's expedition, and afterwards settled in Winchester, where he acted as sheriff. Having large landed interests in the neighborhood of Pittsburgh, he made his home on Chartier's Creek, and was a delegate chosen by the West Augusta people to represent them in the Virginia Convention (1774); through illness, however, he was unable to attend. The company that he marched to Pittsburgh were largely Frederick County militia. Neville remained in command until June, 1777. Being then made colonel of the 4th Virginia continental regiment, he served throughout the Revolution in the Eastern department. After the war he returned to his Western home, being chosen member of the supreme executive council of Pennsylvania. He was inspector of revenue at the time of the Whiskey Rebellion (1794), during which dis-

point 100 for Fincastele, these last & very Deservedly have met with oposition, many Schemes of Jobing may be Discovered here but this is no new thing— resolves are entred into for ye Encouragement of making Saltpeter, Sulphur [and] Gunpowder The Delegates to ye Genl Congress that meet next month are Pay[ton]. Randolph, B. Harrison, R. H. Lee, T. Jefferson, T. Nelson, F L Lee, G^o Wythe. A Committee of Safety who are to answer to the Executive part of Govm^t Consisting of 11 persons are appointed visz. E^d Pendelton, G^o Mason, Jno Page, Richd Bland, F. L. Lee, Paul Carrinton, Dudley Diggs, Wm Cable [Cabell], Carter Braxton, James Mercer, Jno Tabb. An Ordinance is in great forwardness for paying off last years Expenses. our proportion of the Continental army to ye lth [first] Jan^r. 150 000, ye Regulars minute men militia &c &c &c will leave us at ye End of the year in a Debt not easily Discharged, I perhaps put it too much in my former Letter, it however will be very Great, The Colony [ies] are by Congress Divided into three Districts for ye Conveniency of treating with the Indians & Gentlemen appointed for that purpose.[47] Carlton

---

turbance his house was sacked and he subjected to much violence. He died on Montour's Island in 1803.—ED.

[47] July 12th, 1775, the Continental Congress determined to organize three departments for Indian affairs, of which the Pittsburgh and Western Virginia region constituted the central. The next day commissioners were chosen for that department in the persons of Benjamin Franklin, Patrick Henry, and James Wilson. In September following, Lewis Morris was appointed in the place of Franklin, who was unable to attend, to conduct the treaty at Pittsburgh; and Dr. Thomas Walker was chosen in the place of Patrick Henry, who declined the commissionership. These three congressional com-

has been Labouring with the Canadians to assist him in Disstressing the Coloneys but has not been very Successfull, there is great reason to believe the New Englanders under Gen¹ Schuyler is in possession of Montreal, & Niagra by this time, the Canadians are Said to wish this, if so it will be an Easy Acquisition as Carlton has not above 600 troops to opose to our army, however this may be, you may depend an Army attempts it.

as to other news yᵉ paper will Inform you all I can say, I wis[h] you all Hapiness & am Dʳ Sir

Your most Humble Serᵗ

THOS LEWIS[48]

monday 21th The Ordinance for the regular troops the minit men & militia passed as well as that for Seteling the Articles of War passed this day & was Despatched to yᵉ press An Ordinance for a Committee of Safety, And one for regulating various Elections will be Completed this Day & to morrow One for paying of Last years Excise & raising or striking money & the means of Sinking the Same is in Some forwardness. it is to be hoped this week will put an End to this Session of which (between [us]) I am heartily Sick

To Col. William Preston

---

missioners (Wilson, Morris, and Walker) proceeded to Pittsburgh, where, in connection with the delegates chosen by Virginia for the same purpose they conducted the required negotiations.—ED.

[48] For a brief biographical sketch of Thomas Lewis see *Dunmore's War*, p. 312, note 30.—ED.

TREATY AT PITTSBURGH, 1775

[Original Ms. in possession of Dr. William C. Rives, Washington, D. C., a descendant of Dr. Thomas Walker.]⁴⁹

At a meeting of the Commissioners Appointed by the Honorable the Convention of the Colony of Virginia for holding a Treaty with the Western Indians

---

⁴⁹ The following complete text of the treaty negotiations at Pittsburgh in the autumn of 1775, is furnished us by the courtesy of Dr. William Cabell Rives, of Washington, D. C., into whose possession the manuscript came with others belonging to Dr. Thomas Walker, from whom he is directly descended. Dr. Walker was the chairman of the Virginia treaty commission, and one of the three congressional commissioners. He appears to have been entrusted with the full minutes of the treaty, also with James Wood's diary of his journey to summon the tribesmen thither. The report of the treaty does not appear to have been before printed in its entirety. In 1847 Lyman C. Draper visited Castle Hill, the ancestral home of the Walker-Rives family in Albemarle County, and was permitted by the then owner to inspect this manuscript, which he found "very neatly written and having the autograph signatures of the Virginia commissioners."—Draper MSS., 5C28. Draper made copious extracts.

John J. Jacobs, author of *Biographical Sketch of Captain Michael Cresap* (Cumberland, 1826), was in possession of a copy of the manuscript minutes of this treaty, furnished him by John Madison, secretary of the Virginia commissioners. The excerpts which Jacobs made for his work (pp. 69-71) are all that have been published therefrom. The present editors, noting Draper's citation from the original document, entered into correspondence with the Rives family, and found that they had preserved this important manuscript entire, and in the condition that Draper found it in 1847. Dr. Rives exercised the greatest care that the transcript should be exact in every particular, and has shown much interest in its present publication. He also informs us that Mrs. William C. Rives, in "A Tale of our Ancestors," published in her book, *Tales and Souvenirs of a Residence in Europe* (1842), uses the names of several Indian chiefs, which she doubtless obtained from the original of this manuscript. The editors consider themselves fortunate in being able to place before their readers the full text of a negotiation fraught with such consequences to the Revolution in the West.—Ed.

September the Twelfth One Thousand Seven Hundred and Seventy five.

The Indians not being Arrived and the Commissioners being Informed they were [on] their Road thought proper to dispatch Mr John Gibson[50] with the Indian Allaniwisica with the following talk to meet and hasten them

Young Brothers Cheifs and Wariors of the different Tribes of Indians on your Way to the Treaty at Fort Pitt We the Commissioners of the Long Knife sent to treat with you our Brothers to the Westward have been Waiting at Pittsburgh the place we Appointed several days and are very impatient to see you we have sent John Gibson and our Young Brother Allaniwisica[51] to meet you on your Road to desire you will come up as soon as you can that we may see you and brighten the Chain of Freindship which we both now have hold of we have many good things to say to you when we meet and shall send Provisions to meet you at Logs Town[52] Should

---

[50] For a brief sketch of Gibson, see *Dunmore's War*, p. 11, note 19.—ED.

[51] Probably the same Indian as the one more frequently called Elinipisco, a son of Cornstalk, who participated in Dunmore's War. In November, 1777, he visited Fort Randolph, where his father was already in custody, and was killed by a mob of vengeful frontiersmen.—ED.

[52] Logstown was an important Indian site, about eighteen miles below Pittsburgh, on the right bank of the river. Its French name was Chiningué, Anglicized as Shenango. This was originally a Shawnee village, but gradually became a large mixed town—an important trading site. Conrad Weiser made a treaty here in 1748; in consequence whereof the French expedition under Céloron, the following year, found the village chiefly in the English interest. Croghan also, in 1751, traded and treated here. Washington stopped at Logstown

you have heard E[vil] Reports from any person we desire you will not beleive them but be Assured our hearts are good towards you *A String of White Wampum*

September 15th, At a Meeting of the Commissioners as well those Appointed by the Honorable the Continential Congress as those Appointed by the Colony of Virginia Thomas Walker Esqr in the Chair

A string of Wampum and Talk was delivered from the White Mingo[53] to the Commissioners by Capⁿ James Wood one of the Virginia Commissioners who received it from Mr. Dorsey Penticost[54] by whom it was sent importing that he had been shot at by two Men in long white hunting Shirts near the Mouth of Pine Creek[55] with an Intention as he Imagined to kill him that being greatly alarmed and Supposing all the Indians near this place were Murdered he kept himself hid that day and Night in the Woods

---

on his embassy of 1753; but by the following year the French had gained complete ascendency. They built for the Indians a village of log huts, where, in 1758, Post succeeded in gaining a hearing for the English cause. After the fall of Fort Duquesne (1758) this village was abandoned, but Pontiac's conspiracy being ended, its former possessors gradually came back for trade. John Gibson had his chief trading house at this site, and Washington mentions it in the diary of his journey in 1770. By 1784 the site was abandoned. It is now part of Economy township.—ED.

[53] White Mingo was a Seneca chief, who lived not far above Pittsburgh on the Allegheny. His signature appeared on Bouquet's treaty (1764), and he died before 1777.—ED.

[54] For a brief biographical sketch of Dorsey Pentecost see *Dunmore's War*, p. 101, note 47.

[55] Pine Creek flows into the Allegheny from the northwest, where the town of Sharpsburg now stands.—ED.

where finding all things Quiet he Ventured to his Camp and finding his family safe went to Col⁰ Croghans[56] from where he sent the String and talk

Resolved that Cap ⁿ James Wood Mr. John Walker Mr. George Morgan and Mr. Lewis Morris take with them Simon Girty and John Montour for Interpreters[57] and visit the White Mingo that they go with him to the Place where he says he was shot at and report to this Meeting whatever they can discover concerning this Affair Resolved that a String of White Wampum and the following talk be delivered the White Mingo by the above Mentioned Gentlemen

Brother the White Mingo We have heard with very great Greif and concern your Message informing us that the day before Yesterday you were shot at by two Men in long White hunting Shirts they must have been very bad People indeed you know there are some such in all Nations but you ought not to

---

[56] For a brief sketch of Col. George Croghan see *Dunmore's War*, p. 7, note 12.—ED.

[57] For a brief sketch of Simon Girty see *Ibid.*, *p.* 152, note, 4.

John Montour was the son of Andrew, the famous half-breed interpreter who accompanied Weiser and Washington on their Western journeys and who was captain in the French and Indian War. John's mother was the granddaughter of the Delaware chief Olumpias, and in her right he was considered a Delaware chief. He was born in 1744, probably near Pittsburgh. When twelve years of age his father took him to Philadelphia, where he was educated at the expense of the state. He was with Dunmore in 1774, and adhered to the colonists' cause during the Revolution, although his fidelity was more than once doubted. In 1782 Montour received a captain's commission, and as late as 1789 was living on Montour's island. This island, now known as Neville, is five miles below Pittsburgh; it is five miles in length, the largest of the islands in the upper river.—ED.

judge of the Sentiments and Conduct of your Brothers the White People from those of a few Wretches among them we will do every thing in our Power to discover who have done this very Wicked Act We will offer a very large Reward for finding them out and bringing them to us and so soon as they shall be found we will take Care that they be imprisoned and Otherwise Punished as they Ought to be They must have been Enemies to us as well as to you Otherwise they would not have done any thing to create Jealousy between us but we hope this Message and the String will Effectually remove it you may return to us with Safety and we Shall be glad to take you by the hand.

Molly Hickman a Delaware Woman[58] Appearing before the Commissioners informs that last Night about Midnight as a Mingo Man and a Shawanese Man was Walking near the Orchard there were four or five White Men following them in close Conversation that the Mingo Man Understanding what they said Acquainted the other they were threatning them & they had best make thier Escape upon which they Separated and run off and the White Men pursued them but they got over the River one Some distance above and the other at the Lower end of the Orchard that the Mingo Man went off Early this Morning that the Shawanese were still there but Apprehending they would share the same fate with some of the Delawares last Year

---

[58] For other Delaware Indians of this name, one of whom acted as escort and interpreter for Frederick Post in 1758, see Thwaites, *Early Western Travels*, i, pp. 220, 227, 235.—ED.

Doctor Walker Col⁰ Morris Col⁰ Lewis Col⁰ Stephen and Col⁰ Wilson went over to the Indian Camp to enquire into the truth of the above report and found that the Indians had Misapprehended the White People from their small Acquaintance with the Language

---

September 16th The Gentlemen Appointed to Visit the White Mingo made the following Report In Obedience to the Order of Yesterday the persons Appointed to visit the White Mingo immediately proceeded to discharge their trust they were met by the White Mingo at the Waterside where he Accosted them thus "When I first saw you coming I was Affraid and had thoughts of running away" he Appeared to be Quite Calm and Shewed no Symptoms of fear from thence they went to his House and after resting awhile delivered the Message and string to which he gave the following Answer "I thank my old Brother of Virginia Pennsylvania &ᶜ for their enquiry into this Matter when I was first fired on I thought it was the Act of some inconsiderate foolish People and did not imagine the Great People knew any thing of it I thank God that he has been pleased to frustrate their designs and has permitted me to live a little longer I am perfectly satisfied and not the least uneasy" they went to the place where he said he was fired at after some search found his Blanket and hat about One hundred and twenty Yards from the Spot they could not see where the Ball struck and he said he never heard

Col. George Morgan

From a silhouette in the possession of his great-grand
daughter, Mrs. Helena C. Beatty of Washington, Pa
Reproduced by permission, from Bausman's *History
of Beaver County, Pa* (New York, 1904)

it they then invited him to come to Town with them if he was uneasy in his mind he said he was not uneasy and would come to Town to morrow when they came to his House his wife was Just returned from Horse Hunting in the same Woods as they went they met with Coyashotas two Wives and another Squa coming from the same place who showed no sign of fear (Signed)

JAMES WOOD
JOHN WALKER

The White Mingo in Answer to the Message from the Commissioners desired to return his thanks to them for sending it and to us as the Bearers he repeated nearly what he had heard and said it should not make him Angry or Uneasy that he Attributed it to some bad people only and that he would come to the fort tomorrow he shewed us the Ground where he said he was shot at and the Place where he threw away his hat and Blanket both of which we found but no mark of a ball tho the tracts of a Man in Mocasins were to be seen where he said the Man shot from

(Signed) GEORGE MORGAN[59]

---

[59] George Morgan, son of Evan, was born in Philadelphia in 1742, and while a young man joined the firm of Baynton, Wharton & Co., well-known Indian traders, and in 1764 married a daughter of Baynton. The firm lost heavily by Pontiac's conspiracy, for which they were recompensed at the treaty of Fort Stanwix (1768). This grant laid the foundation of the Indiana Company, for which Morgan was secretary and agent many years. Morgan early visited the Indian country, and made himself popular with the tribesmen—a voyage to the Illinois and down the Mississippi as early as 1766 being recorded. In 1768 he was living in the Illinois, but left there some time before the outbreak of the Revolution. His

The White Mingo upon the Speeches being interpreted to him returned thanks to his Brother of the Big knife and his Brothers of New York and Pennsylvania for their kind speech he said he was [now] Easy in his own Mind as to their being Unfreindly to him or having any design to injure him that he supposed they were some evil minded persons who wanted to make a breach between the People of his Colour and his White Brothers but he thanked God that he had rescued him from the hands of such Villians and permitted him to live a little longer with regard to his being fired upon he says that on Wednesday as he was paddling down the River a bullet struck just by him which he did not conceive to be fired at him at that time but thought it was some person a hunting had carelessly fired that way that he landed and met with two Men Cloathed in White hunting Shirts with Guns upon their Shoulders that he went up to them in a freindly Manner and offered to shake hands with

---

appointment by Congress in April, 1776, as Indian agent for the Middle Department brought him again to Pittsburgh, where he remained in this capacity until his resignation in the spring of 1779. He then rejoined the Eastern army, wherein he attained the rank of colonel. At the close of the war he settled in Princeton, N. J., there becoming a leading citizen and a trustee of the college. In 1788–89, Morgan was occupied with a plan for settling a colony on the Spanish side of the Mississippi, and founded there the settlement of New Madrid. Having failed to secure proper authorization from the Spanish authorities, the proposed colony was abandoned. In 1796 Morgan removed to Washington County, Pa., where he built an estate called "Morganza." There the Aaron Burr plot was first detected and reported. Morgan died at his Western home in 1810. His Indian name was "Taimenend." Dr. Samuel P. Hildreth of Marietta, Ohio, once possessed Morgan's journals, and published extracts therefrom in his *Pioneer History* (Cincinnati, 1848).—ED.

them and that they passed on without taking any Notice of him that he then began to suspect that the Bullet was Aimed at him and that something had happened to his freinds below that he walked along the Bank and discovered a great Many White People and that he was then sure that something had happened and turned back to his Cabin that as he was descending a hill in the Wood he saw two Men dressed in the same Manner as those he had seen before and that he Observed one of them presented at him that he immediately turned about and run upon which the Man fired and that he did not return to his Cabin until some time on Thursday that the White Mingo went with us to the Place where he said he was fired at and Shewed us the Place where he stood and the Man who fired at him that I saw the steps of the White Mingo and that Cap^n Wood as I Understand saw the Prints of the two Men that we found the Matchcoat and hat which he dropped and returned them to him

(Signed) LEWIS MORRIS Jun[60]

Pittsburgh Septr. 16th 1775

Resolved that it be recommended to the Indians to encamp near to each other and that each Incampment

---

[60] Lewis Morris, of the famous New York family of that name, was born in 1726 and graduated at Yale College twenty years later. On the outbreak of the Revolution he joined the patriot cause, was elected to Congress in 1775, and made a commissioner of Indian affairs. In that capacity he visited Pittsburgh, and held the treaty of 1775. In 1776 he was one of the signers of the Declaration of Independence, and retiring from Congress served in the New York legislature (1777–78), and in the state militia, where he attained the rank of major-general. He died at Morrisania in 1798.—ED.

with the Approbation of the Commissioners make Choice of an Interpreter to stay O'Nights to inform the Commissioners the names of such White Persons who shall go among them to disturb them

Resolved that Advertisements be set up in the Most Public Places ofering a reward of Two Hundred Dollars to any person or persons who shall discover the two Men or either of them that Shot at the White Mingo on Wednesday last

Captain James Wood reported his Journal in his late Expedition to invite the Indians to this Treaty Ordered that the said Journal be Copied in these Proceedings which is as follows

Diary 1775

24th June the Honorable the Council and House of Burgesses Appointed George Washington Thomas Walker James Wood Andrew Lewis John Walker and Adam Stephen Esquires Commissioners for holding a Treaty with the Ohio Indians impowering the Treasurer to pay the Expence Accruing provided the same did not Exceed the sum of £2,000 the Evening of the same day the Commissioners were Informed that the House directed them not to Apply more than One Thousand Pounds towards the Negotiation at the same time they directed me to proceed immediately to the different Tribes of Indians as well to give them an Invitation to a Treaty as to remove any bad impressions which might be made by Chenusaw[61] one of the Shawanese Indians who had Escaped from

---

[61] Chenusaw was one of the hostages taken by Dunmore, after the treaty of Camp Charlotte; see *Dunmore's War*, p. 305.—ED.

Williamsburg Upon my Appointment to this Service I moved the house to know how far I was to go in an Explanation of the disputes with Great Britain in Case the Indians should make any Enquirey into that Matter which I was well assured they would Col⁰ Bland then moved the House that I should be directed to Explain the whole dispute to the Indians to make them sensible of the Great Unanimity of the Colonies to Assure them of our Peaceable Intentions towards them and that we did not stand in need of or desire any Assistance from them or any other Nation which Motion was agreed to by the House Nemine Contradicente

25th I left Williamsburg and proceeded on my Journey having stayed three days at home in prepareing for it

9th July I Arrived at Fort Pitt where I received Information that the Cheifs of the Delawares and a few of the Mingoes had lately been Treating with Major Connolly agreeable to Instructions from Lord Dunmore and that Shawanese had not come to the Treaty agreable to their Appointment upon Examining the Proceedings with the Delawares and Mingoes I found that they had been given assurances that a General Treaty would be soon held with all the Ohio Indians upon which I thought it Adviseable to dispatch an Express to the Convention with the following Letter directed to the Honorable Peyton Randolph Esqʳ

Sir—On my Arrival at this Place I found that Majʳ Connolly had finished a Treaty with the Delaware and Mingo Cheifs who had assembled agreable to

Lord Dunmores Appointment and were returned well satisfied with Assurances that a General Treaty would be soon held with them and the Other Ohio Tribes It seems from the Governors Instructions to Maj^r Connolly that he only intended a few of the Cheifs should be called together in order to make them easy till a treaty could be properly negotiated with them I am now waiting to see the Cornstalk who is on his way and is Expected here tomorrow or the next day the Reason that the Shawanese did not Attend at the Treaty lately held is not known but generally beleived to be owing to Two French Men who were at their Towns and desired to speak to the Cheifs of that Nation in Council as soon as I see the Cornstalk I purpose setting off for the Shawanese Towns in hopes of being able to Counteract any diabolical Schems formed by the Enemies of this Country to remove any bad Impressions which may have been made on the Minds of these Savages and to Satisfy them concerning their Hostages from thence I shall proceed to the Wyandots Towns[62] where it is said the

---

[62] The Wyandot were of Huron-Iroquois stock, being of the sub-tribe of Tobacco-Huron, or Petun. Nearly destroyed by the Iroquois in the early seventeenth century, they fled westward, and placing themselves under French protection, settled about Detroit early in the eighteenth century. Gradually they straggled eastward along the southern shore of Lake Erie. In 1747 one band, under the leadership of chief Nicolas, built a tŏwn at Lower Sandusky, and the following year made an alliance with the English. During the French and Indian War, however, the Wyandot adhered to the French, took part in Braddock's defeat, and joined Pontiac's conspiracy. A few young warriors joined the Shawnee in Dunmore's War but the tribe as a whole held aloof. Their towns lay along the Sandusky River, and throughout the Revolution were under the influence of the British at Detroit.—ED.

same Frenchmen have lately been in Council with that Nation and to return by way of the Delaware and Mingo Towns

I find that the Indians have been led to expect a General Treaty and that they would as Usual receive Presents upon a Compliance with the Terms imposed by Lord Dunmore so that I am realy Apprehensive we shall not be able from the Sum Allowed by the Assembly to make the different tribes a Present that will Answer their Expectations Considering the Excessive dearness of Provisions in this part of the Country and the high Advance we must Necessarily pay for Goods from the Great Scarcity now in the Country from these Considerations I would beg the Gentlemen of the Convention to consider whether It would not be adviseable to direct the whole Sum of Two Thousand Pounds allowed by the Resolve of the House should not be laid Out to the best Advantage for this Necessary purpose I am well Assured it will have an Exceeding good Effect and that a lasting peace may be Established with all the Ohio Indians

By the same Express that brings this the Committee of West Augusta purpose sending to their Delegates the Proceedings of the late Treaty held with the Delawares and Mingoes together with a Copy of thir Resolves prior to the Treaty In Justice to the Committee (among whom are Many respectable Characters) I must beg leave to Observe that they have been Attentive to the Interest of their Country on this important Occasion as no kind of provision was made by Government towards providing Necessaries for the Indians who were Called to a Council by the Governor the Committee at a Considerable Expence provided a Quantity of Provisions with a present in Goods which were distributed Among the Indians and which I beleive gave them General Satisfaction on the other hand if they had not thus taken up the Matter the Certain Consequence must have been that the Indians would have returned dissatisfied and a General discontent would have prevaled among the different Tribes

The Committee as well as Major Connollys most inveterate Enemies all agree that he Conducted this Affair in the Most Open and Candid Manner that it was transacted in the presence of the Committee and that he laid the Governors Instructions on this Occasion before them I shall be Extremely happy if my poor Endeavours on this or any future Occasion should in the smallest Degree Contribute to the Service of my Country I have the honor to be &c as soon as I dispatched my Letter I sent for White Eyes[63] and Killbuck[64] Chiefs of the Delawares and Kyashota[65] and

---

[63] For a brief sketch of White Eyes see *Dunmore's War*, p. 29, note 48.—ED.

[64] Killbuck was a grandson of King Newcomer, having been born at the Lehigh Water Gap in the decade between 1730 and 1740. He removed West with his tribe, and was noted for his friendship with the whites and his respect for civilization. About 1788 he was baptized by the Moravians under the name of William Henry, and lived at their town of Goshen until his death in 1811. A lineal descendant by the name of Killbuck is today a missionary in Alaska.—ED.

[65] Guyashusta (Kiasola, Kyashota) was the principal chief of the Six Nations on the Allegheny. During the French and Indian War he was hostile to the English, and the chief conspirator on the Ohio during Pontiac's plot (1763). He signed with Bouquet the treaty of 1764, and kept it loyally, taking

the White Mingo Cheifs of the Mingoes and delivered the following Speech sent by Thomas Walker and Andrew Lewis Esqr two of the Commissioners to the Cheifs and Warriors of the Shawanese Wyandots Delaware and Mingo Nations.

Brothers we are Appointed by your elder Brothers of Virginia to meet you in Council to finish the treaty began by Lord Dunmore last Year we hope to put an End to all differences between your People and ours so effectually that your Children and ours may live in the Strictest friendship till the Sun Shall shine no more or the Waters run in the Ohio

Brothers your Freind Cap^n James Wood who is Appointed one of the Commissioners on this Important Occasion will deliver you this talk by whom you will be informed of the Imprudent Behaviour of your Brother Chenusaw who we hope has got safe to you before this the Manner in which he went from us gives us reason to fear he may give you some alarming Accounts but we hope Cap^n Wood will satisfy you that we are your freinds and have been kind to your people the Wolf[66] and Newau will come with us to the Treaty at Fort Pitt where we hope to meet you on the tenth day of September to Compleat this great Work and must request you to give Notice to all your Neighbouring Nations that are Concerned we desire you will bring with you all the Prisoners and be fully prepared

---

no part in Dunmore's War of 1774. During the Revolution he endeavored to maintain neutrality, dying at Cornplanter's village on the Allegheny about 1795.—ED.

[66] The Indian name of the Wolf, another hostage, was Cuttena (Cuttemwha).—ED.

in every respect to fulfil your agreement with Lord
Dunmore to which White Eyes Answered

Brother I return you as well as our two Brothers
that sent it thanks for the good talk you have now delivered us and you may depend I will make it my business to send the String now delivered to me to all my freinds and make no doubt but they will receive it in the same freindly and thankful Manner I do The White Mingo then Spoke as follows
Brother I am very thankful to you and your two Brothers in Virginia for your good talk and String now delivered I am certain It will give all my freinds the same Pleasure which it gives me to meet you at the time Appointed for holding the treaty at this place and you may be assured they shall be told of it

10th July White Eyes came with an Interpreter to my Lodgings he informed me he was desirous of going to Williamsburg with Major Connolly to see Lord Dunmore who had promised him his Interest in procuring a Grant from the King for the Lands claimed by the Delawares that they were all desirous of living as the White People do and under their Laws and Protection that Lord Dunmore had engaged to make him some Satisfaction for his Trouble in going several times to the Shawanese Towns and serving with him on Campaign and likewise the damage he has sustained by some of our Men Plundering and destroying his Effects that he was a very poor Man and had Neglected to raise Corn by endeavouring to serve us and that his wife and Childerin were now almost starving for Bread he told me he hoped I would advise him whether It was proper for him to go or not

I was then Under the Necessity of Acquainting him with the disputes subsisting between Lord Dunmore and the People of Virginia and engaged whenever the Assembly met that I would go with him to Williamsburg and represent his Case to the Assembly and made no doubt they would Amply reward him for his Services and damages sustained he was very thankful and Appeared perfectly satisfied with the promise I made him

16th July the Cornstalk Nimwha[67] Wryneck Blue Jacket Silver Heels[68] and about fifteen other Shawanese arrived they immediately got drunk and Continued in that situation for two days

18th The Shawanese being assembled I made The following Speech to them *Brothers the Shawanese* I am now on my way to your towns by directions of the great Council of Virginia my Business is to give

---

[67] Nimwha (or Munseeka) was a Shawnee chief, brother of Cornstalk, whom he succeeded as head of the tribe. He took part in Pontiac's Conspiracy, and was present at Bouquet's treaty (1764) as well as those of Fort Pitt (1768 and 1775). In 1778 he led the detachment that captured Daniel Boone, and the following year headed the besiegers of Fort Laurens. His death occurred early in 1780.—ED.

[68] An early mention of these two noted chiefs, Blue Jacket and Silverheels. Blue Jacket was principal chief of the Shawnee during the Indian wars, defeated Harmar and St. Clair, and was defeated by Wayne in 1794. He took part in the treaty of Greenville, and soon after retired to the neighborhood of Sandwich, Ont., where he died about 1810. He was said to have been appointed a brigadier-general in the British service. Silverheels rescued several Pennsylvania traders on the outbreak of Dunmore's War, and at the risk of his own life escorted them to Pittsburgh. While in a fit of intoxication, he was killed by Indians.—ED.

the Cheifs of your Nation an Invitation to meet Commissioners Appointed by them in a general Council at Fort Pitt in 53 days from this time in order fully to Confirm the peace agreed upon last year with Lord Dunmore your Brothers Cuttemwha and Newau are well and you may depend upon seeing them at the time Appointed for your Meeting about forty days ago Chenusaw left us without any provocation that we know of as soon as we found he was gone we dispatched many Men on horseback with Writen papers directing all our People to treat him kindley and to let him Pass to you without receiveing any hurt your Brother Cuttemwha desired me to tell you to be Strong and to come at the time which I Appoint
A String of White Wampum

I then delivered Messrs Walker and Lewis's speech with a String of Wampum soon after which Cornstalk made the following Answer *Brothers the Bigknife* I am greatly oblidged to you as well as to all my Elder Brothers of Virginia for their good talks and Intentions towards their Younger Brothers the Shawanese I look upon what you have said in the Manner as if delivered by your great Council and am as happy in seeing you as if they were all present I shall deliver your talks to the Cheifs on my return and make no doubt but they will meet you at the time Appointed

The Cornstalk after delivering the speech told me he thought it would be best for me to go to the Shawanese Towns least Chenusaw should return and make any bad reports he then informed me that some of the Shawanese were desirous of going to Winchester in order to meet their freinds Cuttemwha and Neawau and to talk with our trading People and desired I would write to my freinds to treat them kindly I then wrote the following letter to the Committee of Frederick

GENTLEMEN—You will receive this by Major Connolly with him three of the Shawanese Cheifs purpose going to Winchester in Order to see their freinds and to talk with some of our Tradeing people if the Hostages should not yet have Arrived I would beg leave to Recommend that an Express be immediately dispatched to Doctor Walkers to bring them up as the treatment these Indians receive will be taken particular Notice of as well by them as the Whole Nation I beg the Attention of the Committee on this Occasion I am &c

at 5 o'Clock this afternoon I sett off from Fort Pitt with Simon Girty an Interpreter encamped ten Miles below on the River Bank

19th July sett off before Sunrise Crossed Big Beaver Creek near the Mouth travelled about 45 Miles this day the Course nearly West

20th Started very Early met Garret Pendergrass[69] about 9 o'Clock who informed us that he left the Delaware Towns two days before that the Delawares were

---

[69] See the affidavit of Pendergrass in *Virginia Magazine of History and Biography*, xiii, p. 423. Garret Pendergrass settled at Harrodsburgh in Kentucky, and in 1776 was commissioned to go with James Harrod on a mission to the Indian towns. In March 28, 1777, he was killed and scalped by prowling savages within sight of the Harrodsburgh fort.—ED.

just returned from the Wiandots Towns where they had been at a Great Council with the French and English Officer and the Wyandots that Monsuer Baubee[70] and the English Officer told them to be upon their Gaurd that the White People intended to strike them very soon that tho' their fathers the French were thrown down the last War by the English they were now got up again and much Stronger than ever and would Assist their Childeren (the Indians) as they formerly did about two days after met two Delaware Squas who upon interrogations gave the same Account travelled about forty Miles this day and encamped on a Small run

21st July started very Early in the Morning at one O'Clock arrived at the Moravian Indian Town

---

[70] Duperon Baby (called by the English Baubee) belonged to a prominent Canadian family, one branch of which had established itself in trade at Detroit, before the English conquest. After that event, Baby declined the oath of allegiance, and desired to retire to France. Having changed his opinion, he became a loyal British subject, and during Pontiac's conspiracy furnished much assistance to the English garrison. His influence with the Indians was large, and during the Revolution and succeeding Indian wars the Detroit commandants utilized it for the British cause. Baby was commissioned colonel of militia and deputy Indian agent, with a large salary, being also given a considerable grant of land. He attended all Indian councils, but seldom personally went on the warpath, although he is said to have commanded the Detroit militia in the campaign against Wayne (1794). Marrying Susanne Reaume, he had a considerable family. One daughter married Col. William Caldwell, and a daughter by an Indian mother married Blue Jacket. His son James became prominent in British councils, and served in the War of 1812-15. Upon surrender of Detroit to the Americans (1796), the Baby family settled in the neighborhood of Windsor, Ont. Col. Duperon Baby died about the time of this removal.—Ed.

Examined the Minister (a Dutchman)[71] concerning the Council lately held with the Indians by the French who Confirmed the Accounts before related six Miles from the Moravian Town Passed a Small Delaware Town a Delaware Man rode with us to New Comers Town[72] where we Encamped having travelled about 30 Miles

22ᵈ July set off Early in the Morning for Koshocktin the Cheif Town of the Delawares Passed White Eyes' Town about 10 o'Clock Arrived at Koshocktin at 1 O'Clock taken to the Council

---

[71] Probably Wood was now at Schönbrunn, some three miles southeast of New Philadelphia, in Tuscarawas County, Ohio. This was built in 1772 by mission Indians, largely of the Delaware tribe, but was deserted in 1777. Reoccupied in 1779, it was soon abandoned for New Schönbrunn, on the west bank of Tuscarawas River. Another Moravian village, known as Gnadenhütten (tents of grace) was on the site of the present Ohio town of that name. The senior missionary in charge was David Zeisberger. Born in Moravia in 1721, his parents emigrated to Saxony when he was five years of age, and later (1736) to Georgia, where their son followed them in 1740. After three years of work among the Creek Indians, Zeisberger was sent to Pennsylvania, where at Bethlehem he studied Indian languages, fitting for his future work. He passed some years among the Iroquois, but finally became identified with the Delawares. Their migration to the Ohio Valley (1771–72) was arranged by him, and he remained with his converts in the vicissitudes of their fate, until his death in 1808 at Goshen, Ohio. During the Revolution he attempted to maintain neutrality, but aided the commandant at Pittsburgh with frequent and important information.—Ed.

[72] Newcomerstown was on the north bank of the Tuscarawas, within the limits of the present town of that name in Tuscarawas County. It was the chief town of the Delawares after their removal to the Muskingum. The small town between that and Gnadenhütten may have been Salem, a third Moravian town, near the present village of that name.—Ed.

House[73] found Many of the Indians drunk and King New Comer a Sleep[74] waked the King at Dark and Delivered the following speech to him in the Presence of Wingenum[75] Young Killbuck and a Number of other Warriours *Brothers the Delawares* your Elder Brothers in Virginia in their Great Council have Appointed me to come to this Place in Order to Assure you that their hearts are good towards you that they are desirous of brightning the Antient Chain of Freindship between you and them and for which they have Appointed Commissioners to meet you and the other Nations in a General Council at Fort Pitt in [blank in MS.] days from this time when they will be glad to meet the Cheifs of your Nation and will use their best Endeavours to give you a hearty Welcome

Brothers I have heard with great Concern that

---

[73] Coshocton (Indian name Goschachgunk) lay in the forks of the Muskingum and Tuscarawas on the north side of the latter stream. It was built about 1775 and was composed of log-houses and a large council-house ranged along a regular street, and forming a considerable village. It was the chief town of the Turtle clan of the Delawares, and the capital of the tribe until its destruction by Brodhead in 1781. White Eyes's Town lay on a plain some ten miles south of the Tuscarawas, and east of Coshocton.—ED.

[74] Newcomer (or Netawatwes) was principal chief of the Delawares, succeeding Beaver in that office about 1772. He had formerly dwelt on the Susquehanna, and signed the treaty of Conestoga in 1718. Upon his removal to the Ohio country, he lived first on the Cuyahoga, settling later upon the Tuscarawas, near the site of the present town named for him. The aged chief died at Pittsburgh in 1776, while attending a treaty at that place.—ED.

[75] Wingenund was an important Delaware chief, later hostile to the Americans. About 1778 he removed his village to the Sandusky, where he assisted in the torture of Col. William Crawford in 1782.—ED.

you have lately been in Council with the French and Wyandots and that you have received a Speech from the French and a belt and String of Black Wampum as there has long subsisted the Greatest Freindship between you and us I desire and insist that you will make me Acquainted with any thing which may have been said to you by the French or any others to the Prejudice of your Elder Brothers of Virginia *A String of White Wampum*

23ᵈ of July the King and Cheifs of the Delawares met in the Council House and delivered the following Answer to my Speech of Yesterday *Brothers the Bigknife* your Brothers the Delawares are very thankful to you for your good talk to them Yesterday and are glad to find their Brothers hearts are good towards them and that they will be joyfull in meeting them at the time and place you Mention *Brother* in Order to Convince our Elder Brothers of Virginia that we desire to live in freindship with them I now deliver you this Belt and String they were sent to us by an English Man and French Man at Fort Detroit with a Message that the People of Virginia were determined to strike us that they would come upon us two different Ways the one by the Way of the Lakes and the other by the Ohio and that the Virginians were determined to drive us off and to take our Lands that we must be constantly on our Gaurd and not to give any Credit to whatever you said as you were a people not to be depended upon that the Virginians would invite Us to a treaty but we must not go at any rate and to take particular Notice of the Advice they gave which proceeded from Motives of real

Freindship and nothing else *Delivers the Belt and String*

I then hired a Man to go with me to the Seneca Towns set off in a hard rain passed thro' a Town of the Muncys and made them Acquainted with my business kept up White Womans Creek Crossing it Six times and Corcosan Creek once lodged at Mohickins old Town now Inhabited by Delawares[76] travelled about 38 Miles this day the Course nearly West

24th July set off very early in the Morning travelled very Constant till twelve O'Clock when we Arrived at Indian Nicholas's and then Proceeded on till Night and encamped near a Small run rain all Night Travelled about 45 Miles the same Course as Yesterday

25th set out very early in the Morning rode Constant till 5 o'Clock in the afternoon when we Arrived at the Seneca Town[77] where we found Logan The Snake the Big Appletree with Several of the Min-

---

[76] White Woman's Creek, now known as Walhonding, was so named from Mary Harris, a captive who adopted Indian ways, and lived in this vicinity as early as 1751. See Darlington, *Christopher Gist's Journals* (Pittsburgh, 1893), pp. 41, 114.

The Munsee town here noted is shown on a map in Hector St. John de Crèvecœur, *Lettres d'un Cultivateur Americain* (Paris, 1787), iii, p. 413. It was on the north bank of White Woman's Creek, just above Killbuck's Creek. Corcosan Creek is noted on this same map as Caucussing, now known as Mohican River from the town here noted by Wood. The town lay on the west bank where the stream joins the Walhonding.—Ed.

[77] This town has usually been identified with Pluggy's Town, but Wood visited that place later. From the courses and distances travelled it would appear to be the Mingo or Seneca town where Logan in 1778 was found by Simon Kenton; it

goes who were lately Prisoners at Fort Pitt they all
Appeared to be Prety Much in Liquor and very inquisitive
to know my Business called them together
and made the same speech to them which I had before
made to the Delawares they made no other Answer
but they would Acquaint the rest of their Nation
with what I had said and discovered that the Indians
were very Angry Many of them Painted themselves
black we Encamped near the Town about ten
O'Clock at Night one of the Indians came and
Stamped upon my head as I lay a Sleep waked
and saw several Indians with Knives and Tomhawks
a Squaw informed us privately that they intended
to kill us advised us to hide ourselves in the
Woods which we did till Morning when we returned
again into the Town Logan repeated in Plain English
the Manner in which the People of Virginia had
killed his Mother Sister and all his Relations during
which he wept and Sung Alternately[78] and concluded
with telling me the Revenge he had taken he then
told me that several of the Mingoes who were long
Prisoners at Fort Pitt[79] wanted to kill us and asked

---

was situated on the trail between Wapatomica and upper
Sandusky, in what is now Hardin County, Ohio. See Draper
MSS., 2BB3.—ED.

[78] This statement that Logan could repeat his wrongs in
"plain English" is interesting in view of the discussion over
the authorship of his famous speech. See *Dunmore's War*,
p. 305, note 21, and references therein cited.—ED.

[79] These were the captives taken by Dunmore after the
treaty of Camp Charlotte, in which the Mingo refused to acquiesce.
See *Ibid*, p. 303. They were kept at Fort Pitt during
the winter of 1774–75, but in the spring were permitted to
escape.—ED.

me whether I was affraid to which I answered I was not that we were two lone Men where [who were] sent to deliver a message to them which we had done that we were in their Power and had no way to defend ourselves that they must kill us if they thought proper to which he replied that we should not be hurt

26th July at 9 O'Clock in the Morning hired two fresh horses and set off for the Wyandot Towns travelled very fast and Constant till 7 O'Clock in the Evening when we Arrived at the Town sent off Runners for the Cheifs who were distant about twenty Miles

27th July at One O'Clock the Wyandots sent to my Camp to Inform me the Cheifs were Arrived and ready at their Council House to hear what I had to say to them and that two of the Tawaas[80] were there and would be ready to Carry my speech to their Nation went to the Council House and delivered the following Speech to the Wyandots and Tawaas

Brothers the Wyandots and Tawaas your Brothers of Virginia in their great Council desirous of brightning the Chain of Freindship between you and them have Appointed Commissioners to meet the Cheifs of the different Nations of Indians on the Ohio and Lakes at Fort Pitt in forty six days from this time and have ordered me to come to this place to Assure you that their Hearts are good towards you and that they hope to agree upon a peace with all the Indians so their Childeren and ours may hereafter live in the Greatest Freindship to give you a kind Invitation to

---

[80] This council occurred at Upper Sandusky. For the Tawaas (Ottawa) see *Dunmore's War*, p. 273, note 90.—ED.

their Council fire and that they will Endeavor to give you a hearty welcome *Brothers* It is with Great Concern I have lately heard that some people who I consider to be enemies as well to you as to us have endeavoured to make your Nations believe that the People of Virginia intended to strike you this you may be Assured is the Greatest falsity as I can with truth assure you that they desire to live in Strict Freindship with all Indians while they continue peaceable with us

Brothers the Tawaas It is with great pleasure I take the Opportunity in the name of my Countrymen to return you thanks for the kind Treatment given by your Nation to one of our young Brothers who was delivered into your hands Last Summer by the Shawanese and to Assure you that if any of your people should ever fall into our hands they will meet with the same freindly treatment[81] *A String of White Wampum Each*

The War Post then Answered *Brother the Big Knife* We have heard what you have said and desire time till to Morrow afternoon to consider it when we will meet you again in the Council house

In the afternoon War Post and five or six other Indians came to my Camp they said they were come to talk with me as freinds that they always Understood that the English had but one King who lived over the Great Water that they were Much Surprized to hear that we were at War with ourselves and that there had been several Engagements at Boston in which

---

[81] This refers to Ezekiel (misprinted Ephraim) Field, for whose capture see *Ibid*, pp. 113, 114, note 65.—ED.

a great Number of Men were killed on both sides
that as he had been told many different Stories they
would be glad to know the Cause of the dispute or
whether we Expected or desired their Assistance I
then began and gave them a true and Just Account
from the beginning of the disputes with Great Britain
and Assured them that we did not stand in need of
or desire any Assistance from them or any other Nation but that we wished them to Continue in peace
and freindliness with us by Observing a Strict neutrality as we had not the least doubt that all differences between ourselves would be soon Accomo-
dated at the same time I made them Acquainted with
the great Unanimity among the Americans and that
they were now become so strong as not to fear any
power on the face of the Earth In this Conversation
I discovered that the Huron Indians had been led to
beleive that the People of Virginia were a different
and distinct Nation from the other Colonies and that
by going to War with us they need not fear the Interposition of the other Colonies this I think I Effectually removed by making them Acquainted with the
Proceedings of the Continental Congress and that the
Colonies were bound and Obliged to defend each
other against Attacks from Whatever Quarter they
might come these Questions were likewise put to me
at other times by the Shawanese Delawares Mingoes
and Tawaas and Answered in the same Manner

28th July went to the Council house at two
O'Clock agreable to the Appointment of the Wyandots when Rotunda or the War Post in the Presence
of Coronyatta Surrahawa Aughunta and other War-

riors of the Wyandots, and Ninnis and Mangagata of the Tawaas delivered the following Answer to my speech of Yesterday *Brother the Bigknife* you tell us you were sent to our Towns by the Great Men of Virginia to let us know that there is now a large Council fire kindling at Fort Pitt that it would be ready in forty six days and we should hear there every thing that was good *Brother* we have listned to what you have said with great Attention and Considered it well we think it is good and will immediately send it Over the Lakes to our Cheifs[82] and will be ruled by them in our determinations *Brother* I have nothing farther to say but that it is always a Custom with us that Whatever News we hear we immediately send it to our head Men as we shall on this Occasion. after delivering the Answer Rotunda told me that he heard the People of Virginia were now building a Fort on Kentucke and intended to drive off all the Indians and take Possession of their Lands I told him that I never heard of any Fort being built on Kentucke but that our People were settling very fast in that Country which they had an Undoubted right to do the whole Country to the Eastward of the Ohio as low down as the Cherokee River was purchased from the Six Nations at the Treaty at Fort Stanwix and that since which the People of Virginia had purchased the Pretended right of the Cherokees that we Should be able to make them sensible of this at the Treaty to be held at Fort Pitt and

---

[82] The chief settlements of the Huron or Wyandot were opposite Detroit, north of Lake Erie. It was proposed to consult these chiefs before coming to a decision.—ED.

that they might rest Assured that we had no thoughts of encroaching any farther than we had already purchased and honestly paid for he then enquired after news and desired to know whether we intended to take Fort Detroit from the Regulars this I told them I knew not but beleived the Americans looked upon it to be a place of no Consequence to them and that they would not Concern with it here I took an Opportunity of telling them that we had already taken Tyconderoga and Crown Point without any loss and that we had beaten the Regulars in every Engagement with very Considerable loss on their sides and very inconsiderable on ours I then told him I was well Acquainted with the Steps taken by the Officer Commanding at Fort D'Troit and Monsieur Baubee to prejudice them against the Americans in General and Virginia in particular I then produced the Belt and String delivered to me by the Delawares and asked him if he knew them here they all appeared to be much Surprised but Acknowledged that they did upon which I proceeded to repeat what was said when they were delivered all of which they Acknowledged Except that the French were concerned in it they said Monsieur Baubee was present but that he did not interfere but added that the Englishmen told them that the Virginians would take the whole Country if they did not all join together against them I told War Post that I was well Acquainted with the whole Matter that I had got it out at the different Towns by degrees first from the Squaws and then from the Men he then desired me to give him a Copy of the Speech which I made in the Council Yesterday that no part of it might be forgot   this I readily complied with and we parted in the most freindly Manner[88]

---

[88] John Dodge, a Connecticut trader at the Sandusky village, gave the following additional particulars of Wood's mission to the Wyandot towns: "In July, 1775, Captain James Woods called at my house, on his way to the different Indian towns, where he was going to invite them, in the name of the Congress, to a treaty to be held at Fort Pitt the ensuing fall; I attended him to their villages, and the savages promised him they would be there. Captain Woods also invited me to go with the Indians to the treaty, as they were in want of an interpreter, which I readily agreed to. Soon after the departure of Captain Woods, the Commander of Fort Detroit sent for the savages in and about Sandusky, and told them that he heard they were invited by the Americans to a treaty at Pittsburgh, which they told him was true; on which he delivered them a talk to the following purport: 'That he was their father, and as such he would advise them as his own children; that the Colonists, who were to meet them at Pittsburgh, were a bad people; that by the indulgence of their Protector, they had grown a numerous and saucy people; that the Great King, not thinking they would have the assurance to oppose his just laws, had kept but a few troops in America for some years past; that those men, being ignorant of their incapacity to go through with what they intend, propose to cut off the regulars in this country, and then you Indians, and have all America to themselves; and all they want is, under the shew of friendship to get you into their hands as hostages, and there hold you, till your nations shall comply with their terms, which if they refuse, you will all be massacred. Therefore, do not go by any means; but if you will join me, and keep them at bay a little, while the King, our father will send large fleets and armies to our assistance, and we will soon subdue them, and have their plantations to ourselves.'

This talk so dismayed the Indians, that they came to me, and said they would not go to the treaty, at the same time telling me what the Governor of Detroit had said to them. On this Mr. James Heron and myself, having the cause of our country at heart, asserted that what the Governor had said was false, and told them that the Colonists would not hurt a hair of their heads; and if they would go to the treaty, that I, with Mr. Heron, would be security, and pledge our property to the amount of 4000 l. for their safe return. This, with the arrival of Mr. Richard Butler with fresh invitations, induced some of them to go with me to the treaty."—Almon's *Remembrancer*, viii, p. 73.—ED.

I then sent Messages by the Tawaas to the Tawixtawees, Picks and other Nations inhabiting the Mimamis and Wabash Rivers with Invitations to meet at the Treaty[84]

29th July set off from the Wyandots Town for Pluggys Town travelled very fast and Constant Eight hours most of the Way thro' extensive Plains and Meadows Course South East

30th Started before sun rise travelled down the Scioto River till twelve O'Clock when we Arrived at the Town found Pluggy[85] was from home and all the Indians drunk and very troublesome left a String of Wampum and Speech for Pluggy purchased some dried Meat from an Indian and then set off for the big salt Licks[86] where I Arrived at Dark found five Seneca Hunters incamped and an old Squaw in a Cabbin where we took up our Lodging

31st July left the Salt Licks at 7 O'Clock in the Morning in Company with a Seneca Man and Woman who were going to the Shawanese Towns travelled Eight and a half Hours very Constant when

---

[84] Twigtwee (Tawixtawee) was the English term for the Miami Indians, a large tribe of Algonquian stock, who for the most part were living along the Wabash and Maumee rivers. They had chiefly been in the French interest before 1763, but then became English partisans, hostile to the American colonists. For the Picts see *ante*, note 30.—ED.

[85] Pluggy was a Mohawk, who with a band of unorganized, undisciplined followers had migrated westward about 1772 and settled upon the present site of Delaware, Ohio. He was in the French and Indian War, and counselled with Dunmore at Fort Pitt, September, 1774. In a raid into Kentucky in December, 1776, Pluggy was killed during an attack on McClelland's Station.—ED.

[86] This was the town raided by Crawford in October, 1774. See *Dunmore's War*, p. 304, note 17.—ED.

TREATY WITH WESTERN INDIANS 57

we Arrived at the Shawanese Towns[87] where I spoke to Kishanosity or the Hardman desired him to call the Cheifs of the different Towns together as soon as Possible that I had something to say to them from the Great Council of Virginia the Hardman[88] then informed me that Chenusaw had returned home the night before and that he had brought the most alarming Accounts from Virginia (viz') that the People of Virginia were all determined upon War with the Indians except the Governor who was for peace but was obliged to fly on board of a ship to save his own life that the hostages found they were to be made Slaves of and sent to some other Country that the White People were all preparing for War and that they shewed him many Indian scalps among which Cuttemwha knew his Brothers that the Hostages determined if Possible to make their Escape and Accordingly sett off in the Night all of them together that the next day he being behind the other two at some distance was seized by three Men that he heard them determine to kill him on which one of them proceeded to Load his Gun while the other two held him by the Arms that before the Man loaded the Gun he found Means to disengage himself and made his Escape leaving his Gun and every thing also that he soon after heard Several Guns and was possitive that Cuttemwha and Neawau were both killed as he had been

---

[87] The principal Shawnee towns were located in the Scioto Valley, between the present Chillicothe and Circleville. See *Ibid.*, pp. 290, 292, 301, notes 5, 7, 14.—ED.

[88] See description of a visit to Hardman in 1773 by Rev. David Jones, *Journal of Two Visits to west side of Ohio* (N. Y., 1866 reprint), p. 52.—ED.

Sixty days travelling and had heard nothing of them I told Kishanosity that most of what Chenusaw had informed him was false and that I would be glad he would send for him which he did as soon as he came I explained the whole Matter to him and a Number of other Indians and Informed them that Cuttemwha and Neawau were both well and on the Road and that they were bringing his Cloaths and every thing which he had left behind him and that it was very unlucky for him he did not turn back as the others had done to have got a horse and Saddle to ride home as they had several of the Indians were employed in Conjuring the whole night during which they kept up a Constant howling like Wolves till day light

1st August Kishanosity sent me word he had sent for the Cheifs of the other Towns and that they would meet me in the Council house to Morrow Morning Employed ourselves the remaining part of the day in enquiries of the Squaws concerning the Speeches and belts sent to the Shawanese by the French at Fort D'Troit who all gave the same Accounts we had before heard with this addition that the Picts and Tawixtawees had Accepted the Belts but that the Shawanese had dug a hole in the Ground and buried them never to rise again

2d August at 10 o'Clock a runner came and Informed me the Cheifs were Assembled in the Council House ready to receive me upon which I went and was received in the most freindly manner when I delivered the following speech to Kishanosity in the Presence of the Shade and Snake the Milkman

Shawanese Ben and many other Cheifs and Warriors *Brothers the Shawaneses* your Elder Brothers of Virginia in their great Council have appointed me with five others to meet all the Cheifs of the different Nations of Indians on the Ohio and Lakes in forty one days from this time at Fort Pitt in Order to Brighten the Chain of Freindship between them and the People of Virginia and have ordered me to come to this Place to assure you that their Hearts are good towards you and that they will be glad to meet the Cheifs of your Nation fully to Confirm the Peace agreed upon last fall between Lord Dunmore and the Shawanese and Expect you will be fully prepared to Comply with your part of the Conditions at that time I am very Glad to see your Brother Chenusaw is returned safe he left us without any reason that we know of but Imagine it must be Owing to some Mistake or other as soon as we found he was gone we sent many People on Horseback with written papers directing all our people to treat him kindly so that he might return to you in Safety your Brothers Cuttemwha and Neawau are well they are now on the way and you may depend will be safely brought to the Treaty Cuttemwha desired me to tell you to be Strong and to come at the time I appoint and to bring some of your wise Women along with you *A String of White Wampum*

after delivering the Speech I called for Chenusaw but was Informed he was ashamed to Appear I then at their Desire Explained the nature of the dispute with Lord Dunmore and Convinced them that Chenusaw had not told them the truth and also Explained

to them the dispute with Great Britain in the same
Manner which I had before done to the Wyandots
and other Nations of Indians the Hardman then
made the following Answer to my Speech

Brother the Big knife I am very thankful as well
as all my freinds here present for your good speech
delivered to us at our Council fire It gives us great
Pleasure to think that our Brothers the big knife have
not forgot us and that we shall have an Opportunity
of talking to them in Freinship at the time you now
Mention we are much Oblidged to our Brothers of
Virginia for their Care in directing all their People
to let our Brother Chenusaw come to us without receiveing any hurt his coming away in the Manner
he did proceeded from Mistake in not Understanding
your Language we are fully Satisfied with what you
have told us and hope you'll not think hard of us for
his bad behaviour after which Kishanosity and other
Cheifs enquired after News whether a great Many of
our Young Men were not going to Boston to War
against the English Red Coats and if we had not several Engagements with them to which I answered that
but few Men were to go from Virginia as there were
a great Sufficiency of Men in New England to Man-
age all the Regular Troops in America or which they
were Able to send and as for the Engagements there
had been several in all of which we had beatten them
with great loss on their side and very small on Ours
but that we were in daily Expectation of all differences being setled between the two Countries to the
Satisfaction of both. The Shade then Informed me
that he had Just returned from the Miami River that

he met Catfish and a Number of other Delawares on
the Ohio with many things which they had Robbed
the Inhabitants of on the Great Kanhawa that he
gave me this Information least his Brothers the Big
knife should blame the Shawanese for it Kishanosity
then Complained of the Encroachments of the Virginians he said they were now settling in Great Numbers in the Midst of their Hunting Grounds on the
Kentucke River and that many of our people Crossed
the Ohio killed and drove off their Game he then
Asked my Advice whether they should go and talk
to the People on Kentucke about it to which I replied
that I thought it would be very Improper least some
of our bad people might do them an Injury but advised them to let the Matter alone till the Treaty
when I made no doubt but we should be able to make
them sensible that we had already purchased the
Lands on Kentucke River from the Six Nations at
the Treaty of Fort Stanwix and as to our Hunters
Crossing the River and Killing the Game we should
do every thing in our power to prevent it in future
he then desired me to beg their brothers the big knife
not to listen to any bad stories which they might hear
as he had great reason to Beleive that David Duncan[89] would make many false reports that he had
been talking a Great deal to the foolish Women and

---

[89] David Duncan was an important Pennsylvania trader in the Indian country in the early Revolution. His home was at Shippensburgh, and at the outbreak of Dunmore's War he was rescued by White Eyes from danger of death. In the later years of the Revolution he made his home in Westmoreland County, and acted as contractor for military supplies at Fort Pitt.—ED.

paid no regard to what the Men said to him I then told him that I had been Informed that the Commanding Officer at Fort De Troit and Monseiur Baubee had sent a Belt and String of Black Wampum to their Nation with a Speech that the people of Virginia Intended to drive them off and to take their Lands recommending them and the other Nations to Join together in Order to Oppose them and at the same time advised them not to Listen to any thing which might be said to them by the Virginians that they were a people not to be depended upon all of which the Shawanese Acknowledged they said that whatever they had heard or received from them they had Dug a hole in the Ground and Buried them never to rise again I was then Informed by a Mohicon Indian[90] who spoke good English that he had Just Returned from Kacayuga where he saw a Greater Number of Indians than he had ever seen before and that

---

[90] The Mahican (Mohegan) Indians, a large branch of the Algonquian stock, were encountered by the whites in Connecticut and on the Hudson River. The western division were frequently in alliance with the Iroquois, and after selling their lands to the Dutch (about 1680), roamed throughout the Western country. The French called them Loups (Wolves), from one of their clan totems, and they had a village on the Detroit River before the building of the French fort at that place (1701). Gradually they drew toward the Delawares, with whom they were cognate, and about 1746 a considerable band of Mahican settled in Wyoming Valley, Pennsylvania. Thence they removed with the Delawares to the Ohio region, and settled near them, although in separate villages. After the Revolution, this western branch became amalgamated with the Delawares. The eastern branch remained in Connecticut until after the Revolution, some of them serving in the Continental armies. The Christianized portion of the tribe, under Samson Occam, became part of the Brothertown Indians, who removed first to New York and finally to Wisconsin.—ED.

we might Expect Warmer Work this fall than had ever happened before I was likewise Informed by James Bavard a Trader in the Shawanese Towns that the Indians were Constantly Counseling and that the Women all seemed very uneasy in Expectations that there would be War I then set off from the Shawanese Towns on my return Called at the Kiocopo[91] Town and then proceeded twenty Miles and Encamped

3ᵈ August sett off before sun rise rode hard and Constant til Seven O Clock in the Evening met a Shawanese Man who Informed me that one of their Nation was lately Killed on Kentucke River and that the white People said it was done by the Southern Indians Travelled about Forty Miles and Encamped rains hard all Night

4ᵗʰ August rains hard set off early Travelled about thirty Eight Miles stopped at a Delaware Womans Cabbin where I staid all night nothing to eat the two days past but Blackberry's

5ᵗʰ August set off in a hard rain very Early Travelled four Hours when I arrived at Captain White Eyes's Purchased some Meat from an Indian set off for New Comers Town at which I staid two Hours proceeded to the Lower Moravian Town[92]

---

[91] Kiscapoo (Kiskapookee) was the settlement of the Shawnee clan by that name. At this time it was located about a mile west of the Scioto, in the upper part of the present Pickaway County, Ohio (see accompanying Crèvecœur map). In 1773 Richard Butler had a trading house at this town, and somewhat earlier there was born here the famous Shawnee chief Tecumseh. This clan of Shawnee were especially hostile to American colonists.—Ed.

[92] This was Gnadenhütten, for which see *ante*, p. 45, note 71.—Ed.

where we Arrived at Dark taken to the Cabbin of an Indian and Hospitably Entertained

6th August (Sunday) went to Church with the Indians at which were present about One hundred and fifty of them, who all Behaved with the Greatest Decency and Decorum the Minister who resides at this Town is a German of the Moravian Sect has Lived with them several Years has Acquired their Language and taught most of them the English and German he prayed in the Delaware Language Preached in the English and sung Psalms in the German in which the Indians Joined and Performed that part of Divine Service in a Manner really Inimitable the Church is a Decent Square Log Building with Plank floars and Benches Ornamented with Several Pieces of German Scripture Paintings has a Small Cupola with a Bell and a very Indifferent Spinnet[93] on which an Indian played the remaining part of the day employed in Hunting for our Horses Unsuccessfully

8th August at two O'Clock in the afternoon found our Horses and Immediately set off Travelled about Twenty Miles and Encamped

9th August set off early in the Morning travelled about forty five Miles and encamped at dark

10th August my Horse failed came to an Indian Hunting Camp where I hired an Horse of an Indian Woman and left mine in her Care to be brought to Fort Pitt in Ten Days Travelled about forty five

---

[93] Possibly the first musical instrument of this sort ever used in Ohio.—ED.

Miles when I arrived at Mr John Gibsons[94] where I staid all Night

11th August   sett off after Breakfast and Arrived Fort Pitt about 3 oClock in the afternoon where I found several Senecas who had Just come from a Treaty which had been held at Niagara by Guy Johnston[95]   I Interrogated them but found that they had got their Lesson not to make any Discovery's   they said that the Indian Agent told them to lie still and not to Concern with the Dispute between the People of Great Britian and America[96]

12th August   I sett off from Fort Pitt for Win-

---

[94] Gibson's trading house was situated at Logstown; see *ante*, p. 26, note 52.—ED.

[95] Guy Johnson was nephew and son-in-law of Sir William Johnson, whom he succeeded in the Indian superintendency on the latter's death in 1774. Born in Ireland in 1740, he came early to America, led provincial troops in the French and Indian War, and possessed a fine estate known as Guy Park, in New York state. A professed Loyalist, he fled to Canada at the beginning of the Revolution, where he assisted with his Indian allies in the defense of that province. During the winter of 1775-76 he visited England, coming again to New York in August, 1776. He was later in Canada, retaining his Indian superintendency until 1783. He died in London, 1788. Johnson was not present at a treaty at Niagara in the summer of 1775. Wood was misinformed in regard to his presence at this place. For a full account of Johnson's movements during the summer of 1775, see his letter to Dartmouth in *N. Y. Colon. Docs.*, viii, pp. 635-637. See also the letter of Col. Adam Stephen in *Amer. Archives*, 4th series, iii, pp. 777, 778, wherein he says that the tribes living on the Allegheny had been to a treaty at Niagara, and others to Caughnawaga, near Montreal, to meet Guy Johnson.—ED.

[96] At the Oswego conference in May, 1775, Guy Johnson urged neutrality upon the western portions of the Iroquois tribesmen; but in July, he received orders from Dartmouth to induce the Six Nations to take up the hatchet against the rebellious colonists.—*N. Y. Colon. Docs.*, viii, p. 596.—ED.

chester where I Arrived in five days the Committee recommended that I would send off an Express to the Convention at Richmond who were still sitting which I did the next Morning with the following Letter Directed to the Hoñble Peyton Randolph Esquire.[97]

Sir—I am just now returned from my Expedition to the Indian Towns and have Inclosed you Extracts from my Journal which Contains every Material Occurance that happened Dureing my tour through the Nations of Shawanese Delawares Senicas and Wiandots the Cheifs of which have Engaged to Attend the Treaty at Fort Pitt the 10th of the next Month from every discovery I was able to make the Indians are forming a General Confederacy against the Colony having been led to beleive that we are a people Quite different and distinct from the other Colonies I Intend myself the Honor of Waiting on the Convention if they should not rise before the 25th in Order to give them every Information in my power I wou'd beg leave to make an Observation that there is no Garrison at Fort Pitt that the Inhabitants in the Neighbourhood of it are in the most defenceless situation and that there will be in my Opinion at least five

---

[97] Peyton Randolph (1721–75) was president of the Virginia convention, as well as president of the first Continental Congress. He died while in attendance on the second Congress in October, 1775. A life-long patriot, he had while King's attorney for the colony of Virginia resisted what was considered the usurpation of Governor Dinwiddie. He was prominent in opposition to the Stamp Act, and chairman of the first committee of correspondence. His death was a loss to the American cause.—Ed.

Peyton Randolph

After the painting in Independence Hall, Philadelphia

hundred Indians at the Treaty[98] I have the Honor to be &c

September 20th 1775

The following is the Information given by the Doctor a Mohawk who was sent to Invite the Six Nation People on the Ohio to a Treaty at Pittsburgh on the part of Virginia from the Upper Town Six Cheifs will Attend but he is not Certain what Number will be down from thence in the whole but they may be Expected in two or three days that they designed to meet at the White Mingos house and would come down from thence in a body Simon Girty who interprets for the Doctor and who delivered the invitation speech to him desired him to endeavour to discover the Intentions of the Indians he was sent to whether the French were tampering with them and what proposals were made by them which he Undertook to do on a promise of Secresy and reports that the Commanding Officer at Niagara[99] and Guy Johnson had invited them the Senecas to a Treaty at Niagara where he put them in mind of their Antient

---

[98] The Virginia convention recognized the services of James Wood by passing a resolution (Jan. 6, 1776) to the effect that having been two months on the mission entrusted to him by the house of burgesses, and having had his life endangered, by the exercise of all his abilities he had engaged the chiefs to attend the treaty; and because of the difficulties and dangers he had undergone, was accordingly voted an honorarium of £250.—*Amer. Archives*, 4th series, iv, pp. 110, 111.—ED.

[99] The commandant at Niagara was Col. John Caldwell, who came to America in 1755 with the 7th Infantry. He was stationed at Fort Niagara from 1774 to November, 1776 when he retired from the army. His name among the Indians was Oguhaenjes.—ED.

Freindship with their Father the French telling them that their Hands were then each made of Silver and would never be injured by Rust he told them they would probably soon be called to a Treaty at Fort Pitt but that they ought not to go to it nor regard anything the Bigknife might say to them for tho he had a very smooth Oily Tongue his Heart was not good that he would soon want to Cross the Great River which is their Line perhaps at Kanhawa or at Pittsburgh on pretence of keeping a Store at De Troit or Cayahoga[1] or some other place and would tell them they would then get Goods very Cheap but they should not beleive him he only wanted to deceive them and take their Lands from them which they knew was now only a small strip that they should on no Account allow him to Cross the Big River for if they did they would surely be undone they put them in Mind of the Treaty they had lately been at at Fort Pitt[2] where the big knife gave them very good Words but they were from the Lips only and not from the Heart, which they might be Sensible of, for when they were going away he gave them little or no Goods, and when they Asked for Powder to hunt with on their way home, they got only one Double Handful, and the reason he would give them no more was, that he wanted it himself to use it against them, that they are now fighting with the Great King over

---

[1] Cuyahoga River, whose mouth is the site of Cleveland, was a well-known rendezvous of the Ottawa, who had a village upon its banks. It was also a considerable trading station, frequented by many tribesmen.—ED.

[2] Referring to Connolly's treaty in June; for which see *ante*, p. 19.—ED.

the Water, from whom they get all their Powder, that they have not more than will serve him for Three Years, and then they must submit as Neither Powder or Cloaths can be made in this Country, but that they have Plenty of both and if they would keep hold of the Chain of Freindship which their Father put into their hands, they would not want. they then gave them a Keg of Powder & Lead in Proportion, and some Goods, they were desired if the Bigknife People should Cross the Great River to send off their head Men to them and tell them to go back to their Country, they should tell them so three times and if they would not Stop nor go back they then should send to him (the Command^g officer at Niagara) and he would speak to them and if they would not pay any regard to what he said he would gather all his People and fight them they must not be Allowed to Spoil this great Island which the good Spirit had allowed for them it might happen that he might be thrown down in the Struggle but if he fell they must fall with him for the Big knife had been pushing them back for a long time and would not rest till he had got all this Country but now he and they were so linked together they would be never Separated but must stand or fall together that their father had long ago sent his Heart to them in a Belt but they did not mind it but rose up with the English and threw him down and thought they had killed him but he was only knocked down and not killed and kept his Eyes Open all the time determined to rise again whenever his Children should be imposed upon that they were now imposed upon by the English for which Reason he had got on his feet again and would bring his Ships and fight them on the Sea Co[a]st and they ought to send out their People and kill them where ever they could find them and between them they would soon root them out and get Satisfaction for all their Injuries

---

September 24th   James Rogers an Adopted Shawanese informs the Commissioners that last summer several Messages were received by the Shawanese from the Chipeways Tawaas Wyandots and the French and English at De Troit   the design of them was to know if the Shawanese and Virginians had made a firm peace to diswade them from it and threatning to strike them if they did as they intended to strike the Virginians   that a Message had been sent from the Towns after the Cornstalk when on his way to this place desiring him and the Young Men to return for they would be cutt off at the Fort   the Cornstalk would not go back but advised the Young Men to it they would not return without him and are all coming on   that he is not Acquainted with the disposition of the six Nations but he has heard they have scolded the Chipeways and Tawaas   that we may Judge of the Shawanese by this Circumstance if they are Anxious to hurry the Business over and get soon away their designs are not good   his information about the Six Nations he got from some Shawanese who had been in their Country and lately returned   the purport of the speech sent by them to the Chipaways and Tawaas was that they had tied up their hands and likewise their own from doing any Mischeif to the White People and notwithstanding three of their Towns meant to break loose and reproved them for it severely that the Report of their design made the Shawanese very uneasy as they meant to Maintain a firm peace with their Bretheren which may be interrupted by it that he had a good Opportunity of knowing the Sentiments of the Shawanese and is sure they do not intend Mischeif but they may be persuaded to it by other Nations or driven into it by fear but he thinks unless the Shawanese join with them the Chipeways and Tawaas will not commence hostilities that the Indians have a suspicion that we have a Number of Armed Men Collected at no great distance from this place with a design to fall upon them when they come to the Treaty which gives them much Uneasiness that we may judge of the Sincerity of the Cornstalk from his discovering the Sentiments and designs of the other Nations which if he does not do but only says in General terms that all is Peace we may reasonably suspect him.

Mr John Gibson Informed the Commissioners that he had Just received a Letter from Major John Connolly directed to him with a Speech from Lord Dunmore to White Eyes a Delaware Cheif requesting him that he would Communicate the same to White Eyes that he thought it a duty which he Owed his Country to lay them before the Commissioners and that they were at Liberty to make what use they pleased of the Letter and Speech which are as followeth

PORTSMOUTH Aug 9th 1775

D<small>R</small> S<small>IR</small>—I have safely Arrived here and am happy to the Greatest Degree having so fortunately Escaped the Narrow Inspection of my Enemies the Enemies to their Country to good Order and Government I shou'd Esteem myself defective in Point of Freindship towards you shou'd I Neglect to caution you to Avoid an Over Zealous Exertion of what is now so rediculously called Patriotic Spirit but on the Contrary to deport yourself with that Moderation for which you have been always remarkable and which must in this Instance tend to your Honor and advantage you may be assured from me Sir that the Greatest Unanimity now Prevails at home and that the Innovating Spirit Amongst us here is looked upon as Ungenerous and Undutifull and that the Utmost Exertion of the Powers of Government (if Necessary) will be Used to Convince the Infatuated People of their folly I cou'd I assure you (Sir) give you such convincing proofs of what I assert and from which every Reasonable person may conclude the Effects that nothing but Madness cou'd Operate upon a Man so far as to overlook his duty to the present Constitution and to form unwarrantable Associations with Enthusiasts whose ill timed folly must draw down upon them inevitable distruction His Lordship desires you to present his hand to Captain White Eyes and to assure him that he is sorry that he had not the Pleasure of seeing him at the Treaty or that the Situation of Affairs prevented him from coming down Beleive me D<small>r</small> Sir that I have no motive in writing my Sentiments thus to you farther than to endeavour to Stear you Clear of the Misfortunes which I am Confidant must Involve but Unhappily too Many I have sent you an Address from the People of Great Britain to the People of America and desire you to Consider it Attentively which will I flatter myself Convince you of the Idleness of Many Declamations and of the absurdity of an Intended Slavery

Give my love to George and tell him that he shall hear from me and I hope to his Advantage Interpret the Inclosed Speech to captain White Eyes from his Lordship be Prevailed upon to shun the Popular Error and Judge for yourself Act as a good Subject and Expect the rewards due to your Services I am &c

   (Signed)   JOHN CONNOLLY

BROTHER CAPTAIN WHITE EYES—I am glad to hear your good speeches sent me by Major Connolly and you may be assured that I shall put the one end of the Belt which you have sent me into the hands of our Great King who will be glad to hear from his Brothers the Delawares and will take strong hold of it you may rest satisfied that our foolish young Men shall never be permited to have your Lands but on the Contrary the Great King will Protect you and Preserve you in the Possession of them Our Young People in this Country have been very foolish and done many Imprudent things for which they must soon be sorry and of which I make no doubt they have Acquainted you but I must desire you not to Listen to them as they wou'd be willing that you shou'd Act Equally foolish with themselves but rather Let what you hear pass in at one Ear and out of the other so that it may make no Impression on your Heart until you hear from me fully which shall be soon as I can give farther Information

Captain White Eyes will please to Acquaint the Cornstalk with these my Sentiments also as well as the Cheifs of the Mingoes and the other six Nations

your Sincere freind and Elder Brother
(Signed)   DUNMORE

September 26th The Shawanese being Arrived the Commissioners received them with Drum and Colours and a Salute of small Arms from the Garrison and having Conducted them to a Council House Erected for the Occasion after a Short Pause the Cornstalk spoke as follows

Brothers of Virginia Listen to what I am going to say Captain McKee[8] was many Years ago Placed by

---

[8] Alexander McKee was a native of Pennsylvania, who early began trading with the Indians on the Ohio, and by 1772 was appointed deputy-agent under Sir William Johnson. In 1771 he was justice of the peace for Bedford, later for Westmoreland County. At the beginning of the Revolution he inclined to the Royalist side, and was privately given a commission by Dunmore as lieutenant-colonel of a battalion to be raised near Fort Pitt. This enlistment was never accomplished, and he contrived to quiet the suspicions of the patriot party so that under parole he was allowed his liberty. In August, 1777, he was confined at Pittsburgh for a brief time, and an effort was made to remove him to an Eastern post This he adroitly evaded, and March 28, 1778, left for Detroit accompanied by Matthew Elliot and Simon Girty. The Eng-

our Wise People at this Council fire to have the Care of it and all our Young people look on him in that light we desire he will still have an Ear to our Mutual Interest as we think he ought to have as great a regard for ours as yours and hope he will have an Ear Open to Each of us *A String of Wampum*

The Cornstalk after Observing that the Gentlemen from Congress were not present said It Appears to me that you are not all as one person as I Expected to find you

Col° Lewis then Spoke as follows *Brothers* agreeable to Appointment we came here Sixteen days ago we have been Impatiently Expecting you and are rejoiced you are now come we have rekindled a Council fire at this place we now take you by the hand and heartily welcome you to it we hope our Meetings in future will be so Frequent that this Council fire will not be Suffered to go out as we have been so long detained here and have much also to do we hope you will as soon as you are rested from the Fatigues of your Journey Proceed to Business and in the Mean time furnish us with all the Intelligence you can respecting the Approach of the Other Tribes

---

lish authorities made him captain in the Indian department, and after 1778, deputy agent. He had large pay and considerable honor and authority, and led several expeditions against the American frontier. After the Revolution he became a colonel, and was accused of continuing to incite the tribesmen against the borderers. Certain it is, that he encouraged the forces against Wayne, and that the battle of Fallen Timbers (1794) was fought within sight of his house and store on the Maumee. After the evacuation of Detroit by the British (1796), McKee removed to Malden, Ont., where he died Jan. 14, 1799, of lockjaw.—ED.

from your Quarter We have the same respect for Captain McKee you have he has still the Care of this Council fire as will be hereafter Explained to you you will find we are more United and one People than ever *A String*

The Cornstalk then Informed the Commissioners that he thought the Delawares and Wiandots might be Expected to morrow Nimwha a Chief of the Shawanese then Addressed the rest of that Nation who were Present he told them they had now the Satisfaction of shaking hands with some of the Wise People of Virginia for which they ought to be very thankful

---

At a Meeting of all the Commissioners for Indian Affairs as well as those from Congress as those from Virginia September 30th Resolved that all the Commissioners for Indian Affairs do meet all the Indians of the Different Tribes in the Council House so soon as all the Nations Expected Arrive that a proper Speech be prepared to be delivered to them by Lewis Morris Esqr which Speech is to Contain the Usual Ceremonies Observed at Treatys with Indians and then to refer them to the Commissioners of Virginia to settle the Particular Business of their Department and that as soon as the same should be finished the Commissioners from the Continental Congress will Speak to them in the Name of the thirteen United Colonies who they represent

The Mingoes marched to the Council House with their Flag they Saluted a little before they Entered

Lewis Morris

After a photograph in the possession of his grandson,
William A. P. Morris, of Madison. Wis.

by firing their Guns which was returned by the Garrison when they were seated in the Council House The White Mingo spoke as follows *Brothers* There was a Small Council fire kindled here not long since by some of Virginia who are now here you sent a Speech up and down the River Informing all the Nations you Intended to kindle a large Council fire here at this time when all who would come shou'd be Welcome some time after we received this Message from our Brothers the Big knife our Brother Onas[4] sent us a speech desiring us to Make haste we have Brother Onas and likewise our Brothers of the big-knife fast by the Hand fifty of us are come as we promised and now produce the Speech which you then sent to us

Colº Morris then Spoke as follows *Brothers* we are very Glad to see you when the Chiefs of the other Nations who we Expect Arrive we shall be glad to see you all at this great Council fire and will then Open to you the design of this Treaty in the Mean time you shall be Amply Provided with Provisions to make your stay Agreeable and we will have such of your Guns and Tomhawks which are out of order repaired *A String of Wampum*

Colº Wilson[5] then desired the White Mingo to de-

---

[4] Big Knife was originally the Indian appelation for the people of Virginia, a term later used for the Americans as a whole. For its origin see Thwaites, *Daniel Boone* (New York, 1902), p. 111, note.

Onas was the Indian term for the governor of Pennsylvania, and was first applied in 1682 to William Penn.—ED.

[5] James Wilson (1742-98), a prominent Pennsylvania statesman, was born and educated in Scotland. Coming to America he settled in Pennsylvania (1766), where he supported the

liver the Invitation speech sent by him to the Mingoes which he did and is also as follows *Brothers* Listen to what we are now to say to you *A String   Brothers* a very large Council fire has been lately kindled at Philadelphia in the Country of your Brother Onas round this Council fire have sat Great Men sent to speak and Act for all the following Colonies Viz' New Hampshire, Massachusetts Bay, Rhode Island, Connecticut, New York, New Jersey, Pennsylvania the Counties of New Castle, Kent and Sussex upon Delaware, Maryland, Virginia, North Carolina, South Carolina and Georgia these Great Men have Consulted and deliberated Concerning a Controversy that has Arisen between the White People who live on this Island and some of the English who live on the other side the Great Water and they were induced by the Antient Harmony and Freindship subsisting between the white People and you to Inform you of the Cause of this Quarrel and in what Manner they wish to behave they will advise you nothing but what will Contribute to your Peace and Advantage as well as their own they have Appointed a Treaty to be held with you and have directed that you shall receive some presents in their name in Order to Convince you of their kindness for you and to Preserve Peace and freindship between the white People and you we who

---

patriot cause, and was delegate to the second Continental Congress. By this body he was chosen commissioner to hold the Indian treaty at Fort Pitt. In 1776 he signed the Declaration of Independence, and held many important offices, including membership in the Federal constitutional convention (1787), and in the Pennsylvania convention (1789-90). Appointed by Washington (1789) to the supreme court of the United States, he held that office until his death.—ED.

are three of the Counsellors round the Great Council fire at Philadelphia are Authorised to hold the Treaty with you in the name of all the Great Council you may beleive our Words in the same Manner as if they all spoke to you

We have Chosen Pitsburg to be the Place and the 10th day of next Month to be the time of holding the Treaty and give you this Notice expecting and Inviting the Cheif Counsellors and Warriours of your Nation at the Treaty that we may behold you face to face Let no false and Wicked Reports that may have been spread abroad Among you by those who are both Enemies to us and to you Prevent you from coming We and you Sprung from the same Ground and live together on the same Island we Ought to live together and have Confidence in Each Other we will not Deceive you that what we have now said to you may be Confirmed and that you may give heed to it we deliver to you by the hands of your and our freind and Brother the White Mingo this String *A String* as the two other Commissioners are not yet Arrived I on their behalf as well as in my own name Subscribe the foregoing Message

(Signed) JAMES WILSON

at Pitsburgh the 25th day of August 1775

At a Meeting of the Commissioners for Indian Affairs as well those Appointed by Congress as those from Virginia 2d October One Thousand Seven Hundred and seventy five

Captain White Eyes and the Delawares not being

yet Arrived the Commissioners Consulted the Cheifs of the Mingoes Wiandots Shawanese Tawaas, King Custaloga and Captain Pipe of the Delawares[6] whether they should proceed to Business or to wait the Arrival of White Eyes and the other Delawares who all gave their Opinion that a Message shou'd be sent to Hasten them whereupon the Commissioner dispatched Thomas Nicholson[7] Interpreter with a Delaware Indian to meet them with the following speech

Brothers the Delawares We have Anxiously waited your Arrival and hope we shall have the Pleasure to see you very soon as our Brethren the Six Nations Wiandots Ottawas and Shawanese with part of you[r] Nation are now here in Conference with them we have agreed to send one of our Young Men and one of yours to meet you and to request that you will come on as fast as Possible that we may begin our Business *A String*

---

[6] Custaloga was a prominent chieftain of the Wolf clan of the Delawares. He removed early to the Ohio, participated in Pontiac's conspiracy, and in 1764 treated with Bouquet. In 1773, Sir Wililam Johnson informed the colonial secretary that Custaloga with one hundred of his followers had retired to the Wabash River.

Captain Pipe was a war-chief who had been hostile during the French wars, and was an enemy to the peace party, as well as to the missionaries settled among his tribe. He dissembled during the first part of the Revolution, but by 1778 removed his village to the Sandusky, within the sphere of British influence, and was zealous in compassing the death of Capt. William Crawford (1782). He was present at the treaties of Fort McIntosh (1785) and Fort Harmar (1789), but apparently died before that of Greenville (1795).—ED.

[7] For a brief notice of this person see *Dunmore's War*, p. 13, note 26.—ED.

TREATY WITH WESTERN INDIANS

At a meeting of the Commissioners on the Part of Virginia the 7th day of October 1775 *Present*
Thomas Walker James Wood Andrew Lewis John Walker Adam Stephen Comrs

The Wiandots having never been condoled with Agreeable to their Custom since the last War for the loss of their freinds who fell in Battle the Commissioners sent for them into A Private room early this Morning and delivered to them the following speech of Condolence

Brothers the Wiandots and Cheifs of the Cochanawagas on Scioto[8] you may remember when Lord Dunmore and your Bretheren of Virginia Assembled the Nations of Indians at this place last year he Acquainted them he was obliged to March a body of Men into the Shawanese Country as he had a dispute with them and desired all other Nations would keep out of the way but some of your young Men were so foolish not to Listen to your Wisemen but wou'd join the other foolish People and Accidentally got killed we now take the Tomahawk out of your hands and Assure you it was not our Intention to strike your Nation and bury it deep in the Ground that no Uneasiness or remembrance of it may Enter into your Minds that your hearts may be at rest while you sit at our Grand Council fire with these few goods we Cover

---

[8] Caughnawaga was a mission Indian village—chiefly of converted Mohawks—on the south side of the St. Lawrence, just above Montreal. The Indians of this and similar mission villages were frequently utilized by the French in war-parties. After the overthrow of the French power, many of these Indians removed west and settled among their kindred tribesmen.—ED.

the Graves of these Unhappy young Men which fell in Battle and desire that it may never more be remembered *A String to Each Nation*

The following Goods were given as a present of Condolence (Viz') two Bundles Each Containing as follows one for the Wiandots and the others for the Cochanawagas 4 Black Strouds 4 Ruffled Shirts 4 pair of Leggins 4 Matchcoats 1 Blanket one half to be tied up and directed to Cochanawaga the other to be delivered to the Wiandot Cheif

---

At a Meeting of all the Commissioners for Indian Affairs October 7th 1775 Present Lewis Morris James Wilson Thomas Walker James Wood Andrew Lewis John Walker Adam Stephen Com^rs

Captain White Eyes and the Delawares being Arrived and the Cheifs of the Wiandots Six Nations Delawares Shawanese and Tawaas being Assembled in the Council House Col° Morris delivered the following speech to them *To the Six Nations Wiandots Delawares Shawanese and Ottawas Cheif Warriors and Brothers* It gives us Joy to see you now meet together at the Invitation of all your English Bretheren who live on this Continent and who have Appointed a Great Council to be held in the great City of your Brother Onas that being the most Convenient place in the United Colonies It is from that Council we are sent to renew and more perfectly Establish the Antient Freindship that has Subsisted between you and us we therefore Bretheren bid you Welcome to this Council fire and with these strings we wipe the

Dust and Sweat Occasioned by the Fatigues of your Journey we likewise wipe off from your Memories and Clear your Ears from any Wicked reports which may have Tended to Interrupt you and our peace and the peace of our Wives and Childeren that you may Plainly hear and Understand what we say to you *A String to Each Nation*

Bretheren with these strings we dry up your Tears for the Loss of your Freinds who have died since your last assembly at this Place we remove all Greif from your hearts on this Account that your minds may be at ease whilst we deliver our Embassy to you from our great United Council of Wise men now Assembled at Philadelphia which we hope you will hear with as much pleasure as we shall deliver it and we Collect the Bones of your Deceased freinds and Bury them deep in the Earth and Transplant the Tree of Peace over them that our Freindship may not be Interrupted nor our Minds disturbed at the Sight of them *A Large String to Each Nation* with these strings we Clear our Council House and desire no discontent may be allowed to Enter therein but that we may Consult together with Honest Hearts for your and our Mutual Peace and Happiness *A String to Each Nation*

Bretheren as our people of Virginia first proposed Meeting you here and Called you together on Business which relates more Particularly to them though we are all Interested in it as we are one people and one flesh and Blood we shall say no more to you at this time untill you finish that Particular Business with them which we hope the good Spirit will put it

into their and your hearts to do in the Most Freindly
Manner as Bretheren who wish to live in Love and
Peace ought to do It is however Necessary to In-
form you that what we may now say is from all the
Wisemen of all our United Colonies who are as one
Man and that Virginia is one of them and as the
right Arm so that you must not beleive those who tell
you that the Virginians are a Distinct People The
Country of your Brother Onas is also one of the
thirteen United Colonies and it is in his great Town
where the Wisemen from Virginia and all the other
Provinces now sat in our Grand Council therefore
Bretheren we desire you to pay Attention to what we
have said the day after tomorrow we will be ready
to hear your Answer and then our Bretheren from Virginia will Open to you their Particular Business
when you and they have finished we who represent
not only the Colony of Virginia and Pennsylvania but
all the other Colonies as already Mentioned and are
sent from their Grand Council now siting will speak
to you again and we hope that not only you and we
but your and our Childeren and their Childerens
Children will hear of and remember this our Meeting with Pleasure and that they will Distinguish it
by the Name of the Blessed Council of Peace *A
Belt to Each Nation*

Captain White Eyes addressed himself to the Indians in the following Words *Brothers* you have
now heard what your Brothers the White People have
said to you It Ought to give you great Pleasure and
I beg you will be Strong and meet them at the time
they direct he then delivered the following Speech

to the Commissioners *My Dear Brothers* On Monday Morning we will meet you again with our Answer we will then let you know who are the People Pitched upon to Negotiate with you we beg you will be strong and be Punctual to your Appointment we wish some Method cou'd be taken to prevent rum being given to our People that has been the sole Cause of this Meeting not being fuller Unless this is Altered it will Greatly impede our Business

---

At a Meeting of all the Commissioners for Indian Affairs 9th October 1775 The Cheifs of the Different Tribes of Indians having Assembled agreeable to the Appointment of Saturday Captain White Eyes spoke to the Indians as follows *Uncles the Six Nations and Wiandots our Grand Children the Ottawas and Shawanese* The time we purposed to speak to our Brothers the White people is Elapsed it is Owing to a Misunderstanding which happened this Morning among ourselves our Uncles the Six Nations propose Speaking in the Morning I shall now speak on Behalf of the Wiandots the Shawanese the Tawaas and my own Nation he then Addressed the Commissioners in the following words *Brothers* we are much obliged to you that as soon as we Appeared you wiped the Sweat from us so that we were Quite refreshed you wiped the Tears from our Eyes and removed all bad Impressions from our hearts so that we are Quite at Ease you have also told us that you have gathered all the Bones of our Deceased relations and Buried them deep in the Ground and planted a tree upon them that our Children or foolish young People may never see them to their Disquiet In the name of our Uncles the Wiandots our Grand Children the Shawanese and Tawaas and our own Nation I Acquaint you we are much rejoiced and return you our Sincere thanks *A String*

Brothers Listen to me I now Inform you that we are Extreemely rejoiced at what we heard the day before Yesterday from you and that all the White People Account themselves as one Body and that Virginia is not alone for the future when we look on you we shall Esteem you all one People our reason *Brothers* why we say we were very much rejoiced to hear you are United is when our Brothers the White People first came upon this Island I thought they and us shou'd be the only people who shou'd live on it we made room for you to set down by Us Accordingly

Brothers I have now Acquainted you what we thought when you first Arrived on this Land I now think our Treatment to you then is the Cause of the King over the Big Water Striking you at this time I therefore desire you not to think much of it but think good untill we hear from him I now also Acquaint you that my Uncles the Wiandots have bound themselves the Shawanese Tawaas and Delawares together and have made us as one People and have also given me that Tract of Country Beginning at the Mouth of Big Beaver Creek and running up the same to where it interlocks with the Branches of Guyahoga Creek and down the said Creek to the Mouth thereof where it empties into the Lake along the Side of the Lake to the Mouth of Sanduskey Creek and up the same to the head untill it interlocks with Muskingum down the same to the Mouth where it Empties into the Ohio and up the said River to the Place of Beginning* I also now Acquaint my Uncles the Six Nations that my Uncles the Wiandots have given me that Tract of Country as we have now Acquainted you what Lands belongs to us I desire you will not Permit any of your foolish People to sit down upon it that I cannot suffer it least other Nations shou'd be Uneasy.[10] *A Belt of Wampum*

Brother I am Extreemly rejoiced to hear what you said to me the day before Yesterday and also to hear you call upon God to witness and Assist us in future meetings to talk of the Freindship which is between us and the reason of my being rejoiced is that we are poor and Ignorant and know but little of Gods Wisdom but you have him in your heart and are more capable of Judging than we can be and as you have made Mention of that heavenly freindship which proceeds from God I am very much pleased and take hold of it and the reason of my being so ready and willing to take hold of it is that our wise forefathers began the Blessed Work I also

---

* White Eyes is speaking for his entire tribe, but in Indian parlance the singular pronoun is generally used. He has here defined the limits of Delaware territory.—ED.

[10] This no doubt is the speech to which Heckewelder refers in *Narrative of the Mission of the United Brethren among the Delaware and Mohegan Indians* (Phila., 1820), pp. 140, 141, when he says that White Eyes defied the Six Nations and made the most bold and daring address ever made in an Indian council by an individual chief. The Iroquois had considered the Delawares as their subject people. White Eyes, thinking that the latter would join the British, took the opportunity to assert the Delawares' independence.—ED.

inform you that I am Extreamly rejoiced and think it was God Almighty that has put it into your hearts to offer us this and that you did not despise us tho poor and Ignorant *A Belt*

I now *Brother* Assure you I am very Much rejoiced you offer me your hand to take hold of I Gladly Accept it and shall not let it fall to the Ground and I hope God Almighty will Endow me with Wisdom to treasure it up in my heart as my Brothers the English do we now desire you *Brothers* to be strong and finish the Business we are come about that we may be able to Inform the other Nations what we have been about and when we have finished this good Work there will never be any Occasion of Difference between our Childeren and your Childeren but that they will have reason to remember it and call it the Blessed Council of Peace *A Belt*

Brothers I am very much rejoiced that you Acquainted me it was a long time since we had met and as some of our great Men might have died desired we would inform you who Acted in their Place we now inform you that there are three tribes of us[11] Kalalamint Walapachakin and Ohokon or Capn Pipe are the Cheifs Appointed for the Delaware Nation *A Belt*

Brothers Listen to your young Sisters the Delawares Women we are very Much rejoiced to hear

---

[11] Referring to the three clans of the tribe, whose totems were respectively the turtle, wolf, and bear. The first of these was accorded the headship of the tribe; the last named were usually called Munsee (Munceys).—ED.

you and our Children renewing the freindship between you and them this is what your Sisters have said to you and our paying Attention to them is the reason why we did not go to War with any Nation whatsoever as God Almighty did not Create us to War with one Another we now also desire you will Acquaint your Mothers our Elder Sisters the White Women what we have said and when any of our Children shall be born in future we will point to heaven and tell them these our sentiments. *A Belt from the Women*

Col⁰ Morris then Answered *Brothers* we are obliged to you for your Speech we are well pleased with it tomorrow we Expect to hear the Six Nations

The Tawaas Cheif Shaganaba[12] Addressed the Commissioners in the following Words *Fathers* I thank you that you have Wiped the Tears from my Eyes the Sweat from my body and thoroughly cleansed me I was at first Unwilling I Acknowledge to come to this Treaty from evil reports I had heard and which I have now found to be falsehoods my father and many other Cheifs have lately Tasted of Death Accept my hearty thanks for your kind Condolence on that Occasion I Present you my right hand in token that I rejoice to see you United nore shall my Children be Untold of it Accept this String of Wampum as a Pledge of my Sincerity and Freindship my Fathers knew you but Unhappily are no more I have now found the road to your Hospi-

---

[12] Shaganaba was the son of the renowned Ottawa chief Pontiac.—ED.

table Mansions nor shall it be Untrodden by my People in the future[13] *A String*

At a Meeting of the Commissoners for Indain Affairs as well those from Congress as those from Virginia October 10th 1775 Present Lewis Morris Thomas Walker James Wilson James Wood Andrew Lewis John Walker Adam Stephen Com^rs

The Indians of the Different Tribes being Arrived at the Council House at 12 ºClock Chau Chau Chau sadea Or the Flying Crow a Cheif of the Six Nations Addressed the Commissioners in the following words *Brothers* Listen you have wiped the Sweat from our Bodies and Cleared our Hearts and throats that we heard your good speeches with pleasure and have us now fast by the hand we now Clear your hearts that you may hear us with Attention and Proceed with your good Speeches to which we will be very Attentive *A String*

Brothers Onas, listen to me likewise *my brothers the big knife* Listen to me we received a Speech from each of you Inviting us to this Council fire as soon as they reached us we rose up to come you there told us you wou'd be glad from your hearts to see us at this time we are glad in our hearts to meet you the Great Men from Onas and Virginia and Esteem you as Much as if all the Great Men

---

[13] Another and more eloquent version of this speech is given in *Amer. Archives*, 4th series, iii, p. 1542. It is also to be found in Draper MSS., 3D, chap. xiii, where it is given as a specimen of Indian eloquence.—ED.

James Wilson

After an engraving in the possession of the Wisconsin
Historical Society

from the Sea side who sent you were Present *A String*

Brothers Onas and Brothers the big knife Listen to me I have first spoke what is Customary on such Occasions you have desired us to Speak our Sentiments I have nothing to say at Present I came to Listen to what You have to say to us and hope you will say Nothing but what is good and from your Hearts that all my Brothers present may hear you and rejoice when I have heard you I will Consider and give you an Answer *A String*

The Half King of the Wiandots[14] then Spoke *Brothers of the Big knife* Listen to me when I received the Message sent me by my Brothers the big knife our Cheifs were Just returned from a Council held at the House of Sir William Johnston they were very much Fatigued and sent word to my People on this side the Lake to Accept the Invitation and to go to the Council and Listen which is the reason you now see us here What I have heard I like very well and I shall Attend to what more you have to say and our Cheifs will I hope when we return be very well Pleased with it Likewise I hope God Almighty will Allow us to return to Our Own Nation in Safety *A Black String*

Brother the Bigknife I am glad to hear what you

---

[14] The Half-King was an important Wyandot chief, head of the Sandusky branch of the tribe, his village being at Upper Sandusky. In 1777 he declared against the Americans, and headed the raid that defeated Foreman, as well as that which assailed Fort Randolph in 1778. He was also prominent in the defeat of Crawford in 1782. He appears to have died before Wayne's treaty in 1795.—ED.

have said to us to our Nephews the Delawares to our Young Brothers the Shawanese and Tawaas and to our Elder Bretheren the Six Nations I am also rejoiced that on our Arrival you wiped the Sweat from us you dried up our Tears that you set our hearts at Ease and that you Cleared our Ears that we might hear the good things you have to say to us I make no doubt our Cheifs who sent us here will be Equally rejoiced at our reception when they are Informed of it on our return[15] *A Black String*

The Cornstalk a Shawanese Cheif came forward to the Council Board and Addressed the Commissioners as follows *Brothers* I imagined all Matters were settled last fall and that we were as one People I now find that there is a bad Wind Blown up I know not from whence it has Arisen but I desire the White People will search into it I hope they will not let that Interrupt the Good work we are now about. If we are Strong and finish the good work we have began our Children now Growing up will live in peace but if we regard what wicked or foolish People do it may be an Impediment to our liveing in Freindship when we received the Message from our Brothers the Bigknife and the other Colonies we Immediately set off with a good heart to meet them determined to think of Nothing bad that Passed Expecting the Good things our King had sent Us to hear at this Meeting wou'd be the Means of our

---

[15] John Dodge, who at the request of Wood accompanied the Wyandot, reports to the following effect: that upon their return to Sandusky they found their tribesmen preparing for war, which the account of their deputies quieted.—Almon's *Remembrancer*, viii, pp. 73, 74.—ED.

Children enjoying a lasting Peace at the Conclusion of the War with Lord Dunmore last fall we Mutually Promised if any thing shou'd happen bad on Either side to Inform Each other of it I now *Brothers* Inform you that some of my foolish Young Men have Burned Several Houses at the Mouth of the big Kanhawa they were Pursued by the White People and came home quite Naked having Lost their Cloaths Blankets &^{c} It happened about ten or 12 days ago; To morrow I will send off two of my Young Men to direct my People to sit still and do no mischeif while we are doing Business I will likewise Inform the Wiandots and Tawaas and hope you will send to your young people and direct them to do ours no harm untill this Business is finished I Intended last Night to have sent off my Young Men this Morning but Considering the Weather is Cold I detained them this day to see if our Brothers wou'd not take Pity on them and give them something to Cloath them and Provisions for their Journey when the Messenger who brought me this Account came off the Cheifs were getting some of the White People who were at the Towns to write and a Man to bring it up we Expect therefore that you will have a written Account in a day or two *A String*

Col^o Morris then spoke to the Different Nations of Indians as follows *Brothers* we are well Pleased with your Speeches of Yesterday and to day and thank you for them and will withdraw till our Brothers the Virginians have finished their Particular Business with you we are Very Glad to see you so desirous of taking fast hold of the Chain of

Freindship and hope the Great and Good Spirit will Preside among you and Guide you to your Mutual Satisfaction

The Gentlemen from the Congress then withdrew and the Commissioners from Virginia Opened their Business with the following Speech delivered by John Walker *To the Mingoes Wiandots Delawares Shawanese and Tawaas Freinds and Bretheren* we are sent here by the Grand Council of our Country, the big knife, to take you by the hand and Welcome you to this Council fire, to which we have Invited all the Ohio Indians and other Neighbouring Nations: you have Accepted the Invitation and we are heartily Glad to see you, this Council we hope, will be called the Blessed Council of Peace, and the Fame of it handed Down thro' all Generations *A String to Each Nation*

Brothers having now met in Council agreeable to the Appointment of our respective Nations, we do with this belt remove from our Roads all Obstructions, that both your and our People may have free and Easy Access, and we hope they will be so Troden by our Mutual Freindly Visits, that they will be forever kept open *A Road Belt*

Brothers we do with this Belt Brighten the Chain of Freindship between us, with it we rub off any Rust it may have Contracted, and desire you may Continue to hold fast by one End of it, so long as the Clouds shall Produce Rain, or the Earth Corn on our part you may depend it will never be let go, unless you wrest it out of our hands, by Commencing Hostilities against us; in which Case you must know, that you will be but as one Child fighting against its family of an Hundred *The Chain Belt*

Brothers we wish to Cultivate so strict a Freindship with you as that your Enemies shou'd be Considered as ours, and our Enemies as yours; However, as we are able to fight our Own Battles we only request of you (as you love us, and regard your Own Welfare) to Continue in Peace and Suffer the Tomhawk which is so deep Buried to lie Still and the Tree which is Planted thereon to grow and flourish in such Manner, that both your and our Childrens Children, may reap the fruits of it.

Brothers you have no doubt heard of the dispute between us and some of our Fathers evil Counsellors beyond the Great Water,[16] in this dispute your Interest is Involved with ours so far as this, that in Case those People with whom we are Contending shou'd Subdue us, your *Lands* your *Trade* your *Liberty* and all that is dear to you must fall with us, for if they wou'd Distroy our flesh and Spill our Blood which is the same with theirs; what can you who are no way related to or Connected with them Expect? and further, 'Suppose you were Inclined to Join our Enemies, how Cou'd you Act in Conjunction with them? they Cannot Pass through us tc your Country Neither cou'd you get to them. Notwithstanding all this, we only ask of you to Stay at

---

[16] See the allegory by which the dispute was explained to the tribesmen under the figure of a cruel father's treatment of his little son, in Heckewelder's *Narrative*, pp. 137-140. See also *Amer. Archives*, 4th series, iii, pp. 482, 483.—ED.

home, to take Care of your Women and Children, and follow other Usual Occupations: we are not Affraid these People will Conquer us, they Can't fight in our Country, and you Know we Can; we fear not them, nor any Power on Earth

Brothers the thirteen great Colonies of this Extensive Continent, Comprehending in the whole, at least One Million of Fighting Men, are now so firmly United and Inseparably bound together by one lasting Chain of Freindship, that we are no more to be Considered as Distinct Nations, but as one great and Strong Man, who if Molested in any one of his Members, will not fail to Exert the Combined force of his whole Body to Punish the Offender, we have already sent some of our Men to Assist our Bretheren at Boston, and so far as the Contest has been hitherto Carried on we have Proved Successful our Enemies are Confined to their Ships and entrenchments and we Expect will Shortly be Almost all Starved or Slain and that the few who shall Escape from famine and Sword will be forced to fly to their own Country for Shelter

Brothers we can with Pleasure Inform you that several Indian Nations in the North have Offered to take up the Tomhawk in our favor, that the People in Canada except a few of Governor Carltons[17] Fools are friendly towards us, that they have

---

[17] Guy Carleton (1724–1808), an eminent English soldier, was at this time governor of Canada. He resigned upon Burgoyne's appointment, and was replaced (1778) by Haldimand. In 1782, Carleton was made commander-in-chief for British America, his policy being one of clemency and conciliation.

absolutely refused, when Ordered by him, to Strike us, and that it is not Improbable they will in a Short time deliver him a Prisoner into our Hands.

Brothers If any other Nation or Nations shou'd take up the Tomhawk and Endeavour to Strike us it wou'd be Kind in you to give us Notice and Use your best Endeavours to Prevent the Stroke, for it must be your Interest to live in Peace and Amity with such near and Powerfull Neighbours and this is all we Ask *A String to Each Nation*

Brothers the Mingoes we desire to bury in Oblivion all that has past, and brighten the Chain of Freindship with you whatever happened to some of your Young people last fall, was Owing to their disregarding the Wise Councils of the Six Nations; we hope the good Advice they will receive from you, and them, will Prevent any Mischief in future *A String*

Brothers the Wiandots we have had good Accounts of you from our people who have been Among you they tell us you are a good and sensible Nation we desire you will give Ear to no Idle reports you may hear from the Commanding Officer at Fort Detroit who will Endeavour to deceive you we have already discovered Many of their Falshoods we desire to live in Peace with you, and hope you will Acquaint your Neighbouring Nations with what we have said *A String*

Returning to England in 1783 he again came out to Canada in 1786 as governor, this time under the title of Lord Dorchester. After retaining the office for ten years, he retired from public life.—ED.

Brothers the Delawares we Esteem you a Wise people for not engaging in the War last Summer and you may depend upon our freindship agreeable to Lord Dunmores Promise *A String*

Brothers the Shawanese we have returned you your Hostages safe and Trust they can say nothing but good of us It is our Earnest desire to live in Peace with you, shou'd any of our People Molest you, we will Endeavour to bring them to Justice and shou'd any of yours Molest us we Expect you will Punish them *A String*

Brothers the Tawaas we are exceedingly rejoiced to see you here we have heard much of your Kindness and Hospitality Especially of your freindship to young Feild who was delivered you by the Shawanese, he is well and has a Gratefull Rememberance of your Favors. One Act of Humanity does a Nation more Grace in the sight both of God and Man, than an hundred Cruelties. your Behaviour to young Feild will indear you to all the White People. now you have found the Way to this Council fire, we hope we shall often meet at it to brighten the Chain of Friendship between us we desire you will Listen to no evil reports of our Mutual Enemies, shou'd you hear of any Mischeif Intended us you will do well to Inform us and do all in your Power to Prevent it, and we desire you will Acquaint your Neighbouring Nations of what we have said to you *A String*

To the whole Nations Present we have reason to Beleive great Uneasinesses and Jealousies have Prevailed Amongst you respecting our Intention of making Encroachments on your Lands we take this Opportunity of Assuring you that we have not the most Distant thought of Possessing any part of your Lands you must all be sensible that the Lands on this side Ohio as far down as the C[h]erokee River[18] was Purchased at the Treaty of Fort Stanwix by Sir William Johnston[19] for the King of England who has since sold it to his Childeren on this Continent and which they now Expect to Enjoy in Peace *A Belt*

Brothers we Expect you have brought with you and are ready to Deliver up all our Flesh and Blood our Negroes and all that belongs to us and that you are prepared to make restitution for all Damages agreeable to the Terms Stipulated between you and Lord Dunmore last Fall *A String*

The Flying Crow then Replied *Brother the Bigknife* It gives me great Satisfaction to hear what you have said, it puts me in mind of our wise forefathers Beleive me when I assure you it has sunk deep into my heart I firmly beleive every thing you have said to me and will duly Consider it as its Consequence deserves and will then give you my Answer to it you may depend the Six Nations will be strong in Peace and we hope the Other Nations will be the same

White Eyes then Addressed the Commissioners and the Different Tribes of the Indians in the following Manner *Uncles the Six Nations And Grand Children the Shawanese and Tawaas* I am much re-

---

[18] The Tennessee was frequently known as Cherokee River, because that tribe dwelt upon its upper waters.—ED.

[19] Sir William Johnson, for many years superintendent of Indian affairs, held this important treaty at Fort Stanwix in 1768, and died in 1774.—ED.

joiced at what I have heard from our brother the bigknife

Brothers the bigknife I am extremely rejoiced to hear the many good things you have said to me as my Heart Desires nothing but what is good I lay hold on the least Appearance of it *Uncles the Six Nations and Wiandots and all who are here present* I hope we shall be able to finish the Good work we are now about so Effectually that our Children and our Childrens Children shall be able to live in peace from it and as soon as all my Bretheren have fully Considered of what you now have said to us we Will return an Answer

Corn Stalk then Spoke as follows *Brothers the Bigknife* as you have desired we shou'd deliver you your flesh and Blood and your Negroes we will give you an Answer to morrow respecting that Matter

---

At a Conference Continued and held with the Shawanese on the 11th October 1775 Present Thomas Walker, Andrew Lewis, James Wood John Walker Adam Stephen Commrs

The Cornstalk addressed the Commissioners *My Old Brothers the Bigknife* In our Councils last fall when we were settling every thing we made ourselves one Body and Promised to Each Other at the same time that if any Mischeif shou'd happen through the inadvertency of foolish Young People that we wou'd not keep it a Secreet from one another but Seriously Consider and have it rectified when I left home I Assembled my Young Men and told them

I was going to Treat with my Bretheren the English and if any foolish People shou'd spread any bad reports not to listen to it as I had nothing in my heart but what was good we had not forgot where the Mischeif a rose from the foolish People who are endeavouring to Overset our Freindship I will now Inform you that Just before our Young Men left our Towns twenty Wiandots and Tawaas came there and desired their Brothers the Shawanese to Listen to what they had to say which was this *Brothers* I now desire you to make yourselves ready and to secure your Provisions for it will not be long before a Body of the White People will Strike you they have already divided your Nation by calling one half of you to a Treaty at Pitsburg where they Informed you that they had good to say to you but it was only to deceive you they desired the Warriors to get their Mocoasins ready and to go and Watch the Mouths of Muskingum, Hockhockin the big Kanhawa and Kentucke for there wou'd be a great number of the Virginia Warriors to strike them the King of the Wiandots and wise men who live at Detroit sent them on a very different Errand they told these Twenty Wiandots and Tawaas to go to their Young brothers the Shawanese and as they were Unsetled On Account of the Disputes between their Elder Brothers of Virginia and them they had sent them to Kindle their Council fire Anew and to gather the Bones of their Dead who fell in the War and to Bury them and remove all Grief from their Hearts that they might sit in Peace and Quietness this is what they were sent for and not to spread bad reports when

the Tawaas and Wiandots came to Pluggies Town
the Mingoes Cheif Called the Stone and another Cheif
called the Black Wolf Invited them to a Council and
there put these evil Stories in their heads and made
them forget the good things their Cheifs had charged
them with their telling these foolish things to my
young Men made them go and do harm to my brothers the English unknown to our Chief Kisquaquawha
[who] was sick or he would have Prevented them
I also Inform you that two of the Wiandots and
Pluggies son one of the Six Nations with two of our
foolish Young Men who they Persuaded to go with
them Pretending they did not know the road are
gone to the Mouth of Kentucke to look at the white
People no doubt their taking our Young Men was to
throw the blame on our Nation[20] to which Col°
Lewis replied *Brothers* The Natural Consequence
of what had happened will be that the white People
will go into the Fort at which you need not be
Alarmed we will send to desire our People to keep
their Own side of the River and to do you no harm
and would recommend it to you to send to your
People to do the same The Cornstalk Answered
This is our Intention

Brothers we have now Informed you what we
have heard and your seeing a Number of us here
both Men and Women may convince you we had no
such thoughts in our Hearts when we left our Towns

---

[20] On Dec. 23, just outside of Boonesborough, this party fired upon Col. Arthur Campbell and two lads named Sanders and McQuinney. The former escaped, the latter was killed, and Sanders was never again heard from. See Draper MSS., 4B55.—ED.

Whatever has happened is Owing to the Advice of bad People who no doubt Envy us as they see us and our Elder Brothers the Big knife as one People If it had been known to the Wise People of your young Brothers the Shawanese they would have Prevented it The Cheif who we left to take Care of our Young People was sick and knew Nothing of their going we Acquainted you we were going to send two of our Young Men to our Towns I shall send my own son Allanawissica and Kataawa with Speeches to my Nation as the Weather is grown cold they hope you will give them some Cloathes and Provisions for their Journey

Brothers listen to me when we held a Council last Fall you desired us to deliver up your Flesh and Blood your Negroes your Horses and every thing that belonged to you our Brother Col° Stephen was here and remembers every thing that Passed as soon as we heard it we Immediately Complied and Delivered you up all your flesh and Blood your Negroes and Horses and all that belonged to you not only at that time but when they were Demanded twice before in the Winter I received a Message from the Commanding Officer at the Kanhawa my father the whitefish and myself went through the Towns hunted up the Horses and Delivered him eight when the Governor Demanded our Relations the White People he told us he only wanted them to go and see their relations and they should be at liberty if they did not like to stay with the white People to return to us when we brought them among us they were then Subservient to our Commands but when

we had delivered them up to the White People and
they returned of their Own Accord they were as free
as ourselves and no longer under our Controul when
I went home I Informed them that some of their
white relations were desirous of seeing them and told
them to go and see their Relations they began to
Cry and said they were not Slaves that they shou'd
be forced away for they had it in their own Choice
where they would stay last spring when some of the
Cherokees robbed your People on the Kentucke we
Immediately set off took two of the Horses from them
and delivered them at the Mouth of Kanhawa and
when the Negro Woman made her Escape from that
Place and Came to our Towns on her being Demanded we delivered her when we did this Captain
Russell said he was a little Sorry to Ask so much
but that the Owner insisted upon having the two
Children brought in that he thought it was too much
as they had been all Winter Delivering Horses and
Performing every Promise they had made in the Winter Captain Russell sent five of his Men to our
Towns we Delivered the Negro Wench but told him
as the Children were Bagat by our People we thought
it very hard they shou'd be made Slaves of as the
Negro Woman is delivered up she will soon have
more Children at the same time they Demanded
Horses from us we Informed them we had delivered
up all the Horses we had belonging to the White
People and that Many of our People had delivered
up their own Horses in leiu of yours which cou'd not
be found we likewise told them that ours was not
the only Nation who had stolen their Horses I now

Inform you we have Delivered up all your Horses and all your Negroes Except One Negro Man who runaway from the Mouth of Hockhockan Who threatens to kill either White Man or Indian who shall Attempt to Molest him

Brothers I now Inform you we have delivered up all we possibly can and as we are one People I hope you will not Ask more of us what white People remain among us are their own Masters and may do as they Please the Young white Man who is here has been to see his Relations if he Chooses to stay with them we have no Objection if he Chooses to return we Cannot Prevent him we will endeavour to Persuade him to Either but let his own Choice direct him 'tis true our Manner of living is not like the white Peoples we suppose that is the reason why their freinds are Unwilling they shou'd live Among us

Brothers we now Inform you if any of your flesh and Blood Choose to return to their relations or if any of their freinds come to our Country for them we shall never Attempt to Hinder them and as you Yesterday Cleared the Road of all Obstructions between you and us It will be the Means of making our freindship more firm and Lasting *A String*

At a Conference Continued and held at Pitsburg with the Different Nations of Indians 12th October 1775 Present Thomas Walker Andrew Lewis James Wood Adam Stephen Comm^rs

Thomas Walker Esqr delivered the following speech to the Shawanese in Answer to theirs of Yesterday

Brothers we are sensible you delivered up a Considerable Number of Horses and Prisoners to Lord Dunmore at Camp Charlotte we are likewise Sensible that you delivered some Horses to the Commanding Officer at the Kanhawa in so doing you performed part of what you Promised and so far Supported the Honor and Dignity of the Shawanese Nation you told us Yesterday you had delivered up all our flesh and Blood in this you are Mistaken there are many of our People still among you several of whom are not of a Proper Age to Judge for themselves and therefore ought to be Under the Controul of their Freinds many Negroes and Horses which were taken from us are Still Wanting a Particular Account of them we will give you at any time

Brothers you have promised that our people shou'd be at Liberty to return to their relations and that if any of our Freinds shou'd go to your Nation for their Children or relations who are too Young to Judge for themselves you that are now present will deliver them to such persons we also Expect that you will Assist any of our People that go for Negroes or horses in geting such Negroes and Horses belonging to them or any of us and as you have not fully Performed your Engagements with Lord Dunmore we Expect that you will Continue the Hostages with us or others in their stead until the whole of your Promises are Complied with

Brothers your two Young Men going with the Wiandots and Pluggies Son to Kentucke will Probably Occasion some uneasiness Amongst the Inhabitants of that Place and if they Behave amiss some of them Perhaps may be killed We recommend it to you to advise your People and all the other Indians not to go over the Ohio without Necessary Business and to Consult their Nation before they go also to take with them some white Person of Credit to Acquaint the Inhabitants of their Business *A String*

The flying Crow a Cheif of the Six Nations then addressed himself to the Commissioners *Brothers the Bigknife* Listen to what I now say you told us Yesterday that you had spoke all you had to say and Desired our Answer what we have heard from you is Just and right and we are well Pleased with it and hope that all the Nations present do Approve it likewise and now you shall hear what we have to say to you *A String Brothers the Bigknife* listen likewise *brother Onas* listen you told us in your Speech that you Understood we thought you had an Intention of taking our Lands from us you then Assured us you had no such Desire It is true we all Suspected that you Intended to encroach upon our Lands but we are now Satisfied and believe you have no such Intention as we think that our Brothers have spoke the real Sentiments of your Hearts and not from your Lips only you must no doubt know what Lands we have heretofore Granted you and we Expect that you will not Suffer any of your foolish young Men to settle or encroach upon our Lands the Boundaries you Mentioned were Settled by our respective Cheifs and we hope you will Observe them and make no Encroachments upon us that our Children may Continue to live in Peace and Freindship *A Belt*

Brothres the bigknife and Onas listen to me we

have heard what you have said and like it well and shall Carefully Observe your Advice to us and sit Still we and all the Nations present have now fast hold of the Chain of Freindship and you may be Assured that we will not suffer it to Slip through our hands and hope you have the same Strong hold of it *A Belt*

Kiashota another Cheif of the Six Nations then Spoke *Brothers the bigknife and Onas* listen Every thing you have said We like and return you our Sincere thanks *Brothers Onas and the bigknife* we have not much to say but what we do say I hope you will Attend to I Observe that there are some Differences between yourselves I advise you to be Strong and let no Disputes be Among you that our Council fire may be well Kindled and burn Clear so that when we are hereafter invited to it we may come with Pleasure *Brothers the Bigknife and Brother Onas* I advise you to what is good for yourselves I now Assure you that the six Nations have a strong hold of the Chain of Freindship and with these Belts I bind fast in freindship my Brothers the Wiandots, Delawares Shawanese and Tawaas with you *Three Belts one to each Nation*

White Eyes then Addressed the Indians as follows *Brothers* listen to me you heard me tell our Bretheren the English that I hoped we shou'd finish the good work we had began and as our Brothers desired us to remove all Obstructions out of the road that our Young Men Women and Children might Pass and repass Unmolested and that the Freindship which has been made between us in the presence of

God Almighty may be Lasting and Strong and as we know the Bounds of the Lands Claimed by our Brothers Extends as far as the Mouth of the Cherokee River I for my part will be Strong and Prevent my young Men from hunting thereon for I had rather they wou'd employ themselves in planting Corn in their Own feilds than that any Mischeif shou'd happen by their hunting Delivers the Road and Freindship Belts to the Wiandots

Brothers the day before Yesterday our brothers the English Acquainted us that all the White People in this Island had now become as one Man and desired us to be Strong and to hold fast of the Chain of Freindship that subsists between us and them for our parts we are but poor and Ignorant and desire nothing but to Preserve the Freindship and as we have now told our Brothers the English that we have all taken fast hold of the Chain of Freindship let us be strong and on our Parts let none of us Attempt to do any thing that will weaken it in the Least our old Cheif who you now see here as well as our Other Old Cheif who we left sick in our Town desired us to go and Listen to the Speeches that shou'd be made to us and embrace every thing that was good *Uncles the Six Nations* as you Count yourselves strong in your Heart and as you say Command the Hearts of all other Nations of Indians I now desire you to be Strong and Acquaint them of this Freindship that has been made so that it may not be broke but Continue forever *A Belt to the Six Nations*

Brothers listen to me while I speak to our brothers the English Brothers as we have now renewed and

Confirmed the freindship between us if you Suspect that there is any thing in my heart but what is good and Sincere, I beg you wou'd tell me of it; as I wou'd wish that no evil thing thats done by my People shou'd be kept Secret, and that every one may know that I wou'd not desire any thing bad shou'd be Unknown and as you have Informed us that if any of your People shou'd do us any Injury you wou'd Punish them I also now for my part promise that if any of my foolish Young Men shou'd do any harm to your People that we will punish them as they deserve without delay as I wou'd wish to Comply with the dictates of the Christian Religion and Commands of our Saviour whose hands were Nailed to the Cross and sides Peirced for our Sins as far as I am Capable in my Present Dark State *A Belt*

Dr Walker then Spoke *Brothers* we heartily thank you for your kind Advice and you may depend all we have said to you Proceeds from our Hearts and that we shall Punctually Comply with every part of it you Mention that there Appears to be some difference Amongst us we know of none we are all Heartily engaged in the same great and good Cause and Expect you will fully discover it is so before this Business is finished

Kiashota on behalf of the Wiandots and Tawaas then Spoke *Brothers the Bigknife and Onas* we have heard and all the Nations here present have heard what you have said to us and we think it good we were sent here by our Cheifs to listen to what our Brothers the big knife and Onas had to say and we are well Pleased with what we have heard we shall return after the Treaty and inform our Cheifs of the good Speeches you have made to us

The Cornstalk then spoke as follows *All my Elder Brothers the English* the reason of my addressing you in this Manner is because you have Informed us that all the White People in this Island are now become as one Man as it is evening now and you have Desired us to Consider well of what we have to say in reply to you we will do so and return you an Answer tomorrow

---

The Commissioners agreeable to the request of the Shawanese dispatched the following Letters by Express Directed to all the Inhabitants on the Ohio and its Eastern Branches and to the Officer Commanding at the Mouth of the Great Kanhawa

FREINDS AND COUNTRYMEN—The Shawanese have Informed us in Council that some of their foolish Young People had burnt some Houses up the Kanhawa and Committed other Irregularities without the Knowledge of the Cheif of their Nation Those of that Nation now here have sent off two of their People to their Towns to endeavour to restrain them from Crossing the Ohio and with Particular Orders not to give any disturbance or be guilty of the like Behaviour in future. they have likewise Informed us that there are a party of Different Nations gone to Observe the Settlement on Kentucke we therefore have thought it proper to Inform you of this that you may be on your gaurd and at the same time Acquaint the Inhabitants on the Kentucke by the first

Opportunity we wou'd have you Avoid giving the
Indians Offence and forbear hunting on the Other
side of the River Ohio at the same time you are to
gaurd against Mischeif from them and not tamely
Submit to any Insult wantonly offered by them We
have reason to beleive that on the return of their
Cheifs from this place every thing will be Amicably
settled in the Nation as they Intend to return from
Pittsburg by Water we Charge you not to give them
Offence as we are Certain that the Shawanese here
are well disposed and will Preserve the Peace with
the white People if Possible

   we are your freinds and Countrymen
 (Signed)   Tho' Walker James Wood
       A Lewis A Stephen

P S. all officers and Soldiers in Actual Service on
the Ohio are desired to take Notice that they are by
a resolve of the Convention to receive their Instructions from time to time of Captain John Nevill Commandant now at this place

Captain Nevills Instructions to the Officer Commanding at Kanhawa

Sir—as I make no doubt you have seen the resolves
of Convention before this time wherein I am appointed to the Command of the Troops on the Ohio
I hereby request you to keep your Men in good Order
and well disciplined you are to Support and Protect
the Neighbouring Settlements (if any) keep some of
your Men Constantly Scouting to Prevent surprize
shou'd the Indians break out or Attempt to Annoy you
on the Settlements It is Expected the Indians will

keep their own side of the river unless it be to your
Fort on Business and you are not to Suffer your Men
to Hunt on their side but that ought not to prevent
your Reconnoit[r]ing and geting well Acquainted
with the Country you will use the Indians well give
them no Offence and do not tamely Submit to any
Insult designedly Offered to you by them let me
know what prospect you have of geting flour to serve
your Company as I am Apprehensive it may be got
much cheaper from this Quarter than from your
Count[r]y it will be Necessary that you let me know
what Quantity you have Engaged and at what rate
I am Persuaded Beef Can be got upon Better Terms
from Green Brier than here shou'd any thing extra-
ordinary happen in your Quarter you will be Kind
Enough to loose no time in making me Acquainted
with the Particulars I flatter myself I shall have
the Pleasure of being better Acquainted with you for
the time to come I wish you an agreeable Winter
and am with respect yrs

       JOHN NEVILL

At a Conferrence Continued and held with the Different Tribes of Indians 13th October 1775 Present
as before

The Cornstalk came forward and Desired his
Brothers the English his Elder Brothers the Six Nations and Wiandots his Grandfathers the Delawares
and all that were present to Listen to him *Brothers
the Bigknife* agreeable to the Invitation which you
gave all the Indians here present you see Among the

rest your younger Brothers the Shawanese who as soon as they received your Message came to this Council fire which you have Kindled you told us that you had removed all evil as well from our hearts as your own so that we would be the Better Enabled to renew and Brighten the Chain of Freindship I was Exceedingly rejoiced and as I thought the Great and Good Spirit had directed you in your good Speeches I Immediately Joined heartily with you in it you likewise Informed us that you had gathered together all the Bones of our freinds who fell in the late Unhappy disputes between us that you had Buried them and Planted the Tree of Peace over them so that they might never be seen again to Create any Sorrow or Uneasiness I was very Much rejoiced to hear this as I thought the Great Spirit had directed you and that you had become wise and took pity on your young Brothers the Shawanese and all your other Brothers now present We and also our old Brothers the six Nations Wiandots Tawaas and our Grandfathers the Delawares are very glad to hear the good things you have said and Immediately laid hold on every thing that was good *Elder Brothers the six Nations and Wiandots our Young Brothers the Tawaas and Grandfathers the Delawares* you have heard what our Elder Brothers have said to us all and were well Pleased with it you also heard how they addressed themselves to their Younger Brothers the Shawanese separately because they think there is some thing yet between us and them that is unsetled

Brothers the Bigknife yesterday you desired us to deliver up all your flesh and Blood your Negroes your horses and every thing also that belonged to you and that the Hostages that where [were] with you last Winter must remain with you or others in their stead untill We Performed every thing you Asked of us this is a hard task you have set us and may create some Uneasiness among us

Brothers the Bigknife I now Inform you that we Cannot Comply with your request in sending our Hostages back with you they have been with you since the last fall and some others of my young Men I sent to Visit their Bretheren and conduct them to this place the reason of my telling you that We Cannot comply with your request is that we have at three different times delivered up to you your flesh and blood and as you say there are still some remaining among us I begg that you wou'd send Twenty of your People with us we will conduct them safe to our Towns and if they find any of your flesh and Blood let them bring them away they will then have an Opportunity of seeing your horses or any thing else that belongs to you if they find any they may take them I have already inform'd you that I was all last Winter Collecting and delivering up your Horses

as you seem to think that we are the only People who have stolen your horses I now inform you that there are above Twenty of your Horses Among the Tawittawas *my Grandfathers the Delawares* some of your foolish Young Men who joined our foolish men last summer particularly the Pheasant carried of[f] Eight of our Brothers Horses you know best whether they have ever been returned there is a Woman of my Nation Anipassicowa who has some of your Ne-

groes as she belongs to my Tribe I will speak to
her and doubt not she will listen to me but as her
Children are Sprung from my Grandfathers the Delawares there may perhaps some difficulty arise from
that It is true there are two Negro Children which
were begotten by my People and we are not the only
People who have intermixed with Negroes we are
not Willing to give up the Children there is another
old Negro Woman which you may Get if you will
bring her home upon your backs for she is not able
to walk As we have clear'd the road between us We
desire you as before to send Twenty of your young
Men with us to the Mouth of Hockocking and a few
of them may go with us to the Town and they will
then have an Opportunity of seeing and hearing what
We say to your Relations

At a Conference Continued and held with the Indians at Pittsburg the 14th of October 1775 Present
the same as Yesterday The following Speech was
delivered to the diferent Nations of Indians Present
by Doctor Walker

*Brothers the Six Nations Wyandots Delawares
Shawanese and Ottawas* We have in a former Speech
told you that we were sent by our great Council in
Virginia to deliver to you your Hostages and to receive of you Our flesh and Blood and all our Negroes
and Horses that yet remain amongst you agreeable to
your Stipulations with Lord Dunmore We are sorry
you are come Unprepared to fulfill your part of that
Solemn Contract and that our Brothers the Sha-

wanese seems to be averse to give us the reasonable
Security we required for the delivery of our property
yet in their hands this seems to be the only Obstruction in our Way to compleat the very Great and desirable work now on hand we are not come unprepared to give Our brothers the Strongest proofs
of the great desire we have of living in Amity with
them and We hope you will not stand out so far as
to deprive us of the happiness We promis'd ourselves
in giving you this Testimony of our Generosity and
freindship for We can by no Means give the present put into our hands for you but to such as fulfill
their Engagements or at least comply with them as
far as may be in their Power we are far from desiring impossibilities of you and we hope that you will
yet exert yourselves and gather together all of our
peoples property you can find and deliver them up
rather than say "We permit you to search for them"
how should we know where to find them you took
them from us and from your hands we Expect to
receive them

Brothers the Shawanese you told us on Wednesday the 12th of this Instant that three of your foolish
young men had been at the Kanhawa and burned
some old Useless Houses but that the Fort was not
hurt we now have proof that part of the Fort is
burn'd and all the Houses in it destroyed Except the
Loggs of the Store and that five Indians were seen
going from the fort to a house near it who on seeing
our People run of[f] their blankets were found about
a Quarter of a Mile from the place where the Indians

were seen from that Circumstance it Appears they intended Mischeif

Brothers we have before told you all that we had no intention of incroaching on your Lands which are the real Sentiments of our hearts but if you will Continue to do us Mischeif you must not Expect to be treated with such Lenity as you were in the Year 1764 by Colo Boquet and by Lord Dunmore last fall but on the Contrary if you Oblige us to march an Army into any of your Countrys to do ourselves Justice the fault will be your Own and you may Judge the Consequence and you may rely upon it that the Interposition of any other Nation will be ineffectual to restrain us from taking Ample Satisfaction for any Injury that you may do us

Brothers of the different Nations here present we have now delivered you the real Sentiments of our hearts and recommend it to you to Consider it with Attention we have been long here and have never Observed you Consult Mutually together we now hope that you will and that you determine within yourselves to think of nothing else till you return us an Answer which we shall be ready to receive and hope it will be soon *A String to Each Nation*

Kayashuta then Spoke as follows *Brothers the Bignknife & Onas* I and all present have heard what you have said there is one thing you have demanded of our Younger Brothers the Shawanese which at this time is a little difficult for them to perform that is that they shou'd deliver up all your flesh and blood and Negroes and everything else that they have taken from you According to their Promise made last fall however as I represent the Six Nations and am the oldest and have greater Authority than any here I will endeavour to have it done and for that purpose will send two of my Men and my Nephews the Delawares will send two to their Towns to see that it is done the Wiandotts and Ottawas will likewise Assist their Brothers the Shawanese in Complying with your request, as we all think you demand nothing more of them than what you've a right to ask of them What I have said now are the real Sentiments of my heart and I mean to perform what I have now promised to Morrow Morning we will all Consult together and some time in the day will give you a final Answer

Doctor Walker then Replyed *Brothers the Six Nations* you have spoke like honest Men and we have not the least doubt but you will perform what you have promised

---

At a Conference Continued and held with the Indians at Pittsburg October 16th 1775 Present the same as before

Kayashuda on behalf of all the Nations Present spoke as follows *Brothers the Bigknife and Onas* two days ago We heard the demand you made of the Shawanese requiring them to deliver up all your flesh and Blood your Negroes, Horses and all that they had belonging to you According to their promise made last fall to Lord Dunmore We that are here present will aid and assist our Young Brothers to fulfill their engagements with you therefore I shall send off two of my Men with two of the Delawares and Shawanese to morrow to collect what white Prisoners are Among us as well as the Negroes and Horses that are yet among us belonging to you and will deliver them to you if there should be any defeciency we will hope you will pity us as we shall do every thing in our Power to Comply with our promise *Brothers* you require of the Shawanese to leave Hostages with you untill they comply with their Engagements made last fall We think you are rather too strict with them, we hope you will not insist upon it but be satisfied with the Promises we have all made you that the Shawanese shall comply with your demands as far as lies in their Power and We desire that your Brothers the Big knife and Onas will send two of your Men (who are Acquainted with our Language and Customs) with those whom we send that they may be Eye Witness's of our endeavours to comply with our promise *Brothers* as the Winter is coming on we hope you will give the Young Men we send to the Towns some Cloaths to keep them warm and some Amunition to supply them with Provisions on the Road *Three Strings*

White Eyes on behalf of the Delawares then addressed himself to the Commissioners and Six Nations and English and Said *Relations* I am Quite tired in my heart in Considering how we shou'd Compleat the good Work we are about you have heard what our Bretheren the English have said to us for some days past they have demanded their flesh and Blood Negroes and horses and as yet we have nothing to Establish a freindship that our Childeren might reap the Advantage of it

My Uncles the Six Nations I told you before and now tell you that my heart is small and I think of nothing but what is good and as you sayed your hearts were Strong and that you had the hearts of other Nations in your hands I desired you to Advise the other Nations to be Strong and perform what our bretheren the English demanded of them I for my part do not love to speak lies my young Men may go to the Towns but I am sure they will bring nothing back with them as I have not heard my Grand Children the Shawanese promise their bretheren to deliver up what belonged to them and it is more than a Year since the Shawanese have refused to listen to us It is not hard what our Brothers demand of them their Flesh and Blood their Negroes and their Horses belong to them they Promised Lord Dunmore to deliver them up and therefore ought to perform it *A String*

Nimwha a Chief of the Shawanese then Spoke *Brothers the Six Nations and Wiandots and Grandfathers the Delawares* listen while I speak to my brothers the big knife *Brothers the big knife* last fall when Lord Dunmore came near to our Towns and we were concluding a Peace he demanded all your Flesh and Blood Negroes Horses and every other thing belonging to you which were with us when you first made your Appearance at this Council fire we heard the Good things you had to say to us and you demanded your People Negroes and Horses from us. I now promise that we will deliver them up to you as we are desirous that we and our Children after us may live in Freindship. *Uncles the*

Six Nations and Grandfathers the Delawares as we are all going for the People and property of our Brothers the English that are Among us there cannot be the Least doubt but we shall Accomplish it now you have heard what we promised *Brothers the Big knife* as we have now Complied with your request in Promising to deliver up your People and property I beg that you and our Brothers from Philadelphia may think of nothing else for the future but how to Preserve the Friendship between us

Doctor Walker then replied *Brothers of the different Nations* as there seems to be a great difference in Opinion Among you at Present we desire you to Consider well of it to night and become Unanimous in what was proposed by the Six Nations otherwise we shall Insist on Hostages being delivered to Us for the Performance of your Engagement with Lord Dunmore at Camp Charlotte last fall

---

At a Conference Continued and held with the Indians at Pittsburg October 17th 1775 Present as before

Kiashota a Six Nation Cheif addressed the Commissioners as follows *Brothers the Bigknife likewise Brothers Onas* listen to what I am going to say also *my Indian Brothers* Listen to me you know you desired the Shawanese to deliver up your flesh and Blood Negroes and Horses you know the Answer we gave you yesterday that we wou'd assist our Younger Brothers the Shawanese and use our Endeavours that they shou'd Comply with your Demand as the Six Nations are the head of all the other Tribes here present I tell you I will be Strong and use my best Endeavours that the Shawanese shall perform the same I say it shall be done and my People will take Care that the Shawanese shall Comply with it all that are come here to this Council fire came to Perform this Good Work and we hope the same will be Settled to our Mutual Satisfaction as I told you yesterday we wou'd send two Men from Each Nation to bring up your flesh and Blood Negroes and Horses we request you wou'd Nominate two of your young Men to go down to the Towns to see this Promise performed I speak for all the Nations here present *A String*

Nimwha in behalf of the Shawanese then Spoke *Brothers* all here present Listen to me. you have heard what Passed at this Council between us and our Brothers of Virginia *Brothers the Bigknife* I now Inform you what was demanded of us shall be delivered up I now desire that our Hearts may be at Ease and I hope that the Great Spirit will take Pity on us so that we will be able to Conclude a Peace and that our Childrens Children may reap the Blessings and advantage of it as you were sent by the Cheifs of your People and we by our Kings to this Council to renew and Strengthen the Freindship subsisting between us let us now be Strong and Accomplish this good work so that every Morning in future when we rise we may think of Nothing but what is good

Captain White Eyes A Cheif of the Delawares Addressed the Indians as follows. *My Indian Brothers*

listen to me I am very much rejoiced to hear your
Promises that you will deliver up the Flesh and
Blood Negroes and Horses which your Brothers the
Bigknife demanded of you and which has Occasioned
this Long Journey to them formerly I was Concerned in the War against my Bretheren the English
but when the Great Spirit took Pity on us and Peace
was Restored and they demanded their flesh and
Blood of us we then sent our Wise People to Lancaster where they Cleared the Council House and delivered up their Flesh and Blood and every thing was
Settled Shortly after other Mischeif Happened Owing to the Advice of Bad People but when we met
Colonel Boquet at Coshocting and he Demanded his
flesh and Blood we then delivered up some [to] him
and sent Killbuck to Sr William Johnston to finish
the Peace there are four of your flesh and Blood
still remaining with us some of whom run away and
came back One Negro which I now promise to deliver at this place in a few days I now tell you my
Uncles the Six Nations that I will bring them myself
and not give any Trouble to you and as some of my
foolish Young Men who Joined in the Unhappy disputes last Year and who brought of[f] some of their
Brothers Horses I know but of three which I will
likewise deliver up and the Owners shall have them
to ride home in a few days as we have now Finished
and promised to deliver up what you demanded I
now Inform for the future if any Mischeif shou'd
happen I will not Join in it but will Immediately
withdraw myself and think of nothing but what is
good there are two Negro Women and two Children

in our Towns in the hands of the Shawanese which
we will also Use our best Endeavours to have delivered up *A String*

Doctor Walker then delivered the following Speech
to the Different Tribes of Indians *Bretheren*
your younger Brothers the Shawanese are Greatly
Obliged to the other Nations for their kind interposition in their favor we are much pleased to find all
the Nations present so heartily disposed to Establish
the Peace of this Country *Brothers* we have heard
your respective promises and Engagements relying
On the Most faithfull Performance thereof we shall
rest satisfied and desire you will all be strong in this
Good Work that the Peace now Established betwixt
us may Endure forever when you bring our flesh
and Blood Negroes and Horses to this place (which
we hope will be soon) we desire you will deliver them
to Captain Nevill Commandant at this Fort we have
a few Presents to make you for your Winter Cloath-
ing and for your Women and Children which were
sent you by your Brothers of Virginia and which is
over and above their Proportionable part of the present you will hereafter receive from the Com[missi]
oners Appointed by the Thirteen Un[ited] Colonies
the Present put into our h[ands] will be delivered
as soon as the Continental Commissioners finish their
Business with you We are now in perfect Freindship with you all and hope to remain so forever *A
String to Each Nation*

The Different Nations of Indians were then Informed that if they were desirous of sending any of
their Children to be Educated among the White

People it shou'd be done without any Expence to them and that if any of them thought proper to Visit our Country they wou'd be taken by the Hand and treated with Hospitality[21]

At a Conference held with the Different Nations of Indians October 19th 1775 Present the same Commissioners as before The Commissioners as well as the Cheifs of the Different Nations proceeded to the Appointment of persons as well on the part of the Colony as the said Indians to Perform that part of the Treaty relating to the Delivery of the Prisoners Negroes and [H]orses which remain among the Indians Mr John Gibson wit[h] one other White Man is Appointed for the Colony of Virginia Kightoi and Kenightie for the Six Nations Tetepuska, Winganum and Joseph Pepy for the Delawares and Allanawissica and Wewelatimiha for the Shawanese It is likewise Engaged by the Indians that Kiashota a Six Nation Cheif and Capⁿ Pipe a

---

[21] The following letter, dated Williamsburgh, Nov. 18, 1775, is printed in *Amer. Archives*, 4th series, iii, p. 1542: "Dr. Thomas Walker, one of the gentlemen appointed by the Convention to treat with the Indians, is returned to this City and informs that all the different nations, who attended the treaty, are peacefully disposed, notwithstanding the endeavours of several persons from Fort Detroit to set them against this Colony in particular. Mr. Walker has brought with him a young Indian (son of the famous Bawbee) to be educated at college." This young chief remained in Virginia until 1779, but upon his return to the Indian country spread among the tribesmen unfavorable reports of the Virginians. See Heckewelder, *Narrative*, p. 206.—ED.

Delaware Cheif shall go with them to the Shawanese Towns and Assist them in the Execution of their purpose

October 21st 1775

> THOMAS WALKER
> ANDREW LEWIS
> JAMES WOOD
> ADAM STEPHEN

BRITISH REPORT OF TREATY

[Lieut. Gov. Henry Hamilton to Gen. Guy Carleton. 45J101 — A. L., draft in handwriting of Hamilton.]

> DETROIT Nov^r: 30th. 1775
> Dec^r: 4th [22]

SIR: I had the honor of writing to your Ex[cellency] by the opportunity of Mr Bolton Master of the Gage Schooner, who is gone down to Canada to endeavor to engage seamen for the service of the Lakes the ensuing season.[23] Since his departure a Delaware savage, named Mahingan John arrived here 23^d. Nov^r: from Pittsbourg where he had been present at a Council of the Virginians assembled there upon the design of engaging several nations to declare in their favor he came to this place in com-

---

[22] In the manuscript the date Nov. 30th has been crossed out, and Decr. 4th substituted, as here indicated.—ED.

[23] The British kept a considerable naval force on the Great Lakes during the Revolution. See papers concerning the equipment, in *Wis. Hist. Colls.*, xi, pp. 193–202. The "Gage" was still in use in 1777. David Bolton later commanded the "Ottawa," and appears to have had charge of all the shipping on the lakes. See *Mich. Pion. & Hist. Colls.*, ix, p. 351.—ED.

pany with a frenchman (one Drouillard)[24] whom Cap.[n]: Lernoult[25] has employed & who was within ten miles of Pittsburg. Drouillard's busyness was to enquire among the savages what was going forward, & to bring the earliest accounts to this place, as also to accompany any savage who might have got Belts to distribute, & to learn the result as well as to contradict false reports &ct. Mahingan John had got belts from the Virginians, which he was to deliver to a Huron chief called Old Calotte, who lives about

---

[24] In the latter years of the French regime, the father of Pierre Drouillard emigrated to Detroit, where the son was born (about 1754). Pierre early became familiar with Indian languages, and was employed in trade with the savages. While among the Shawnee, he had a son, George, who afterwards accompanied Lewis and Clark on their expedition to the Pacific (1804-06). At the outbreak of the Revolution, Pierre was taken into the Indian department as interpreter for the Wyandot nation, receiving sixteen shillings per day until 1783. In 1778, he saved Simon Kenton from the stake, by the payment of $100 in goods. At the close of the war he sought Kenton's home in Kentucky, where the latter rewarded him with a gift of land, and a home in his own house. In 1786 Drouillard visited Congress, and was taken into United States service, being sent to negotiate with the Northwestern Indians. He finally settled on his farm between Sandwich and Malden and died there in April, 1803. He had married (1776) Angeline Labadie, by whom he left several children. Much of the above information was secured by Draper from the heirs of Kenton and Drouillard; see Draper MSS., 17S and 8BB.—ED.

[25] Richard Berringer Lernoult was in 1756 commissioned lieutenant of the 8th (or King's) regiment, and received his captaincy in 1767. Two years later he was stationed in America, and in 1773 sent with a small detachment to Detroit. In 1776 he was relieved, but returned to Detroit Dec. 1, 1777. There he was left first in command on the departure of Governor Hamilton for Vincennes in October, 1778. After the capture of Hamilton, Lernoult had entire charge of the department of the West until relieved by De Peyster in November, 1779. At Quebec he was promoted to a majority and served as adjutant-general for Haldimand, 1780-83.—ED.

Lieut.-Gov. Henry Hamilton

After a portrait in the possession of Clarence M. Burto of Detroit

10 leagues from this place who is much in the English Interest, and who has declared he will not allow those Belts to go any further, but that they should be buried with him. We expect him here early in the Spring and shall endeavor to keep him in the same disposition. We have had accounts of your Excellency's success against the Rebels upon which I beg leave most sincerely to congratulate you[26]   As Mahingan John is to be at a Council next Spring at Pittsburgh, he has been made acquainted with some of the particulars which are sufficient to undeceive the Delawares and Shawanese, which latter from the purport of the enclosed papers your Excellency will perceive are not likely to continue upon terms with the Virginians. Indeed any Peace between those people and any of the savage nations is liable to frequent interruptions from more causes than one. The Virginians are haughty Violent and bloody, the savages have a high opinion of them as Warriors, but are jealous of their encroachments, and very suspicious of their faith in treaties, the Virginians having furnished them with frequent cause, seizing their Chiefs & detaining them as hostages, during which time their treatment has not been as mild as good policy should have dictated. In the inroads of the Virginians upon the savages, the former have plundered, burnt and murdered without mercy. Tis to be supposed from the character of the savages, that opportunity only

---

[26] Referring doubtless to the defeat and capture of Ethan Allen, who rashly made an attempt upon Montreal, Sept. 24, 1775.—ED.

is wanting to retaliate, and that there can be but little cordiallity between them. If the affairs of the Colonials decline next year as I think we may reasonably expect, from all I can learn of the disposition of the savages, the frontier of Virginia in particular will suffer very severely. The nation of the Hurons is greatly respected by all the neighbouring nations, and it is probable the expence of presents to them next Spring will be pretty considerable. C[aptain] Lernoult tells me your Ex: had mentioned to him by letter that he should have by this fall or the next spring six Months provisions in addition for this post and that of Missilimalkinak, which considering the proposed addition of seamen, and the Necessity of providing the savages will be very necessary. M^r: Hay who acts as Engineer here, and who understands the Huron language,[27] judges from what the savages say that if the Virginians and Delawares should cross the Ohio next Spring it will be as early as April. The Virginians have several Emissaries in pay and have given away in presents and

---

[27] Jehu Hay was born in Chester, Pennsylvania, and in 1758 enlisted in the 60th (or Royal) American regiment. In 1762 he was promoted to a lieutenancy, and sent to Detroit with a detachment of troops. There he served during Pontiac's conspiracy, and in 1766 was made Indian commissary. In 1776 he became deputy Indian agent, and major of the Detroit militia. Having accompanied Hamilton to Vincennes, he was taken prisoner (1779) by George Rogers Clark, and sent to Virginia, where he was finally exchanged in 1781, and passed via New York to England. In June, 1782, Hay was again in Quebec, where he was appointed lieutenant-governor of Detroit to succeed De Peyster. He did not, however, reach Detroit until the summer of 1784, and died a year later while occupying his office. Hay had much influence with the Detroit Indians, by whom he was known as "Touraighwaghti."—ED.

Provisions to the amount of three thousand Pounds, I have desired M`r`: Hay to give me a copy of his letter to Capt`n`: Claus[28] which I have the honor to enclose to your Ex: as it may save the time of Capt`n`: Claus communicating to you what it contains. A Canadian one Desnoyers[29] carries the Express, accompanied by a Chipawaa Savage,[30] they are to call at Niagara and pass by the way of Oswegatchie[31]

---

[28] Col. Daniel Claus was born in Germany in 1727. Arriving in Philadelphia in 1749, he met Conrad Weiser, a well-known Indian interpreter, and accompanied him among the Six Nations. Claus's proficiency in acquiring Indian languages attracted the notice of the governor of Pennsylvania who commissioned him to learn Iroquois, during which time he resided with Sir William Johnson and King Hendrick, the Mohawk. In the French and Indian War Claus was commissioned lieutenant of the 60th regiment, and deputy Indian agent under Johnson. At the close of the war, having married Johnson's daughter, he became superintendent for the Canadian Indians, an office which he held until 1776. Having then been superseded, he visited England, returning in 1777 with a new commission as deputy Indian agent. In that capacity he accompanied St. Leger's expedition (1777) and was in constant service during the Revolutionary War. At its close, while in the mother country to recover his estate confiscated by the Americans, he died in Cardiff, Wales, 1787.—ED.

[29] The Desnoyers were a prominent Detroit family, one member of which, living on the east side of the river, warned the English officers of the intended siege by Pontiac. Pierre Desnoyers and wife are noted in the census of 1779.—ED.

[30] The Chippewa are a large branch of the Algonquian family, whose first representatives were met by the French at Sault Ste. Marie—hence their French name, Saulteurs. Upon the founding of Detroit, one branch was attracted to that vicinity. Their chief habitat was, however, the shores of Lake Superior and the country north, where large bands of this tribe are still extant.—ED.

[31] Fort Oswegatchie was on the site of the mission and fortified post of Abbé Picquet, a Sulpician missionary, who began an establishment in 1749, called "La Presentation." By the time of the French and Indian War, he had attracted to this place a force of nearly a thousand Iroquois. Being surrendered

to Montreal, they have directions to go to General Prescott,[32] and wait for your Excellency's orders. As soon as the season grows something milder (for we have now very severe frost with snow) I shall review the Companies of Militia and make your Excellency a report of the state in which I shall find them. As it may possibly happen that Captain Bolton (whom I have already mentioned) has been detained by bad weather, or some unforeseen accident, I send a duplicate of Captn: Grant's[33] return of Naval stores wanting for the Vessels, that if possible they may come by the first Batteaux. The Traders at this Place have presented me a petition (respecting the carrying place at Niagara) to be laid before your Excellency, which I send by the Express. I am not a proper judge of the reasonable [ness] of

to the English in 1760, they rebuilt the fort and named it Oswegatchie. A garrison was maintained therein until after Jay's Treaty in 1794. The fort was on the site of the present town of Ogdensburgh, N. Y.—ED.

[32] Richard Prescott (1725–88) became major of the 33rd infantry in 1756. In 1773 he came to Canada, and with the rank of brigadier-general was in command at Montreal in 1775. When Montgomery captured the city, Prescott attempted to escape down the river, but was intercepted and made prisoner. Exchanged the following August (1776), he was sent in December to command in Rhode Island, where he was again made prisoner by the Americans. Prescott was accused of much harshness in his treatment of American prisoners, and was greatly disliked.—ED.

[33] Capt. Alexander Grant of the 42nd infantry was in Detroit as early as 1774. He commanded a vessel on the Great Lakes during the entire Revolutionary War, and later became commodore of the British fleet, as well as serving as magistrate and councillor for the district. In 1812 he was still in command, after fifty years of service. He died at his home at Grosse Pointe about 1815, aged above eighty-five years. His naval service was efficient.—ED.

their demands and objections, but by all accounts the present occupyer has behaved with uncommon Diligence, activity and spirit, and I take the liberty of representing him to your Excellency as a very proper person, at the same time, that I by no means insinuate the facts alledged by the traders to be falsely stated. Mr Stedman told me when on the spot, that having been used to transport the loading of Batteaux, estimated at so many Barrels, or so many Packs, these Barrels & packs at a certain weight, he found *some* traders had added to the size of the former & the Weight of the latter, so that he came to a resolution of having all goods weighed in scales at the landing, & to take payment accordingly which would prevent imposition. It is not to be supposed however that the parties concerned are to be judges of the rates or to fix them themselves. I told them they were not to expect at such a time as this that regulations were to be alterd, or another carrying place thought of on the opposite side (which is the Idea of the Merch^s: in Canada as I am informd,) but that they might expect Government would in due time attend to their representation. I shall not at present take up your Excellency's time with a detail of matters relating to the civil state of the Settlement, when it is signified to me that it may be seasonably done, I shall take the liberty of laying before your Excellency such things as call more immediately for redress.

I am informed by a person of Character here (M^r: Hay acting Engineer,) that when Colo^l: Bradstreet took Possession of this place & Missilimakinak[84] he took to the last place a number of Canadians with Arms to assist in taking Possession of the Post, & to cut fuel & do other services for the Garrison, they were promised half a Dollar p^r: day, but never got payment, tho they had neglected their harvest & returnd half naked. such a precedent must be of the worst Consequence and I mention the fact to your Excellency as it has left a deep impression on those who were sufferers from such a dishonorable breach of word and Credit. I beg leave to remind your Ex: of a young man named Ferguson or Farquharson, apprentice to M^r: Dobie Merch^t at Montreal, who was extremely active as a Volunteer on the Sorel, and who gave the strongest proofs of his zeal for Government, I had promised him to speak in his favor to your Excellency, but my sudden departure from Montreal would not allow me to be as good as my word, I hope to be excused for taking that liberty now, as I really look upon him to be a young man who would not be a disgrace to the service,

---

[84] Col. John Bradstreet, although English born, spent most of his mature life in America. Distinguishing himself for gallantry at the siege of Louisburg (1745), he received promotion in the army; and in the French and Indian War was for some time in command at Oswego. His most noted exploit was the capture of Fort Frontenac (1758). After Pontiac and his braves had besieged Detroit for nearly fifteen months, Bradstreet arrived in August, 1764, with an army of twelve hundred overawing the recalcitrant chiefs. Having made a treaty with the Indians, Colonel Bradstreet sent a detachment of three hundred troops under Capt. John Howard to reoccupy Mackinac, or Fort Missilimackimac, as it was then called. With them went two companies of Canadian militia, composed of fifty men each. Bradstreet was made major-general in 1772, but died two years later at Detroit.—ED.

& whose talent seems to lye that way, he speaks french very well and is not forward.

The following Paragraph is copied from the torn pieces of a paper which coverd the Talk of the Virginians to the savages at Fort Pitt, and which I suppose beeing deem'd by some of the council as too acrimonious has been corrected and crossed out as I have done exactly[85]

I have sent this copy to your Excellency because tho not deliverd at the Council it shows how hardly they can restrain their inveteracy against the Savages, and how little cordiallity there can be in their Professions on either side. it does not appear that the savages have returned Belts or Strings for those presented them by the Commissioners, nor have we any account of the answer given by them to the Talk of the Commissioners. a copy of the minutes is sent to Niagara, & will be forwarded in the Spring to Missilimakinak

HENRY HAMILTON[86]

Copy of a letter to Genl. Carleton Dec^r: 5th. 1775

wrote the same day to Genl. Gage an acc^t. of the meeting at Fort Pitt on the 7th. Oct^r: kept no Copy

same date to Genl. Gage Boston [87] Genl. Prescott, Montreal Lord Rawdon Boston [88] Captⁿ: Gambel Montreal [89] Colo^l. Caldwell Niagara

---

[85] Here follows a copy of Dr. Walker's speech of Oct. 14, as delivered to the tribesmen, without any omissions; see *ante*, pp. 116–118. Hamilton was incorrect in his surmise that this was too acrimonious to be delivered.—ED.

[86] Henry Hamilton, of Irish descent, entered the British army in 1754; two years later he received his lieutenancy, and served with the 15th infantry, at first in France and then with Amherst at Louisburg (1758), where he was slightly wounded. His regiment had part in the battles around Quebec, and later

CONNOLLY'S PLOT

[The first document is an extract from a letter dated Georgetown, Md., Nov. 26, 1775, published in *Pennsylvania Packet*, 1775, transcribed in Draper MSS., 2JJ, book E, 30-33; the second is from the same source, Dec. 4, 1775, 2JJ34, 35.]

Agreeable to what I wrote you by ———, I set out on Tuesday morning last for Frederick-Town, and when within eight or nine miles of that place, had the pleasure to hear that Major Connolly with three companions were taken about five miles above Hagar's Town, on their way to Fort Pitt; Connolly

---

served in the West Indies. In April, 1775, he was appointed lieutenant-governor of Detroit, where he arrived Nov. 9 of the same year. He was accused of cruelty in instigating the Indians to war, and when captured by George Rogers Clark at Vincennes (1779) was sent to Virginia in irons. His exchange was not arranged until 1780, when he returned to England via New York. In 1782 he was appointed to succeed Haldimand as governor of Canada, an office which he held until 1785. In 1790 he was made governor of Bermudas, and in 1794 of Dominica. During the latter incumbency he died (1796) on the island of Dominica.—ED.

[87] Gen. Thomas Gage (1721-87) entered the army in 1741 and first served in Flanders. Coming to America with Braddock (1754), he continued here throughout the French and Indian War, and at its close (1763) was made commander-in-chief of British forces in America, with headquarters in New York. Having returned to England in 1772, he was sent two years later to subdue the rebellious province of Massachusetts. Not succeeding in this he resigned (1775) and returned to England.—ED.

[88] Francis Lord Rawdon (1754-1826), later Marquis of Hastings, was a brilliant young nobleman who came over with Gage and served against the colonists until 1781. His most noted command was in South Carolina. He was active in English politics, and in 1812 became governor-general of India, in which post he remained ten years.—ED.

[89] Thomas Gambel was a lieutenant when he came to America in 1762. He had received his captaincy in August of the year in which Hamilton writes. See his letters from Quebec in *Amer. Archives*, 4th series, iv, p. 962.—ED.

has been this summer at Boston, where he presented a plan of operations for the next spring, to General Gage, which met the general's approbation, and he was now on his way to put it in execution.[40] He is made Lieutenant Colonel Commandant, was to proceed to Fort Detroit, where Captain Lord, who is now at the Illinois with two companies of the Royal Irish,[41] was to meet him with the field pieces and

---

[40] Upon reaching Lord Dunmore, off Yorktown in August, Connolly made such an impression upon the late governor's mind by his plan to advance against the colonists from the Western frontier, that the latter sent him by sea to Boston. There Gage approved his plan, and had he gone as was first proposed by way of Quebec and the Great Lakes to Detroit, it might have been successfully carried out—to the great injury of the American cause. The capture of Montreal and Arnold's expedition against Quebec, blocked the Canadian enterprise, whereupon Connolly made his way back to Lord Dunmore, and attempted to reach the West through Virginia and Maryland. He was, however, too well-known and too strongly suspected to escape the vigilance of the patriots, who were warned by his letters to John Gibson and White Eyes (see *ante,* pp. 72-74), and arrested him as here stated on the night of Nov. 19.—ED.

[41] Hugh Lord was commissioned captain in England, in 1762. In 1770 he was assigned to the 18th Royal Irish regiment then in America, and probably went to Illinois with Lieut.-Col. John Wilkins, whom he superseded in command of that country in 1771. Wilkins was very unpopular with the habitants. Lord, on the contrary, made himself much liked by them. During his administration (1772), Fort Chartres was abandoned, because of being undermined by floods, and the garrison withdrawn to Kaskaskia, christening their stronghold Fort Gage. Lord was in Detroit until 1777. The following year he was promoted to a majority and assigned to the 75th, which took no part in the American war. In 1783 he was retired on half pay, but in the Napoleonic wars was major of the 7th Royal Irish, and commandant for the island of Jersey. He died June 2, 1829. His withdrawal from the Illinois early in 1776 doubtless was caused by the failure of Connolly's plan. See the latter's letters in *Amer. Archives,* 4th series, iv, pp. 617, 618.—ED.

stores that are there. Connolly was to raise a regiment, as many Indians and partisans as he could; to enable him to do this, he had power to engage to every person that entered into the service three hundred acres of land when the troubles are over, and whatever other pecuniary rewards he might think proper, was to appoint and commission all the officers under him, which commissions were to be confirmed by Dunmore.

With this force he was to destroy Fort Pitt and Fort Fincastle,[42] if the Americans should make any resistance, and meet Dunmore by the 20th of April next at Alexandria, where he, Dunmore was to land an army under the cannon of the ships of war. Connolly's companions were one Cameron,[43] who is now a lieutenant, with promise of promotion, one Dr. Smith who says he was to be surgeon of Connolly's regiment:[44] the other was Connolly's servant.

---

[42] For an account of Fort Fincastle see *Dunmore's War*, p. 86, note 35.—ED.

[43] Allen Cameron was a native of Scotland, and probably related to the deputy Indian agent, John Stuart; see *Ibid.*, p. 40, note 72. Connolly says (*op. cit.*, in note 40, *ante*) that Cameron had been agent under Stuart, had suffered much for his principles, and had refused offers of military rank from South Carolinian patriots; that he had come to Virginia with dispatches from the governors of East Florida and South Carolina, and knowing Indian character was considered by Lord Dunmore a proper person to join his (Connolly's) expedition. In December, 1776, Cameron made an attempt to escape from the Philadelphia prison, but his rope broke, and he fell fifty feet, being found in an apparently dying condition. He partially recovered, however, and obtained his release in the winter of 1778, when he went to England, his physical condition debarring him from further military service.—ED.

[44] John Ferdinand Dalziel Smyth was a native of Scotland, who came to America a few years before the Revolution, and according to his own account, published as *A Tour in the*

They were brought into Frederick-Town on Wednesday morning, and on Thursday examined before the Committee. On searching their portmanteaus a copy of Connolly's plan was found.[45] Thus you see a part of the diabolical scheme is defeated, but make no doubt but Dunmore will land an army at Alex-

---

United States of America (London, 1784), travelled extensively in all the southern and western portions of the country. He finally bought property and settled in Maryland, whence he was driven at the commencement of the Revolution, because of his Loyalist sentiments. Having visited Lord Dunmore at Norfolk, he was induced to embark in Connolly's expedition. A brief account of his arrest is given in *Amer. Archives*, 4th series, iv, p. 616, note. Having made a bold escape, and a subsequent push for Fort Pitt, charged with Connolly's orders, he was again arrested and his papers confiscated, he being sent to Philadelphia for confinement. He finally escaped from Baltimore in December, 1776, reached Lord Howe in New York, and was made captain in the Queen's Rangers. In that capacity he was in the battle of Germantown. Smyth had a facile pen, and wrote several Loyalist ballads and songs. His *Tour* is not to be trusted; he makes therein many unauthenticated statements.—ED.

[45] For this plan, see succeeding document. In his "Narrative," Connolly says that the search of the committee for his papers was at first ineffectual, as both he and Dr. Smyth had destroyed all incriminating documents before leaving Norfolk. Yet "there was a manuscript that had been wrapt around a stick of black ball by my servant, so soiled and besmeared, as to have escaped the search both of ourselves there, and the committee here, who were as industrious as they were suspicious. This paper, which contained a rough draft of propositions, supposed to have been laid before General Gage by me, but which really was not the case, was discovered in consequence of a fresh examination demanded by a Member of Congress, who arrived at the committee some days after we had been taken to Frederick Town, and was published as my confession, though I repeatedly, and with truth, denied the justice of the supposition." Connolly also states that his important papers were concealed in the pillion sticks of his saddle, that his servant obtained access to the shed where they were, and in the dead of the night destroyed all the papers save Connolly's commission, which he managed to have conveyed to him.—ED.

andria in the spring; but as their scheme has thus providentially come to light, hope such preparations will be made, as will enable us to give him the reception he merits.

Proposals for raising an army to the Westward, and for effectually obstructing a communication between the Southern and Northern Governments.

"As I have, by directions from his Excellency Lord Dunmore, prepared the Ohio Indians to act in concert with me against his Majesty's enemies in that quarter; and have also dispatched intelligence to the different officers of the militia on the frontiers of Augusta county, in Virginia, giving them Lord Dunmore's assurances that such of them as shall hereafter evince their loyalty to his Majesty, by putting themselves under my command, when I should appear amongst them with proper authority for that purpose, of a confirmation of titles to their lands, and the quantity of three hundred acres to all who should take up arms in support of the constitution, when the present rebellion subsided, I will undertake to penetrate through Virginia, and join his Excellency Lord Dunmore at Alexandria early next spring, on the following conditions and authority.

"*First*, That your Excellency will give me a commission to act as major commandant of such troops as I may raise, and embody on the frontiers, with a power to command to the westward and employ such serviceable French and English partizans as I can engage by pecuniary rewards or otherwise.

"*Secondly*, That your Excellency will give orders to Capt. Lord, at the Illinois, to remove himself, with the garrison under his command, from Fort Gage to Detroit,[46] by the Anabache [Wabash], bringing with him all the artillery, stores, &c. &c. to facilitate which undertaking he is to have authority to hire boats, horses, Frenchmen, Indians &c. &c. to proceed with all possible expedition on that rout, as the weather may occasionally permit, and to put himself under my command on his arrival at Detroit.

"*Thirdly*, That the commissary at Detroit shall be empowered to furnish such provision as I may judge necessary for the good of the service, and that the commanding officer shall be instructed to give every possible assistance in encouraging the French and Indians of that settlement to join me.

---

[46] There has been considerable controversy over the site of Fort Gage, local tradition having long placed it on the east bank of Kaskaskia River, opposite the town. This appears to have been the actual site of an early French fort, known only as Kaskaskia, which was burned in 1766; and of Fort Gage, a later American fort, occupied in the first years of the nineteenth century. The British Fort Gage, however, was situated in the village itself, on the west bank of the river, in the southeastern portion of the town. When Captain Lord was obliged to abandon Fort Chartres (1772), he removed the garrison to Kaskaskia, and occupied the house that had belonged to the Jesuit missionaries, which he stockaded and called Fort Gage. This was the stronghold captured by George Rogers Clark on July 4, 1778. The name was thereafter changed to Fort Clark.

Lord removed the garrison and most of his effects from Fort Gage to Detroit in May, 1776, leaving Philippe de Rocheblave in command, without a garrison. It has been assumed that Lord's retirement was due to Carleton's desire to concentrate and cut down expense. May not this project of Connolly and its failure account in at least some measure for the abandonment of the Illinois?—ED.

"*Fourthly*, That an officer of artillery be immediately sent with me to pursue such rout as I may find most expedient to gain Detroit, with orders to have such pieces of light ordnance as may be thought requisite for the demolishing of Fort Dunmore and Fort Fincastle, if resistance should be made by the rebels in possession of those garrisons.

"*Fifthly*, That your Excellency will empower me to make such reasonable presents to the Indian chiefs and others, as may urge them to act with vigor in the execution of my orders.

"*Sixthly*, That your Excellency will send to Lord Dunmore such arms as may be spared, in order to equip such persons as may be willing to serve his Majesty at our junction, in the vicinity of Alexandria, &c. &c. If your Excellency judges it expedient for the good of the service, to furnish me with the authority and other requisites I have mentioned, I shall embrace the earliest opportunity of setting off for Canada, and shall immediately dispatch Lord Dunmore's armed schooner, which now awaits my commands, with an account of what your Excellency has done, and that I shall be ready, if practicable, to join your Lordship by the twentieth of April, at Alexandria, where the troops under my command may fortify themselves under my cover of the men of war on that station.

"If, on the contrary, your Excellency should not approve of what I propose, you will be good enough to immediately honor me with your dispatches to the Earl of Dunmore, that I may return as early as possible.

THE FRONTIERS, EARLY IN 1776

[Summary of conditions on the frontiers in the first months of 1776.]

The Virginia Convention met at Richmond Dec. 1, 1775, and adjourned to Williamsburgh, where sessions were held until January 20, 1776. The raising of troops occupied a large part of the time; arrangements were made to settle the accounts of Dunmore's War, and private claims to the fort at Pittsburgh were adjudicated.[47]

Meanwhile according to the reports of the trader, John Dodge,[48] the British commandant at Detroit was urging the Western Indians to war upon the American frontier settlements. Sometime in March, a French-

---

[47] See minutes in *Amer. Archives*, 4th series, iv, pp. 75–112. The claims against the government for Fort Pitt grew out of the purchase made in 1772 by Alexander Ross and William Thompson of the buildings of the fort, when it was abandoned by the British garrison.—ED.

[48] John Dodge was born in Connecticut about 1749. In 1770 he entered the Indian trade and settled in the Wyandot villages on the Sandusky, where he acquired considerable influence over the savages. Charged with leaning to the colonists' side, he was arrested in January, 1776, confined at Detroit, and finally sent a prisoner to Quebec, whence he escaped in 1778 and made his way to Boston. He was received with cordiality by Gates and Washington, and Congress noticed his case; granting him a compensation in land for his losses at Sandusky. Having visited Virginia he made the acquaintance of Jefferson, who appointed him Indian agent for the Illinois country. After his arrival in Kaskaskia, he became the leader of the military party in that county, and was accused of peculation and arbitrary violence with the inhabitants. After 1782 he dominated the settlement, having seized and fortified a commanding site. In 1787 he removed to Ste. Genevieve on the Spanish side of the river and died in that vicinity in 1794. See C. W. Alvord, *Cahokia Records* (Springfield, Ill., 1907), pp. xcv-cxx, xiv.—ED.

man named Lorimier,[49] who had large influence with the Western Indians, left Montreal in company with two Englishmen to visit the upper country and secure adherents for the British.[50]

Reports of this activity on the part of the British gave great uneasiness to the Western settlers, now beginning to seek the rich cane-lands of Kentucky, and cultivating the Virginia valleys leading to the Ohio. Want of ammunition was one of the difficulties, and in May, George Gibson and William Linn led an expedition down the Ohio, in order to procure supplies of powder from New Orleans.[51]

---

[49] Peter Lorimier (Laramie, Lorimie) was a French trader who about 1769 established a trading house on the west bank of the Great Miami, since called from his name Lorime's Creek. He was a prominent interpreter and Indian agent for the British during the Revolution and successive Indian wars. In 1778 he was one of the party that captured Daniel Boone. In 1782, Clark's expedition rifled his post, when he narrowly escaped personal capture. He remained in the British service until about 1793, when with a considerable band of Shawnee he removed across the Mississippi, and was appointed an officer in the Spanish service.—ED.

[50] *Amer. Archives*, 4th series, v, p. 417.—ED.

[51] For the result of this expedition see *post*, 1777.

George Gibson was a brother of John, being born in Lancaster County, Pa., in 1747. Entering a mercantile house in Philadelphia, he made several voyages to the West Indies as supercargo. Early becoming interested in Western lands, he received a large patent on the Cumberland in 1768. At the outbreak of the Revolution he raised a company around Fort Pitt, where his battalion was known as "Gibson's Lambs," and reinforced the Virginia line. His venturesome expedition to New Orleans (1776-77) brought him promotion, and he joined Washington's army as colonel, serving in the Jersey campaigns. Retiring to his home in Cumberland County (Pa.) he became county lieutenant and in that capacity led out a regiment to re-inforce St. Clair, and was killed in the Indian battle of 1791.

Col. William Linn was born in Warren County, N. J., in 1734. In his youth he removed to western Maryland and took

At Fort Pitt, Captain Neville was occupied with garrison duties and Indian negotiations. An expedition against Detroit was considered by Congress, upon the suggestion of Gen. Charles Lee, seconded by Washington; but in the multitude of affairs the project was lost sight of, and because of insufficient means was dropped.[52]

A CAPTAIN'S COMMISSION

[Virginia Committee of Safety to William Harrod. 4NN27 — D. S.]

The Committee of Safety for the Colony of Virginia.

To WILLIAM HARROD[53] GENTLEMAN—By Virtue of the Power and Authority invested in us, by the Dele-

---

active part in Forbes's campaign (1758), being wounded in McDonald's expedition of 1774. When George Gibson enlisted his rifle company (1775), Linn went with him as first lieutenant. He also joined Gibson's New Orleans expedition, performing the difficult exploit of bringing a considerable supply of powder up the Mississippi and Ohio to Pittsburgh (see *post*). In 1777 he was out with Foreman's party, but by his sagacity escaped the massacre, bringing the news of the defeat to Forts Shepherd and Henry. The next year, Linn joined George Rogers Clark's expedition, took part in the Kaskaskia campaign, and settled a station not far from Louisville. In 1780 he was colonel of militia in the Indian campaign of that year, but was shot and mortally wounded by Indians near his home, March 5, 1781.—ED.

[52] See *Journals of the Continental Congress* (Washington, 1906), iv, pp. 301, 318, 373; also *Amer. Archives*, 4th series, vi, p. 403; and *Penna. Colon. Records*, x, p. 525.—ED.

[53] For a brief sketch of William Harrod, see *Dunmore's War*, p. 68, note 14. The commission is issued on a printed form, the words here printed in Italics being written in the blank spaces. The signatures are autographs.—ED.

gates and Representatives of the several Counties and Corporations in General Convention assembled, we, reposing especial Trust and Confidence in your Patriotism, Fidelity, Courage, and good Conduct, do, by these Presents, constitute and appoint you to be *Captain* of the Militia of the *District* of *West Augusta;* and you are therefore carefully and diligently to discharge the Trust reposed in you, by disciplining all Officers and Soldiers under your Command. And we do hereby require them to obey you, as their *Captain*. And you are to observe and follow all such Orders and Directions as you shall from Time to Time receive from the Convention, the Committee of Safety for the Time being, or any superior Officers, according to the Rules and Regulations established by the Convention.

Given under our Hands, at *Williamsburgh* this 7th *Day of March* Anno Domini 1776.

JOHN PAGE
DUDLEY DIGGES
P. CARRINGTON
THO[s] LUD. LEE
JOS. JONES
THOMAS WALKER[54]

---

[54] Members of the committee of safety, who were in charge of the executive department of the government until the election of Patrick Henry as first governor of the state of Virginia, June 29, 1776. This committee consisted of eleven members, those in office at the time of this commission being chosen by the convention on Dec. 16, 1775. All had previously served on the committee, save Joseph Jones of King George County, and Thomas Walker, who replaced George Mason and Carter Braxton.—ED.

INFORMATION REGARDING DETROIT

[Unsigned letter. 3U580.]

DETROIT 2d April 1776

Detroit is garrisoned by 120 Soldiers of the 8th. reg^t commanded by Capt Richard Berenger Lernoult,[55] the soldiers seen indifferant about the present unhappy Disputes. An attack has been long suspected From Fort Pitt and Fasines prepared for Defence of the Citadal. at present there is none suspected for this season. a Serjant and 12 men mounte guard in the town, and A Corporal and 4 men in the Citidal, half their number are centries. Supplies of amunition and provisions are received from canada By the way of Niagara. of the Former there is about a Tun of Powder, ball And Shott in proportion, of the Latter Sufficient to next August or Septr. The French are desirous of remaining neuter, there is no Noblesse among Them to stir them up. the English are in General well disposed, there is two Priest[s], one on the S E side of the river (a Jesuit Pere Poutie) the other In the Fort (a Recolet Pere Semple)[56]

---

[55] Henry Hamilton arrived as lieutenant-governor, Nov. 9, 1775; Lernoult was, however, in charge of the troops of the garrison until sometime in the summer of 1776.—ED.

[56] Père Pierre Potier was born in Belgium in 1708, entered the Jesuit order when twenty-one years of age, and came to America in 1743. After a year spent in studying the Huron language, he was sent to re-inforce the Huron mission at Detroit. This mission had been established at Pointe de Montreal (now Sandwich, Ont.) by Père de la Richardie. Upon the latter's retirement, Potier became superior of the mission, ministering to both Huron converts and French habitants. During Pontiac's conspiracy, he is thought to have furnished useful information to the British garrison. As a philologist he accumulated material on the Huron grammar, and left a con-

The Millitia are Embodid, but not Deciplined or Exercised. their number is about 350 which includes all able To bear arms, their Cap^{ts} are Piere Reaume Joseph Bundes, Jacque Campeau, Bap^t Chapaten,[57] Phillip Dijean,[58] and James Sterling,[59] their intention

---

siderable body of manuscripts—see Thwaites, *Jesuit Relations*, lxix, lxx. His death in 1781 was due to an accidental fall.

Père Simple (Simplicus Bocquet) was priest of the church of St. Anne, 1754–84. This, the first church built at Detroit, was placed by its founders under the care of the Recollects, and was thus maintained until after the Revolution. Father Simple was at his post during Pontiac's conspiracy, and at the time of the Revolution was spoken of as an excellent, kindhearted old man.—ED.

[57] All these were prominent members of Detroit French families. The first Pierre Reaume came with his brother Hyacinthe to Detroit before 1726. Many descendants of both branches spread over the Northwest. Capt. Pierre Reaume was dismissed from the service before 1778, but continued to reside in Detroit some time thereafter.

Joseph Douaire de Bondy came to Detroit from Montreal about 1730. His son Joseph married at the former city in 1758, was still captain of militia in 1778, and was on the tax roll of 1799.

The Campeaus were a prominent Detroit family, whose progenitor came to that place as an armorer as early as 1710. Jacques Junior married in 1760 Catharine Ménard. He had resigned his captaincy by 1778, and Jean Baptiste Campeau had been appointed in his place.

The first Jean Baptiste Chapoton came to Detroit in 1718 as surgeon to the garrison. His son, born in 1721, was active in interceding with Pontiac in 1763. A petition of 1769 shows him as a prominent merchant. He resigned his captaincy before 1778, and was freely accused of sympathy with the American colonists.—ED.

[58] Philip de Jean was probably born in France, coming to Detroit as merchant shortly before the English conquest. Becoming a British subject he was appointed (1767) justice of the peace, and is said to have served the interests of the military

[59] James Sterling came to America with the British forces during the French and Indian War, and served as commissary under Haldimand in 1759–60. At the close of the war he settled in Detroit, where he married into a French family,

are To Remain neuter. The Savages are wavering, and divided, Frequent Councils have [been], and are held with them, By the commanding officer asisted By Jehu Hay Indian Agent at this place. they are desired to Opose Any Body of men that may penetrate into their Country. this is All that has transpired and it does not appear that any general Combination is Formed among them. There is two armed Schooners On the Lake Bellonging to the Crown, mounting 12 Six pounders each, the Largest the General Gage is commanded by James Andrews,[60] the other the Dunmore Is commanded by David Bolton, Besides these, there is two Schooners and two Sloops bellonging to Capt Alex^{dr} who commands the whole Naval

---

commandants while acting in that capacity. In 1779 he was on his way to re-inforce Hamilton at Vincennes, when he was captured by a force sent out by George Rogers Clark, and with others sent a prisoner to Virginia. Having accepted a parole in October, 1779, he visited the Illinois, and was desirous of communicating with his family in Detroit. The conduct of the British authorities exasperated De Jean, who resolved to live no longer under English rule, whereupon he visited France, and in 1786 was naval agent of that government at New London, Conn. The French Revolution involved him in serious financial difficulties, and having retired to the West Indies he died a prisoner on the island of Jamaica in 1795. These biographical details, derived from the Draper MSS., are believed to have been hitherto unpublished.—ED.

---

and became the chief merchant of the place. His knowledge of Indian languages gave him government employ as interpreter, and his popularity with the French led to his being chosen militia captain. Later (1777), he was suspected of sympathy with the Americans, deprived of his office, and sent to Canada to give security for his conduct.—ED.

[60] Capt. James Andrews was a lake captain in the Northwest as early as 1773. He was highly recommended by Governor Hamilton in 1778, being promoted to command the shipping on Lake Ontario, an office which he held until his decease, late in 1780 or early in 1781.—ED.

Department, and one Sloop bellonging to Messrs. McTavish and McBeth[61] Wiiliam Rinhen [?] Commands one of the Sloops called the Angelica[62] the others are At present without Masters. To man the whole there is 30 Seamen and Servants, among that number are very few seamen and not one Gunner, they are generally disatisfied with the Service, and will make a poor resistance. The Vessels commands the Fort, which is only defended by a Stocade of Picquets about 9 Feet out of the earth, without Frize or ditch. The Picquets are mostly cedar, and generaly Sound. There is about 20 Boats at the place capable of car[rying] [Ms. torn] Barrels each, and boards Sufficent to build 60 more.

The armed Schooners are at Fort Erie[63] (an In-

---

[61] Simon McTavish was one of the fur-traders who founded the North West Company. Coming early to the West, he was in 1782 enrolled as a citizen of Detroit. Later, he made his home in Montreal, directing the affairs of the fur-trade in so able but arbitrary a manner that he became known as "le Marquis." After founding a large fortune through what was essentially a trade monopoly, he died at Montreal in 1804.

George McBeath was likewise a Scotchman prominently identified with the Northwestern fur-trade. One of the founders of the North West Company, he operated largely in Wisconsin, with headquarters at Mackinac, making himself useful to the British commandants at the latter post. In 1783 he accompanied Charles de Langlade to Prairie du Chien to hold a conference with the Indians and announce the Peace of Paris.—ED.

[62] The "Angelica" was wrecked on the lakes in the autumn of 1783.—ED.

[63] Fort Erie, at the lower end of Lake Erie, on the west bank of Niagara River, was built in 1764 by Capt. John Montressor, who prepared the way for Col. John Bradstreet's expedition to Detroit. During the Revolution it was maintained chiefly as a supply depot. It was rebuilt at intervals (1778, 1790, 1807), and during the War of 1812-15 was an important factor in the British-American contest. After a spirited de-

significant [fort] garrisoned by 20 Men) during the months of may and June, one of them once took all the others, with Detroit and Michilimacinack falls Presguile[64] is only Ninety miles from Fort Erie.

INDIANS VISIT NIAGARA

[Summary of printed documents in *Amer. Archives,* 4th series, v, pp. 815-820.]

In a letter of Richard Butler[65] dated at Fort Pitt, April 8, 1776, he states that Kiasola[66] with two mes-

---

fense during August and September, 1814, the Americans blew up the fort upon their departure in November. The ruins remained until 1860 or later. The Canadian government has since rebuilt and regarrisoned this fort.—ED.

[64] Fort Presqu'isle was built (1753) on the site of the present Erie, Pa., by a French expedition under the leadership of Captain Marin. In 1758 it was greatly strengthened, but upon the capture of Forts Pitt (1758) and Niagara (1759) was abandoned by the French and secured by the British. The English garrison at this point fell victims to Pontiac's conspiracy in 1763; and here, the following year, Bradstreet held a conference with the tribesmen. The fort was not rebuilt during the Revolution; but in 1793 Wayne reared a block-house on this site, and here he died (1796) two years after his great victory. A garrison was maintained here until the breaking-out of the War of 1812-15, when Erie became an important naval station, being the harbor whence Perry's fleet issued for the battle of Lake Erie. The naval station was not finally abandoned until 1825.—ED.

[65] Gen. Richard Butler was born in Ireland in 1743. When quite young his father brought him to Pennsylvania, where he grew up in the Cumberland Valley. About 1770, with his brother William, he embarked in the Indian trade at Fort Pitt. A partisan of Pennsylvania during the boundary disputes, Butler did not serve under Dunmore, and was opposed to all of

---

[66] Kiasola is another form of the Seneca name Guyashusta, for whom see *ante,* p. 38, note 65.—ED.

sengers from Colonel Butler,[67] commandant at Niagara, came to Fort Pitt recently, with a letter to Captain McKee. As Kiasola was determined to go to Niagara, Agent Butler sent him off with several messages intended to secure the Indians, especially the Delawares, in their neutrality.

The Indians are alarmed at the exorbitant price of goods, which Agent Butler explains as occasioned by the war.

April 9, he continues his letter, with news of the arrival of John Gibson, with several Shawnee, who come bringing in white prisoners, according to the agreement at the treaty of 1775.[68]

Connolly's measures. After the Fort Pitt treaty of 1775, he was appointed by Congress as Indian agent at Fort Pitt, an office held by him until May, 1776, when he was superseded by George Morgan. In July of the same year, Butler was made major of the continental line; becoming lieutenant-colonel in 1777, he became one of the most efficient Revolutionary officers, serving, however, largely in the Eastern army. At the close of the war he retired with the brevet of brigadier-general. In 1784 he was chosen superintendent of Indian affairs, commissioner for several Indian treaties, and while second in command of St. Clair's army, fell in the battle of November, 1791.—ED.

[67] Col. John Butler was a native of Connecticut, who early removed to the Mohawk Valley, and became a trusted assistant of Sir William Johnson, acting as interpreter in Indian councils, and as leader of war-parties in the French and Indian War. On the outbreak of the Revolution he adhered to the Royalist side, and was left in New York by Sir John Johnson when he retired to Canada, in charge of the affairs of the Six Nations. In 1777 he enlisted a company of rangers that devasted the New York frontier, took part in the battle of Oriskany, and led the raid against Wyoming (1778). It is said that his conduct on that occasion lost him the honor of knighthood. After the Revolution he retired to Canada, received a pension from the government, and died at Niagara in 1794.—ED.

[68] See *ante*, p. 126.—ED.

The Indians complain of a survey made recently by Col. William Crawford for John Harvie and Charles Simms,[69] of an island below Pittsburgh, that is claimed by John Montour.

ALARM IN KENTUCKY

[John Floyd to Col. William Preston. 33S291 — transcript made by Draper.]

POWELL'S VALLEY,[70] 1st May, 1776.

DEAR COLONEL—We have been much discouraged on the way by alarms &c, but on our arrival here find the greatest part of the news to be false. I met so many people removing in, as I went down Holston that I thought it best to leave my negro wench & her child on the way. I need say nothing about the mischief that has been done, as Mr Lee, brother to Willis Lee, who is killed, can give you a history of the whole

---

[69] John Harvie was a son of Thomas Jefferson's guardian, who lived at "Belmont" in Albemarle County, Virginia. The younger Harvie represented West Augusta district in the Virginia conventions of 1775 and 1776, and in May of the latter year was chosen one of the Indian commissioners for the Middle Department. Later he was a member of the Continental Congress, and had charge of the prisoners captured at Burgoyne's surrender, whom he quartered near his home in Albemarle. Through Jefferson's good offices Harvie was appointed register of the land office at Richmond, whither he removed at the close of the Revolution, and where he was mayor in 1786. He died at his home, "Belvidere," near Richmond, in 1807. His wife was a daughter of Gabriel Jones, the well-known Augusta County lawyer.

For Col. Charles Simms see *Dunmore's War*, p. 317, note 34.—ED.

[70] For Powell's Valley see *Ibid.*, p. 4, note 6.—ED.

that may be relied on.[71] We are all well, & are 6 in number. Mr Todd[72] overtook us last night. * * *

Capt. Martin's compliments to you.

JNO. FLOYD.[73]

---

[71] Willis Lee of Fauquier County, Virginia, visited Kentucky in 1774 with his cousin, Hancock Taylor, and other surveyors (see *Ibid.*, p. 23), and was wounded when Taylor was killed. Lee recovered, and returned to Kentucky the following year, laying out the site of Leestown, a mile below Frankfort on the Kentucky River. The brother to whom Floyd refers was Hancock Lee, under whom George Rogers Clark was engaged as surveyor for the Ohio Company (1775). Willis Lee visited Kentucky in 1773, and again in 1774 when he joined McDonald's Wapatomica expedition. Having built cabins at Leestown, that had been attacked by Indians (see *post*), he was now returning to Virginia.—ED.

[72] Gen. Levi Todd, born in Pennsylvania in 1756, was educated in Virginia, and went to Kentucky with Floyd in 1776. In 1777, he was first clerk of Kentucky County, and the next year was a lieutenant in Clark's Kaskaskia expedition. After the taking of that town he went on a secret mission to the Spaniards across the river, and then escorted Clark's prisoners to Virginia. In 1779 he commanded a company on Bowman's expedition, and in the autumn of that year laid out a station ten miles above Lexington, but soon removed to the latter place as more protected, and was one of the first lot-holders of that town. In 1782, as major of militia, he collected a force to relieve Bryant's Station, and took part in the battle of Blue Licks, wherein his brother fell. All his life in public employ, he became a brigadier and finally a major-general of militia. From the time of the organization of Fayette County, he was clerk of the court, and a member of both Danville conventions to agitate the new-state movement. He died at his home in Lexington in 1807, leaving a large family. One granddaughter became the wife of Abraham Lincoln.—ED.

[73] For Capt. Joseph Martin, at whose house Floyd no doubt wrote this letter, see *Dunmore's War*, p. 235, note 64. For Floyd, *Ibid.*, p. 9, note 13.—ED.

PROTECTION FOR THE FRONTIER

[Patrick Lockhart to the chairman of the Botetourt committee. 1U16 — A. L. S.]

WILLIAMSBURG 14th May 1776

Sir—Capt John Gibson who arrived here yesterday Informs us that there is a great Probability that they Wayndott Taway & other Indians will be Troublesome on our Frontiers this Summer. They have been to the De Troit & Recd. Presents from the Commandant there; an application was made to the Convention & a Supply of 500lb Gunpowder is ordered for your County which will be forwarded with all Possible Despatch also Barr Lead is to be Procured from Chissells Mines[74] & I hope that if they should Attempt any thing on our Frontiers that Perhaps the Inhabitants will endeavor to Repel them; I shall apply in the Morning to the Committee of Safety who is to send the Gunpowder to the Care of your County Committee & Expects they will write you in regard to it I also beg leave to inform you that a Resolve is past in the Convention that the Money Collected to Purchase Gunpowder &c. is to be return'd to the Respective Persons that paid it & any Ammun[it]ion Furnished is to be a Public Charge therefore I think it might be returned the People at any time that there was an Opportunity on their Producing the Rects given by the Collectors.

I am Sir your mo Hble Servt

PAT LOCKHART[75]

---

[74] For location of these mines, see *Ibid.*, p. 52, note 90.—ED.
[75] Patrick Lockhart was a prominent merchant of Botetourt, who represented his county in the Virginia legislature of 1776.

N. B. Mr Gibson reports that the Shanese & Delawares does not seem to have any Hostile Intention against [us].

P. L.

The Chairman of the Committee of Botetourt.

[Col. William Preston to Col. William Fleming. 1U18 — A. L. S.]

May the 30th. 1776

Sir—I am Just Favoured with Yours of the 27th covering a Copy of a Letter from Capt Lockhart to the Chairman of Botetourt Committee.

Should the Tawaws, Wyandots & those Tribes beyond the Ohio break out, this County and the Inhabitants on Greenbrier will be in a distrest Situation; But if the Shawnesse & Delawares &, Mingoes do not Join them, I can hardly think they would undertake a, War at so great a Distance. However, be that as it will, it is our Duty to endeavour all we can to be prepared for the worst. The Supply of Ammunition given by the Convention will be a great encouragement to the People on the Frontiers who were intirely destitute of that Article.[76]

* * * * * * * *

Tho' the Supply Granted by the Convention will be a great Relief to the Frontiers, yet I cannot conceive

---

His name appears as late as 1789 in the annals of that state, serving as trustee for erecting towns, as member of the James River Improvement Company, and as major of militia for his county.—Ed.

[76] The omitted portions deal with the outbreak of the Cherokee, and the preparation for war in the Southwest.—Ed.

that it will be sufficent in case of a War, which we ought at all Events to be prepared for. Therefore I am of Opinion it would be imprudent not to lay up a larger Stock of Powder, and of Course that the Collection ought not to be refunded, at least for some time. Should there be no Occasion to use the Powder in our Defence, it will at a future Day sell for the same, or nearly so, that it costs; then the Money may be returned & no Man Injured except by laying a little longer out of a very triffle. Should there be Occasion to use it for the General Defence of the Country, then the Public will Refund the Money to the Committees who can readily repay it to the People. These Steps I hope will be taken by our Committee, and I would fain hope will be adopted by Yours.

I expect a Man toNight or toMorrow from the lower Settlement of Holston for Powder If he brings any Interesting News I shall Communicate it to you, and shall always be glad to Co-operate with you in every Measure that may be for the Safety and Protection of the Frontiers.

I have some Intention of going to Botetourt next Week, if I go down, I shall do myself the Pleasure to spend an Evening with you, when we can talk those Matters fully over, & fix on some general Plan for the Defence of the Frontiers untill Instructions can be rec^d from the Committee [of safety], to whom I have forwarded all the Int [Ms. torn] I rec^d from the Westward. In [the mean] time beleive me to be Dr Sir

   Your sincere Wellwisher & hble serv^t
      Wm PRESTON

GARRISON FOR POINT PLEASANT; INDIAN AFFAIRS

[Summary of printed documents.][77]

George Morgan writes to Lewis Morris, May 16 1776, from Pittsburgh, where he has just arrived to supersede Richard Butler in the conduct of Indian affairs. Capt. Matthew Arbuckle[78] with a company of Virginia troops left Fort Pitt, May 15, for the Great Kanawha. The Seneca Indians are to be suspected, and Morgan fears that an expedition from Niagara is being planned against Pittsburgh, because the carrying place (portage)[79] has been lately reconnoitred. In June he expects several Seneca chiefs,[80] with Shawnee and Delawares, and hopes for deputies from the Wabash confederacy.[81]

May 31, 1776, Morgan wrote to the commandant at Detroit to the effect that he had heard of letters

---

[77] The following summary is compiled from *Amer. Archives*, 4th series, vi, pp. 474, 475; and Joseph H. Bausman, *History of Beaver County* (N. Y., 1904), p. 70, which contains extracts from Morgan's letter-book preserved in the Carnegie Library, Pittsburgh.—ED.

[78] For a brief sketch of Capt. Matthew Arbuckle, see *Dunmore's War*, p. 103, note 49.—ED.

[79] The carrying place, or portage, here referred to, would on first thought be that between Erie (Presqu'isle), Pa., and French Creek, where old Fort Le Bœuf had stood. This portage, however, was thirteen miles in length, so that probably Morgan had in mind the Chautauqua portage, which although rougher is shorter; about nine miles by the old road cut by Céloron in 1749.—ED.

[80] See description of negotiations by Seneca chief, *post*.—ED.

[81] The Wabash (Anabache, Ouabache) confederacy consisted of the various branches of the Miami tribe situated on that river, together with the remnants of Mascoutin and Kickapoo tribes that had settled near old Fort Ouiatanon, on the upper Wabash.—ED.

having been sent to him that had not reached Fort Pitt. He informs his correspondent that no colonial army is now on the march to Detroit; but the frontier settlers are prepared to defend themselves should the Indians attack them.

CONFERENCE AT FORT PITT

[Blacksnake's account of a visit to Pittsburgh. 16F109-114.][82]

When I was about fourteen years of my age[83] I have than taken more Notice of our chiefs councils

---

[82] The following account is taken from the life of Governor Blacksnake, dictated by him in 1845-46 to Benjamin Williams, a partially-educated half-breed, at Dr. Draper's request. As it is impossible to verify the dates, the account is inserted at this point as probably referring to the conference which Morgan says he expects with three Seneca chiefs; this meeting must have taken place some time in the summer of 1776. The document is interesting as giving an Indian's recollections of the sort of conferences held at Fort Pitt during this season. The spelling and phraseology have a decided aboriginal cast.—ED.

[83] Blacksnake was a Seneca chieftain, born in pre-Revolutionary times, but still living in 1850, when Dr. Draper visited him at his home in Cold Spring, Cattaraugus County, N. Y. The latter secured a highly-interesting and valuable interview with the aged chieftain, who said that he was born two years before Johnson defeated the French at Fort George (1755), and that he recollected his capture of Niagara (1759), as well as the Devil's Hole massacre (1763). He was appointed war-chief at the Oswego treaty (1777), and took the war-path against Fort Schuyler, being in the battle of Oriskany, the raids on Wyoming, Cherry Valley, Canajoharie, Schoharie, etc. In 1784, Blacksnake attended the treaty of Fort Stanwix, and afterwards visited Congress at New York and met Washington. During the Indian war of 1790-95, Blacksnake kept neutral, and abided by the treaty of Fort Harmar (1789), which he had signed under another name—Blacksnake not being his customary appelation until 1812. During the War of 1812-15, he assisted the Americans against the British.—ED.

affairs, at that times my Recollection than [then] was good. Especially the important Subject and Views of the many Differance Nations and tribes of Indians Residance of one Body,

In the month of April, 1763 [1775] the messenger from Albany arrived at avone, to Notify to our chiefs to attendans to a convention to be held at Pittsbough, for the purpose for communicating, with the Six Nations of Indians, Concerning of the Difficulties Exsisted Between their own Brother great Britain and America. Supose in order to understanding Between Americans and the Indians &c.

Cornplanter and Redjackett[84] was the head men

---

[84] Cornplanter and Red Jacket were two of the best known Seneca chiefs, the former a warrior and a promoter of civilization, the latter an orator and an advocate of old Indian customs. They were, therefore, frequently in opposition, although in the early period of their lives they acted in concert.

Cornplanter (or John O'Bail) was a half-breed, son of an Irish trader and a Seneca mother. He was born in the Seneca country and belonged to the Wolf clan. In the Devil's Hole massacre (1763), Cornplanter was near by as a guard. He finally joined the British cause, was made war-chief at Oswego in 1777, and took part in the battle of Oriskany and the raids on Cherry Valley and Wyoming. In 1779 he commanded raiding parties, one of which attacked Fort Freelands, while the other was defeated at Brady's Bend. In the following year, he captured his own father in a Canajoharie raid, but at his request quickly released him. Having signed the Fort Stanwix treaty of 1784, he became somewhat unpopular with his tribe and visited New York to treat for an understanding regarding the land sales. He was accorded a grant on the Allegheny River, seventeen miles above Warren, where he established a farm, built a saw-mill, and devoted himself to the elevation of his people, particularly preaching abstinence from intoxicating liquors. He died on his farm in 1836.

Red Jacket (or Sagoyewatha—he who keeps them awake) was born near Geneva, N. Y., about 1750. His first participation in public affairs occurred in the Revolution, where he op-

Governor Blacksnake

Seneca chief. After a photograph in the possession of the Wisconsin Historical Society

among the Seneca chiefs and other Nations of Indians connected with the Iroquois, they again Called the Second time to be held a council for to appoint Delegation to attend the convention at Pittsbough and to Re-consideration on the important Subject all the Six Nations and other Nations which is not included as to be belonging to the six Nations all met, at avone a long house[85] Redjacket & Cornplanter Both had considerable influence amongst all others tribes and they concluded themselve it would be Necessary for them to attend the Pittsbough Convention according to invitation So all consented of the Differant Nations to Each one make their own appointments to Delegations to the convention to be held at Pittsbough Chiefs and Warriors, and I was particularly invited

---

posed taking the hatchet against the colonists. He was, however, overruled by the majority, and took part in the affairs at Oriskany, Wyoming, Chemung, and Canajoharie. He was said to have sent messengers to Sullivan requesting peace during the latter's raid (1779). He declined to attend the treaty of 1784, but afterwards visited Washington and was presented with a medal, which now belongs to the Buffalo Historical Society. In both the Indian war of 1790-95, and in that of 1812-15, he sided with the Americans. In his latter years, Red Jacket dwelt near Buffalo, and being addicted to intemperance was deposed from his chieftainship in 1827. He died three years later, and in 1884 his bones were re-interred at Buffalo, where a monument has since been reared to his memory.—ED.

[85] The village which Blacksnake here designates as Avone, was usually known as Canawaugus. It was the most northerly of the Seneca villages, and was located on the west bank of Genesee River in Livingston County, Avon township, nearly opposite the sulphur springs of Avon. The population was at one time estimated at almost a thousand, probably an exaggeration. Relics of the council house could be seen at this place as late as the middle of the nineteenth century, although the town was raided by Sullivan's men in 1779.—ED.

to go long with them, this is the Early part of the Spring the year, 1763 [1775]. So we went to work to make preparations to Start and provides that who is to stay at home, with in a few Days was already and Several chiefs and warriors Started from Avone, and take westerly Course to strik[e] and Came into about Eight miles above the mouth of the Buffalo Creek into lake Erie and we travellerd on lake Shore and went on up as fars Erie village in Pennsylvania[86] was then But a few house this village one or two Stores and a tavern and provision stores and thence from this place South and we Came into a stream above now called midville[87] and thence on Down french creek empdies to Allegany River, So on Down this stream Several Days traval before we Came out to the mouth of this creek, there was But three or four log cabins of white people first settlers at the mouth of this creek[88] there we made a stop and Camp

---

[86] Then known as Presqu'isle; see *ante*, p. 151, note 64.—ED.

[87] Meadville, Pa., not then established; Blacksnake here speaks from later knowledge. The site of Meadville was an early fording-place on French Creek, and there are traditions of a French store-house at this place, but not a permanent fort. In 1788 it was explored by the brothers Mead, and a block-house built, the nucleus of the present town.—ED.

[88] The site of Franklin, at the junction of French Creek with Allegheny River, was first occupied by an Indian village wherein was built a trading-house by John Frazer, a Pennsylvania trader. When the French took possession of the country in 1753, they drove out Frazer, and raised the French flag over his place, as reported by Washington in his journal of that year. The following spring Fort Machault was built, and held a garrison until 1759, when the capture of Fort Duquesne and the attack on Niagara forced the French to destroy their fort and retire. The next year (1760) the English built Fort Venango, forty rods higher up, which was maintained until its complete destruction by the Seneca in Pontiac's conspiracy (1763). Fort Venango was not rebuilt during the Revolution.

Cornplanter

Shawnee chief. Otherwise known as Gyantwahchia, John Abeel, John O'Bail, and John the Cornplanter. After a photograph in the possession of the Wisconsin Historical Society

out Near this Neighborhood for Several Days, for Building Bark Canoes to go Down the River with them as fars Pittsbough while we Stayed at this white Neighborhood, the oldest man use to visit us and Bring Bread timber for us to Eat and we use to give him every time fresh vension we get Some time five or Six Deer Every Day, while we Stayed at this place, untill we got our Bark Canoes was Built sufficient to Carry our Number Down Stream So we Saile on Down stream on the Allegany River, this was got to be about the fall the year 1763 [1775]. So we made stop 7 miles from Franklin over winter at now called big Sandy Creek[89] in the spring 1764 [1776] on the first Day on Journy from Big sandy, we arrived at Pittsbough. Several white men Came to See us, on the Same afternoon the News went to the Commissioners Ears that we are Come, and he visit it us that Evening and he made induced himself to us, for acquaintance Cornplanter and Redjackett Several others chiefs of the Several Differant Nations of Indians proper Delegates, and we conversed with the Commissioner and he told us the object holding a meeting and he wishes to have it opened meeting on the Next morning immediately after Brackvest and made appointment a certain ground to meet, and he

---

The cabins of which Blacksnake speaks must have been soon evacuated, as the Indians grew hostile, and no white people lived on this site until 1787, when Capt. Jonathan Heart built Fort Franklin, a half mile up French Creek. This fort was dismantled in 1796, but a garrison was maintained until 1803 on the site of the town, which was laid out in 1795.—ED.

[89] This stream, flowing through Mercer and Venango counties, comes in from the west, about eleven miles below Franklin.—ED.

Set several men to work at it for the Seats in open f[i]eld, the Next morning after Brackvest and called together, uncle cornplanter give the Company advice to hold one minde and appoint Redjackett for Speaker in the meeting and made all prepaired on our part and we went on the ground, there was a large number asambled, and one of the officers give us a seat in the mid of it. the Commissioner appeared and Called to order he first Said the Commissioner we the white people has been long Desirous to have you to met with us, for the purpose of to make known to you, Brothers, we considerated necessary for us to let you Know and to make you acquainted our circumstances and the Difficulties Existed Between America and the King of great britain the great Britain government use us bad and the American people endeavours to have freedom to Built up our own government the King ordered his armies and warriours to fight us, we are therefore would use my utmost Endeavours to great a Number of our Red Brethren the Six Nations, and others to not Join Either Party for we Determint that we Shall have freedom and independant Nation from the British government if posibly can and let us fight it out our liberty for we will laid Down our lifes for our independence and freedom and we feel interst and Desirious in your wellfairs that you would continue hold on as independent Nations of your people and not to lift it your hands against America or great Britain because he and me alone got into Difficulty and wishes you to Stand notual [neutral] and be Peace to all your White Brethren and if we should lost our liberty, than we always be under the great Britain

Red Jacket

Seneca chief. Indian name, Sagoyewatha. After a lithograph in the possession of the Wisconsin Historical Society

government we are poor the King is Rich But God
look upon us if we are a Right he would help us to
again our liberty and we are outh [ought] to look to
him for our favours, this we shall Endeavour to Do,
and would be glad of your advice and assistance to
Communicate it, the Same with your people at home,
and in Broad among your Red Brethren, this object
amost important to have all understand before hand
&c. this is only the Substance of the Commissioner
Said in this convention, and about intermission at noon,
in the afternoon got [tog]ether again and there was
more people assembled as it was fornoon, before this
we have Consulted the manners the Commissioner had
use to his advise, then the commissioners called to
order and Ready to Receive the answer

Redjackett given answer

Brothers we are suppose you are Ready to hear
the answer we will make of you We are Indians and
Citizens of this Island God made us here to habited
and grewed large a Number and give us all we Need
it, to enjoyed, and we have Several large a Number
of our Red Brethren, and Never had yet wars Difficulties, to any worth while to mention our maker protect it us through lives and provides us all Collors
of his children are under heavens, we all Now give
thank to God who guard us gether together this Day,
and had clean Ears to hear you speaken to us and understand it which we acknowledge it is important to
hear to we therefore would take your a word and
advice with us to our people and laid the subject before them, Because we are not authorize or power

to Completed the object, therefore would leaved it to our people, the Business Shall be Done by majority of them Before we Should make our Determination To upon any important Business, Although all in our Number that are here agreed to use all the influence over our people at home to go into this effect and we Should endeavour to Do all can and we Shall Send you a Delegation to carried the answer which our people will make, Soon after passed their opinion on the subject

Commissioner Reported

"Brothers and friends, we Desire you will hear and Receive what we have now told you, and that will open a good Ear and listen to what are now been Said to you this is a family quarrel Between us and old England, you Indians, are not Concerned in it, we don't wish you to take up the hatchet [for] the King's troops, we Desire you to Remain at home, and not join Either Side: But keep the hatchet buried Deep, in the name and behalf of all our people, we ask and Desire you to love peace and Maintain it and love and Sympathize with us in our troubles that the path may be Kept open with all our people and yours to pass and Repass without molestation, Brothers we live on the same ground with you, the Same Island is our common birthplace we Desire to sit Down under the Same tree of peace with you, &c. &c. this is all I have to Say, To a wanted what I have said before noon and I feel satisfied what you have Said in answer you made, &c. and wish you this afternoon to take a walk with me and visited to a new garrison.

So we all went with him, there was only a few Regular warriors in garrison and a few pieces of cannons and Balls for them the United Commissioner ordered us to go to provision Store to get what we wanted while Stayed in the place. Near at Night Returned to our Camp at the mouth of monongahella and the Next morning we made preparation to Start for home about at noon we got Ready to Start, Some of our Bark canoes we away. 3 canoes we Kept for to Keep our provision in as we came up the River and Some of us Come on foot and Some pushing up our canoes up stream, we came on about 10 miles that Day, and we Kept a going Every Day and Came the month of June 1764 [1776] at avone on Genesee River

DEFENSE OF FINCASTLE COUNTY

[President Edmund Pendleton to Col. William Fleming. 1U19 — L. S.]

WILLIAMSBURG June 20th. 1776.

SIR—Pursuant to the Resolution of the General Convention, you are to direct the March of one Company of your militia, with the proper officers without delay to the County of Fincastle, there to be employed as a Ranging Company for the defence & protection of the Inhabitants, they are to carry with them Ammunition and Provisions Sufficient to last them to the place of Rendezvous, appointed by Colonel William

Russell, who is to command the whole. For and by order of the Committee of Safety. I am, Sir

Your obed^t hble Servant

EDW^d PENDLETON P[resident]⁹⁰

County Lieut: or Comm^d. Officer of the Militia of Botetourt.

[Col. William Fleming to Capt. William McClenechan. 1U21 — A. L. S.]

BOTETOURT COUNTY

SIR—Agreeable to the Resolve of Convention and in consequence of Orders Received from the Honourable President to me directed, as County Lieut^t of Botetourt ordering one of the Militia Companies of this County properly Officered to March immediately to Fincastle County to be imployed as Rangers under the direction and Command of Col^o Wm Russell. You are therefore to March immediately with the first and Second Devisions of your own Company or Volunteers equivalent. You are to be Joined by draughts from Capt Armstrongs, Capt Lockhearts Capt Crockets & Capt Robinsons⁹¹ Companies to form Your Command to Fifty Rank and file exclusive of Serg^{ts} & Drummer You are to march with all Expedition to Fincastle County and Join the Troops at the General Rendezvuse Appointed by Col^o Russell on Holston

---

⁹⁰ Edmund Pendleton was a prominent Virginia statesman (1721–1803), president both of the convention of 1776 and of the Virginia committee of safety. As such he was chief executive officer of the state until the election of Patrick Henry, first governor, in July, 1776.—ED.

⁹¹ For the captains of the Botetourt militia in 1774, see *Dunmore's War*, pp. 44, 45.—ED.

You are to take what provisions will Serve Your Company to Capt Madisons on New River[92] who will Supply You with what is Necessary for your further March. You will take care to keep your Men Orderly on the March and for their own Credit I expect they will behave in a Soldierly Manner by keeping sober, being Alert on Duty and paying a proper Obedience to all Necessary Commands of their Officers I hope you will be in Readiness to March from the Lick on Monday Next with the draughts of your own & the Companies below you the Men of Capt Crocketts & Robinsons Companies are to Join you at Mr Kents. I am Sir Your most Hble Servt

       WILLIAM FLEMING C: L^t
          July 16 1776

To Capt. William McClennachan [93]

[Capt. William McClenechan to Col. William Fleming.
3ZZ23 — A. L. S.]

        HANDS MEADOWS July 24: 1776

SIR—I this day Marched to the above place without the Least difficulty My Men all in high spirits; but am greatly disappointed in Regard to the draughts of Capt. Crocketts and Capt. Robinsons companys——

---

[92] For Capt. Thomas Madison, see *Dunmore's War*, p. 59, note 99.—ED.

[93] Capt. William McClenechan (McClanahan) was born in Ireland in 1733. He came to Botetourt County (now part of Roanoke) from North Carolina, and settled on an upper branch of the Roanoke, southeast of the present Salem. He died in 1819. Big Lick lay about two miles north of his place, and was the point of departure mentioned by Fleming.—ED.

the former five, and the Latter only four: I have seventeen in my own including a serjant. Capt. Lockharts draught nine including a serjant from the same Capt. armstrongs are nine men amounting to forty one privates and tho My Company is not Compleat thought it proper to march with all Expedition and hope my intentions will meet with your approbation.

I am informed this day by Capt John Bowman[94] of a battle fought on holston within four miles of the Big Island between a party of Indians amounting to about one hundred and fifty and a party of our men the savages had on their side killed on the field fourteen and our Loss is only four wounded the above battle was fought on the twentieth of this Instant[95] for further particulars Refer you to Capt Bowman and am sir

              Yours

                W^m McClenechan

---

[94] John Bowman was born (1738) in Frederick County, Virginia, son of George Bowman, whose wife was a daughter of the earliest settler of that region, Joist Hite. John visited Kentucky in 1775, and in the summer of 1776 was at Harrodsburgh, where he served as one of the committee of safety (June 15-20). He must have been on his return trip at the time this letter was written. In the autumn of this year (1776) Bowman was chosen colonel of Kentucky militia, and led thither a company for the defense of the country, arriving in August, 1777. In 1779 he led an expedition into the Miami country, which, however, accomplished little beyond devastation of Indian crops. In 1781 Bowman became sheriff, and county-lieutenant of the newly-erected Lincoln County. He died at his home in that county, May 4, 1784.—Ed.

[95] This is an accurate contemporary account of a battle famous in Western annals, known usually as that of Big (or Long) Island on Holston. For the official report see *Amer. Archives*, 5th series, i, p. 464; see also Roosevelt, *Winning of the West* (New York, 1889), i, pp. 286-290.—Ed.

REPORT FROM NIAGARA; NEUTRALITY TO BE MAINTAINED

[Summary of printed documents in *Amer. Archives*, 5th series, i, pp. 36, 37.]

A conference was held at Fort Pitt, July 6, 1776, upon the return of Guyashusta (Kiasola) from Niagara. Several Delawares and Shawnee were present as well as Capt. John Neville and his officers, Major Trent,[96] Major Ward,[97] and several other inhabitants. Guyashusta reported that on his way to Niagara he was stopped at Caughnawaga[98] for nearly

---

[96] Major William Trent was born in Lancaster, Pa., about 1715. He was in the Pennsylvania service in King George's War (1744-48), and as early as 1749 was employed as a confidential Indian agent. In 1752 he formed a fur-trading partnership with George Croghan, and two years later acted as Virginia commissioner at the treaty at Logstown, thereafter visiting the Miami tribe to confirm the treaty. In 1754 he was commissioned to raise a company and take possession of the forks of the Ohio, whence he was driven by the French. Trent accompanied Forbes's expedition in 1758, and the following year was in the Indian service under Sir William Johnson. As a trader he lost heavily during Pontiac's conspiracy, but was re-imbursed at the treaty of Fort Stanwix (1768). At the outbreak of the Revolution he adhered to the patriots' cause, and was commissioned major, but died in Cumberland County in 1778.—ED.

[97] Edward Ward was closely associated with Trent and Croghan, being a half-brother of the latter. While ensign (1754), he surrendered the forks of the Ohio to the French. In 1756-57 he served as lieutenant, and the two following years as captain of the 1st Pennsylvania battalion, taking part in Forbes's campaign. After the war he was Indian agent for several years, making headquarters near Pittsburgh, where he had business interests. In 1774 he was justice of the peace and in 1775 a member of the committee of safety for West Augusta. In 1776-81 he served as a magistrate of Yohogania County, living opposite Pittsburgh as late as 1787.—ED.

[98] Caughnawaga was a prominent Mohawk Indian village located northwest of Fonda, in Montgomery County, New York. It was the site of the martyrdom of Father Jogues in

a month, by messengers from Col. John Butler, who wished him to await the arrival of the Detroit Indians. After reaching Niagara the Seneca chieftain was told that the conference was finished, but having insisted upon speaking with the British commandant, he informed him that the Six Nations were determined to take no part in the war between Great Britain and America. He likewise informed the officers at Fort Pitt that the Six Nations had intrusted him with the care of their territory in that region, and that they would not suffer either a British or American army to be marched through their lands, and desired that no expedition against Detroit be undertaken. Captain Neville thereupon assured the Seneca that the Americans would not attempt to march an army through his country, without acquainting him thereof, unless they should hear of a British army advancing against them.

FRONTIERS OF VIRGINIA

[Col. William Preston to the President of the Committee of Safety. 4QQ64 — A. L. S.]

FINCASTLE Augt. 2^d. 1776

SIR—I am favoured with your Letters of the 25th and 26th of July covering an Order of Council re-

---

the seventeenth century, and was destroyed by the French Governor Tracy in his invasion of the Mohawk country in 1666. By the time of the Revolution all the region north of the river was known as Caughnawaga, and Dutch settlers had largely invaded the territory. In the raid of 1780 the Dutch settlement of Caughnawaga was burned. This Mohawk Valley town should not be confused with the Indian mission of that name in Canada.—ED.

quiring me to Order a Lieutenants Command to the Lead Mines and to have a stockade fort erect[ed] there. I would beg leave to inform you that Col⁰ Russell, fully sensible of the Importance of that Place, on his first coming up, and on hearing of the Approach of the Enemy, ordered a Lieutenant and thirty Men to the Mines; and on his finding the nearer Approach of the Savages in large Bodies; and having intelligence from the Traders who Escaped from the Indian Towns that they intended to attack that Place,[99] he wrote to me to Order a Captain there and Augment the Party. This I immediately complied with; but before the Captain got [to] the Place a Compʸ of the Bedford Militia, who had been called out had taken Post there and do now Garrison the Fort which was built round the Works by the Militia, the Country People & Chiefly by Col⁰ Collaways[1] People There is now a Sufficent Party to guard the Works and cover the Workmen when out. The Party of Fincastle Militia that had been there I ordered out to the relief of the Inhabitants on Holston. The greatest part of the Way from Wattawgo to the Mines is Mountainous & uninhabited, so that a large Party of the Enemy might easily get in by that Route. Therefore it was Judged that a full Company was but barely Sufficent to guard that Place.[2]

* * * * * * * *

[99] This refers to the Cherokee Indian outbreak.—ED.

[1] This was Col. James Callaway, son of William, who was active in the defense of the frontier during the French and Indian War. James was a resident of Bedford County, appointed by the state to superintend the lead mines and secure their product for the government.—ED.

[2] The omissions relate to the news from the Southwest, and preparation for the Cherokee expedition.—ED.

The only thing that can retard the raising of Men in this & Botetourt; is a general Apprehension amongst the People that the Shawnesse Delawares &c will surely break out. Could there be any assurance that these Nations would not strike this Season I believe a great Body of Militia could be raised in these Counties for this Service. But be that as it will, I have no doubt of raising the Number required.

* * * * * * * *

Be assured Sir that nothing in my Power Shall be wanting to forward this very Necessary Service; and that I shall with Cheerfulness comply with every Order I receive from your Honble Board.

I am your Honours most Obed. & very hble serv^t
                                                Wm PRESTON

[Col. William Fleming to Col. William Preston. 4QQ65 — A. L. S.]

D^r SIR—Mr May[3] did not return from Bedford till Tuesday, on Wednesday & Thursday I was abroad, prevented me writing you sooner. Mr Lynch[4] had no powder but promises to be in your County directly, where he expects to make 50^lbs a daye. Henry Pauling[5] was here this Morning, immediately from Your County, and as he brings nothing new, I am in hopes

---

[3] For a sketch of this pioneer see *Dunmore's War*, p. 21, note 34.—ED.

[4] Charles Lynch of Bedford County, who was a delegate to the Virginia convention of May-July, 1776, and appointed by that body to prepare gunpowder for government use.—ED.

[5] For a brief biographic sketch of Pauling see *Dunmore's War*, p. 187, note 33.—ED.

the first fire of the Indians is extinguished & that the Checks they have met with will be Attended with the good effect of hurrying them home. What we can do in case of an Attack in Botetourt for want of Powder I really know not, as only 100^{wt} of what was sent us, is good for any thing —— and of that I spared as much as I possibly could to the Men for your County. Pauling informs me, You have now a sufficiency of Men, & that he heard no complaint for Powder. My Dr Sir no commands of Yours, nor anything in my power for the preservation of your County shall ever be deemed a trouble. By the Presed^{ts} of July 25th I am ordered to raise 150 men out of this County to Assist in an Expedition against the Cherokees. they are to march to the big Iland on Holston River, then to be under the Com^d of Lt Co^l Russel till an Officer can be appointed to command the whole Force intended for that expedition. On Monday Next I meet the Field officers to proceed to the Appointment of Officers for the Above purposes. I understand 50 men are ordered from Augusta & some considerable number from below. It is reported by Letter from Point Pleasant that two prisoners have been delivered up at Pitsburg lately taken by a party of Mingoes. and that the Shawnise sent them up. I imagine they must have been taken on the Kentucke.[6] Capt Arbuckles

---

[6] These were twin sons of Andrew McConnell, who afterwards fell at Blue Licks (1782). The father was a Pennsylvanian who had lived for some five years in Westmoreland County. In 1775 he planted corn and built a cabin at Lee's Station, and the next winter sent for his family. Some time in June, 1776, Mrs. McConnell sent a bound boy and her two sons, Adam Baxter and William Barber, to bring up the cows

Officers & Men will proceed very soon to the Point. As to the Expedition I can say nothing being a Stranger to the Plan. I am well convinced that carrying the War into the Nation, is the only way to secure our Frontiers and make us respected, but I wish it may be conducted on such a Plan that we may not depend too much on the Efforts of Carolina, but be enabled to Act independent of them. I had an Opportunity of lately seeing Our Acquaintance from the Westward. he is unhappy in having any Misunderstanding between him & you, and sincerely desires a reconciliation. Some little inadvertencies, I hope he will clear up, if he has not already which may restore that harmony which formerly existed. It is a misfortune to square our actions alone, from even the Vatican liberary. He knows not that I ever designed to mention anything to you. I am Dr Sir sincerely Your Friend. And

Most hble Servt
WILL^m FLEMING

Augt 2^d. 76

---

to be milked. The skulking Mingo party killed the bound boy and captured one twin, while the other hid. At the sight of his brother's distress, the lad gave himself up. When the boys reached the Shawnee towns with their captors, they were recognized by Joseph Nicholson (see his mission, *post*), who knew their father. He purchased the lads for a rifle, and they returned to Pittsburgh under the care of Col. George Morgan, who sent them to their uncle William McConnell, then in Westmoreland County. The boys were in captivity about sixty days. The above information was secured from their sister, Mrs. Ezekiel January, and is in Draper MSS., 11 CC. See also *Pennsylvania Packet*, Aug. 20, 1776, *post*.—ED.

FRONTIERS OF VIRGINIA

[Capt. John Stuart to Col. William Fleming. 3ZZ1—
A. L. S.]

GREENBRIER August 2ᵈ 1776

Sʳ.—I have this Morning heard that Capᵗ Vanbiber[7] hath yesterday Recᵈ. Notice there is a Large Number of Indians Discovered makeing for our frontiers, this news hath been handed to me from Vanbiber by Report from hand to hand that makes it out of my power to give a perfect account of the Truth of it, but as there is a great probability there is two Much Certainty in it I thought as our people is in a Defenceless Situation it was Necessary to give you this Notice. we are at a great loss for men as well as amunition to such a Degree that without Some Immediate Relife of Boath should this Report be True I am persuaded our Country will be Soon Layd Waste. I hope you'l think proper to Order so many of Militia to our Assistance as you'l think Sufficent I thing [think] there ought to be

---

[7] John and Peter Van Bibber were of Holland ancestry and removed from Pennsylvania to Maryland, finally settling (about 1771) in the Greenbrier region of Botetourt County. John made an early exploration of Kentucky, passing down the Ohio and Mississippi to New Orleans. In 1773 he was one of a small party of surveyors who explored the Great Kanawha, and left his name on a cliff below the falls, still known as "Van Bibber's rock." Both brothers took part in the Point Pleasant campaign (1774), where a third brother, Isaac, was killed. After this, both served as captains in the militia. Peter had a block-house on Wolf Creek, which was an important frontier outpost. About 1781, the two brothers moved into the Kanawha Valley, and Peter died at Point Pleasant in 1796; John in 1821. Peter's sons Matthias and Jacob were noted in later border warfare, and his daughter married a son of Daniel Boone. The reference here may be to either of the brothers, John or Peter.—ED.

three Companys Made up at least for this frontier that is one on Indian Creek on Muddy Creek and in the Leavels[8] under such proper officers as you Shall think fit to appoint to the Command of them, may be a means of saving many from Distruction. I shall in the mean Time do Every thing in my power towards puting ourselves in a poisture of Diffence untill I have an Answer from you, & I am Much affreid our people being Divided into so many small Companys which consist Chiefly of marryed men &C (the Best of our young men being Taken by Cap[t] Arbuckle) will now make the Turn Difficult for us to Embody to make a good Defence, and should our people pen themselves in little Forts as formerly they did it will be the Readyest method of having themselves Distroyed. N[e]ither do I know there is any method of preventing them from doing so, unless you should order the Officers of the Militia to Draught a party out of Each C[o]. to make one proper fortification for the Deffence of the whole, that is in Different Quarters. I have here 100[ls]. of powder which was Ordered to the point half of which I shall Detain untill I hear from you as I understand Cap[t] Arbuckle is well Supplyed. I hope you'l do what you think Best with all Expedition. I am, S[r]. your Ob. Humb[e] Serv[t].

JOHN STEWART[9]

On the Publick Service
To Col[o]. William Fleming Botetourt.

[8] For these locations see *Dunmore's War*, pp. 181, 319, notes 25, 37. Indian Creek was an affluent of New River, where was a ford used by Indian parties.—ED.

[9] For a brief biographical sketch of Stuart, see *Dunmore's War*, p. 104, note 51.—ED.

[Col. William Fleming to Capt. John Stuart. 3ZZ1 — Draft in Fleming's handwriting.]

SIR—Yours by W^m. Huggen I have Just received I perceive that mine has not reached you. I think it highly Necessary that the Inhabitants should have places of defence prepaired to which they may retire in case of Necessity And these Forts placed as centrual as conveniences will Allow, for which purpose I would have you fix with the Approbation of the other officers of the Comp^y. on some place the most suitable to the People who may be supposed to take Shelter there and build a Fort. You are therefor to take what part of your own Comp^y. & Capt Browns is necessary & effect it as soon as possible. I am apt to think that the Indians discovered on Walkers Creek[10] making this way, may be a party of the Western Tribes on their way home from the Cherokee Nation, that Jerrit Williams gave information, of being there.[11] However the above step will Al-

---

[10] For Walker's Creek, see *Ibid.*, p. 56, note 96.

[11] Jarret Williams was an Indian trader, also an inhabitant of the Watauga settlement before 1773. In Dunmore's War he enlisted in Capt. Evan Shelby's company, and at its close resumed his trade with the Cherokee. In June, 1776, he escaped from their towns, and brought word to the frontier settlements of the invasion which the Cherokee were preparing. His testimony is published in J. G. M. Ramsey, *Annals of Tennessee* (Philadelphia, 1853), pp. 148, 149. He therein says that fifteen of the Northern Indians were at the Cherokee towns with a war-belt, and a party went out to strike the settlers in Kentucky. This is the party which Fleming suggests may have caused the alarm on Greenbrier. Williams was reimbursed by the North Carolina legislature for his losses by the Cherokee War, to the amount of £100. He went out in 1778 as lieutenant of Clark's Illinois regiment, and received

lay the Apprehensions of the Inhabitants. I shall be
expeditious in sending you Assistance I propose
sending out a Sufficient Number to repell them in
case of an Invasion. You are to have your Comp^y.
prepaired in the best manner you can for defence.
And if the Enemy penetrates into the County take
what Number you think proper of them, and call in
the neighboring Capt^s to your Assistance and on a
Junction proceed in Quest of the Enemy Tomorrow
I meet the Field Officers, when, what is further necessary will be concluded on. I shall take every
Method in my power to get a supply of Powder.
And expected before this that Capt Vanbiber would
have brought in 300^w. If he or any other Powder
Maker has any, I wish it would be procured. I have
wrote to the President to get what was sent in from
W^{ms}b^g exchanged for other that is good. Please to
send Coppies of the Inclosed to your Neighboring
Capt^s. I think it proper to have an Eye on the foard-
ings of New River, and if a few smart men were
sent out to watch them from Culbertsons down to the
Warrior's foarding it may be Necessary[12] In other
things that do not occur Act as prudence will derect
you,—till you receive further Orders &c.

              W. F.

Augt 4, 1776.

To The Militia Officers on Green Brier—
As we have the greatest reason to Apprehend an

---

his share of the Illinois grant. He settled on Floyd's fork of
Salt River, in Bullitt County, Kentucky, and passed there the
remainder of his life.—Ed.

[12] For Culbertson's, see *Dunmore's War*, p. 76, note 25.
For the Warrior's Ford, see *Ibid*, p. 322, note 40.—Ed.

Attack on Our Frontiers, You are therefore to have your Respective Companies in the best order possible for Defence And on any sudden immergency You are to make a Junction with Capt. Stewart with all the Men you can conveniently March to go in Quest of & repell the Enemy. In case of Necessity a Field Officer will be on the Spot to regulate the Opperations. You are desired to send me immediate Notice on Your discovering the Enemy or of Murder or Mischief being done.

F.

[Capt. John Stuart to Col. William Fleming. 3ZZ2, 3— A. L. S.]

GREENBRYER Augt. 10th. 1776

SIR—Agreeable to your orders p^r. Wm Huggans, I have Draught'd Ten men from Capt. Browns C^o. & Ten from my Own, with which I expect to have a fort soon compleated at Camp Union, large enought to Contain the greatest part of the Inhabitants of these leavels, the men I shall continue in the Fort for Immediate protection untill you shall think fit to Disband them, and should you send out any more men for our assistance In case of an Invation, should be glad thirty would be sent to Join the above Number to compleat the company, Twenty five of which I shall send under the command of a Lieutenant to Keep Capt. Arbuckles old fort on Muddy creek, & alay the timidity of the people of that quarter. I should think another Lieutenants C^o. on Indian creek & one more further up the Country would not be amiss, with which number the fears of the people would be wholely assuaged & to which our own strength of militia could be readily Join'd, to Repel any considerable number of the enemy that may come. I am from the Report brought lately by some of Capt. Arbucles men from the point much of oppinion we Shall be visited soon by our old neighbors, for whose Reception should they please to keep away a little while we will be middleing well prepared. Capt Saml. Brown hath undertaken to furnish the above men, & any other, that may come on this Quarter with provisions, a proper account of he will keep, & dispose of the fith [sic] quarters &c of Beef which will still save some expense & can be done with [MS. torn] than otherwise for which Trouble I expect he will be Allowed. I have sent out Jacob Lockhart[13] & Josiah McDowell to watch the pass from below the Little Meadow River to the warior fording, & Ge^o. Davidson & W^m. Johnston to watch from Below the forks of the Road towards the head of gauley,[14] I understand Vanbiber hath sent Two out to watch from the mouth of Greenbrier towards the head of

---

[13] Jacob Lockhart was one of the early settlers on Greenbrier, and accompanied Matthew Arbuckle on an expedition to the Indian towns to recover horses, some time before Dunmore's War. In the latter expedition, he served as a scout. He was killed by Indians shortly after the Revolution.—ED.

[14] Two well-known Indian trails were covered by these scouts; the former came up the Kanawha, and then struck across the branches of Meadow Creek to the upper waters of the Muddy, an affluent of the Greenbrier. This route was followed by the invaders who attacked Donnally's Fort in 1778, and was the outward passage of Lewis's army in 1774. The Gauley River route, farther northeast, also led to the heads of the Greenbrier.—ED.

paint creek,[15] which I think is a sufficient number at preasent. I know of nobody nigh me that hath any Quantity of powder that can be Secured. I am told the [that] Cap[t]. Hendersons[16] hath some, which I make no doubt their own prudence will direct them to Keep. I shall be expeditious in giving you notice on the appearance of any of the Enemy and am with Esteem

      Your Obed Humb[l] Serv[t].

         JOHN STEWART

N. B. Should you think the above number of men necessary at preasant I think Cap. Donallys would be a proper place for one Division as it is convenient for a number of people & will cover a great many more.[17]

            J. S.

On publick Service Aug[t]. To Col[o]. William Fleming Botetourt.

---

[15] The western Indian trail around the narrows of the Great Kanawha led up Paint Creek, thence crossed Flattop Mountain, and came back to the main river near the mouth of the Bluestone.—ED.

[16] John Henderson—son of James, who served in the French and Indian War—was born about 1737 in Augusta County. In 1765 he married Anne Givens, sister of Mrs. Andrew Lewis, and soon after removed to Greenbrier, where he established a homestead not far from Lewisburg. In 1774 he served as lieutenant under Captain Herbert, and became captain of militia until December 1776, when he resigned to enter Daniel Morgan's regiment as a corporal in Daniel Gregory's company. Leaving the army in April, 1779, he became justice of peace and died at his home in Greenbrier County in 1787. See *West Virginia Magazine*, April, 1905.—ED.

[17] Andrew Donnally was born in the north of Ireland, removing to America about the middle of the eighteenth century. He went out to the extreme frontier of Greenbrier, and built a blockhouse there in 1771—about eight miles north of the present Lewisburg. Donnally was a man of influence and

[Col. William Fleming to Capt. John Stuart. 3ZZ3 — Draft in Fleming's handwriting.]

Sir—Yours I received by Capt Donnaly. I think it may be prudent to keep a small Command of Men at the Fort on the levels when finished to preserve it. this is all that I have at present in my power to do. till we have more reason to Apprehend an Actual Invasion, the Ordinance for that purpose limits me. but depend upon it as soon as I have, I will take every effectual Measure for the defence of Our Frontiers I am in hopes to have it in my power in a short time to send you a supply of Powder should it be wanted. in the meantime I desire you will endeavour to quiet the Apprehensions of the People as they may depend on being effectually supported, I am Sir

Your Hble Servt

WILL^m FLEMING

Augt 24th. 1776

---

ability. In 1776 he was captain of militia, and in May, 1778, defended his fort against an Indian raid. He is reputed to have been lieutenant of Botetourt County (see *West Virginia Magazine,* July, 1901, pp. 52–56); but if so, he could not have been chosen until after the retirement of Col. William Fleming, who held that office during the Revolution. In 1782 Donnally was a trustee for the founding of Lewisburg; but some time after removed to the Kanawha Valley, where he lived first at Point Pleasant, then on Elk Creek, and later at Charleston. In 1789 and again in 1803 he represented Kanawha County in the state legislature. He died at his Charleston home about 1825. The fort in Greenbrier was destroyed about the same time.—ED.

NEWS FROM FORT RANDOLPH

[Capt. Matthew Arbuckle to Col. William Fleming. 2ZZ78 —
A. L. S.]

FORT RANDOLPH [18] August 15th 1776

WORTHY SIR—As I am Inform'd Your Committee has had Some Complaints Laid in Against me By Some person About Sundry Affairs Transacted By me. In the first place worthy Sir View My Station So Remote from Advice or Councel from any of the Committee's, and Oblige'd to Act According As My own Weak Judgment Tell I Never have Rec^d any Positive Instructions from the Committee of Safety or Your Committee Concerning My Enlisting of men, I have therefore wrote to the Committee of Safety Long Ago to have positive Instructions Concerning this point and have Rec^d. none. then I Sent Officers to Get men Not willing to Leave this Garrison Lest the Indians Should Make a Break which I Did not Know But might Be Every hour, as there had upwards of Fifty of My men Given Me warning According to the Ordinance to Leave the Garrison At the Expiration of their Year, If I was Not to Get men in that time to Come to fill their Vacant places the Garrison Must of Course Break up and Either I misunderstand the Ordinance or it Sais there Shall

---

[18] Fort Randolph was built by Capt. Matthew Arbuckle in the early summer of 1776, to replace Fort Blair (see *Dunmore's War*, p. 310, note 27), which had been burned by the Indians in 1775. It was erected about forty rods from the first fort, and held a garrison until the close of the Revolution. The name was no doubt given in honor of Peyton Randolph, for whom see *ante*, p. 66, note 97.—ED.

Officers Recruit men to fill the Vacont places that They May Be at the Station Before the men Leave it Lest those few that Remains Become a prey to the thirsty Savages and the Garrison Be Destroyd Not having a Sufficient Strength to Keep it against an Inhuman and fierce Enemy As Such I Look upon the Indians when at war But Worthy Sir, My Country Shall Never have to Say I Dare not Stand the Attacks of the Indians or fly the Cause they are So Justly fighting for, on the Contrary I will Loose the Last Drop of My Blood in Defence of My Country when fighting for that Blessed Enjoyment Call^d. Liberty and Should all the Indians Nations Join in Confederacy and attack me here tho I had But Twenty men I would Defend it with My Latest Breath, and Glory In the Cause, and I am Willing when Call^d on By Your Committee or any Other to have My Transactions Examin'd in the Strictest Manner. As to the Best of My Little Judgment I Act all I Can for the Safeguard of My Country and My own honour. I was Inform'd Some time Ago the Shanahs and Cherokee's had taken 3 Women prisoners from Cantuckee and Got one Scalp,[19] I therefore Dispatch^d. three of My Men to Demand the three prisoners (If in possession of the Shanahs) to be Immediately Deliverd up two of the women were Daughters to Colo^l. Calaway at Cantuckee and the other a Daughter of Colo^l Boon's at Cantuckee Likewise and this Day the Men

---

[19] The scalp was doubtless that of James Cooper, a Pennsylvanian who first visited Kentucky in 1775. He was killed near Licking River, July 7, 1776. See *Amer. Archives*, 5th series, i, p. 1228.—ED.

are Return'd Again with one of the Shanah Chiefs and Brother of the Cornstalk's, Who Informs Me that After having taken the Prisoners from Cantuck the white's follow'd and Retook the prisoners and Kill[d] two of their Men,[20] upon this I Inform'd them the fate of the Cherokee's and that our people would without Dispute Cut them all off which Seem to have a Great Effect upon them and they promised to hold to a Lasting peace But this I Dispute as they have Now the Cornstalk away at fort Detroit Treating with the English and are Constantly Backward's and forward's, on that Course So that the peace with them I Look upon it not to Be Lasting and am Ever on My Guard for fear of a Surprise, and the Trader's Gets Quantitys of Goods from the English at Detroit and has for Some time, As the Traders Inform'd My Men while at the Town's they had Rec[d] Sundry of Goods from thence for the Use of the Indians; So any Material Transactions that Occurs I shall Inform you And Remain Your Devoted Humble Servant to Command

MATT[w] ARBUCKLE

---

[20] The capture and rescue of Jemima Boone, and Elizabeth (Betsy) and Frances (Fanny) Callaway is one of the thrilling tales of early Kentucky settlement. The girls were taken July 14, 1776, from a canoe just below Boonesborough, and hurried off to the northward across Licking River. Daniel Boone at once organized a rescue party, which caught up with the fugitives on the third day. The three girls were rescued, and two of the savages were shot, later dying of their wounds. Draper collected much material on this episode, which he embodied in his manuscript "Life of Boone," 4B 77-99.—ED.

INDIAN DEPREDATIONS

[Transcribed by Draper from *Pennsylvania Packet* of August 27, 1776. 16]27.]

PHILADELPHIA, Aug. 20, 1776.

Saturday se'en night[21] George Morgan, Esqr. arrived in this city from the Westward: On the 9th ulto whilst at one of the Shawanese Towns on the Scioto, he received intelligence of three Six Nation warriors having passed by there with two prisoners they had taken sixteen days before[22] from Virginia. Mr. Morgan followed and got to their town before them, prevented the usual punishment of the prisoners on their entry, and insisted on their being immediately delivered up to him, unless they intended this breach of the peace as an open declaration of war. All the headmen of the Six Nations, Shawanese & Delawares, who were called together on this occasion, behaved in a very friendly manner, and joined with Mr. Morgan in his demand made to these warriors, who soon complied therewith, and were promised forgiveness on condition of future good behavior. These warriors told Mr. Morgan they had done no damage, except [unless] they killed a young man they shot at when they took these prisoners; but he made his escape, though they believed the ball entered his breast. The prisoners are twin sons of Andrew McConnell, late of Pennsylvania, who removed last winter to Lees Town on Kenruke [Kentucky] river, and were taken within a few hundred yards of the town. Mr. Mor-

---

[21] August 3, 1776.—L. C. D.
[22] About June 24th.—L. C. D.

gan brought them with him to Pittsburg, and delivered them to their uncle in Westmoreland County in this State.

Since then a small party of Shawanese returning from the Cherokee country, killed and scalped two persons near the Big Bone Lick; they were pursued by a few of the neighbors, who killed and scalped two of the Indians—the others escaped.[28] This breach is also likely to be settled to the satisfaction of all parties, as the headmen had expressed great concern at the conduct of their foolish young people, and promise to do all in their power to preserve our friendship.

A treaty is to be held at Pittsburg with the Western Indians the beginning of October, when, it is hoped, they will listen to and follow their true interests as they have promised to do.

WILLIAMSBURG Vª. Aug. 17—We understand from Fort Pitt that the Northern Indians are not disposed to attack us in that quarter, & have only engaged not to suffer [an army] to march through their country against Detroit; we may hope that there is not much to be dreaded from the terrible combination of Indians we have been threatened with by our enemies.

---

[28] Reference to the killing of Cooper, and the capture of the Boone and Callaway girls, as described in the preceding document.—ED.

THREATENED HOSTILITIES

[Commissioners of Indian Affairs, circular letter to county lieutenants. 1U34 — L. S.]

PITTSBURGH Augt. 31st. 1776

SIR—We Yesterday Evening received Intelligence by a Gentleman from the lower Shawanese Towns, which is very alarming, a General Confederacy of the Western Tribes seems to have been form'd, in order to Strike our Frontier Settlements. The Indians it is said wait only untill their scatter'd Young men can be call'd in, and the Corn be somewhat riper for their Subsistance before they take up the Hatchet. The danger of the Times demand that every measure should be taken to defend ourselves from their Incursions and repel their attacks. We have sent an Express to Congress upon this occasion and have wrote to the Governor and Council of Virginia on the same Subject. We would not wish to alarm too much the minds of the People it must rest with you to intimate the News We have receiv'd to the Inhabitants of your County in such manner as you shall think most eligible and conducive to the Public Weal. We think it our duty to communicate to you and the other Lieutenants of the Neighboring Counties, the critical Situation of Indian affairs, their plan of Operation is that the Chippawas and Ottawas two numerous Tribes should attack this place, and the Shawanese the Settlements on this side the Ohio, a few days will evince their real Intentions, We Therefore Recommend it to you in the strongest Terms to hold your

Militia in readiness to march properly accoutred on the shortest notice as the emergency of Affairs may require your immediate assistance.

We are Sir y^r. most Obed. Serv^{ts}.

THOMAS WALKER
J^{no}. HARVIE
JOHN MONTGOMERY[24]
J. YEATES[25]

---

[24] John Montgomery was a Scotch-Irishman born in Ireland in 1722. About 1740 he emigrated to America and settled at Carlisle, where he was a successful merchant. In the French and Indian War he was commissioned captain in Forbes's army (1758), and was a prominent patriot leader in the early Revolution, in 1774 acting as chairman of the first committee from his county. In July, 1776, he was appointed by Congress to hold the treaty at Pittsburgh, and continued there until November. The next year he was colonel of a Pennsylvania regiment in the New Jersey campaign, and served in Congress, 1782-83. He was justice of the peace for Cumberland County, and aided in founding Dickenson College, dying at his home in Carlisle in 1808.—ED.

[25] Jasper Yeates belonged to a well-known Philadelphia family, and was born in that city in 1745. He was early admitted to the bar, and became an eminent jurist and member of the Pennsylvania supreme court (1791-1817). During the Revolution he resided in Lancaster, and was an active patriot, aiding the colonists both financially and with his legal knowledge. He was a member of the Pennsylvania convention that ratified the constitution, and was a commissioner for the government in the Whiskey Rebellion (1794). During his sojourn at Pittsburgh- as Indian commissioner, he visited Braddock's battlefield and vividly described its appearance and his impressions (see Samuel Hazard, *Register of Pennsylvania*, vi, p. 104). Judge Yeates died at his Lancaster home in 1817.—ED.

PREPARATIONS FOR DEFENSE

[Col. William Fleming to Capt. George Givens. 3ZZ4 —
Draft in Fleming's handwriting.]

Septr. 2^d. 1776

SIR—It is thought Necessary that a Comp^y. should march to the Protection of the Inhabitants of Green Brier. And as the Field Officers have Appointed you to that Charge, you will therefore immediately endeavour to get the Comp^y. compleated, you are to have Lieut^t. Beard from Capt. Hanleys and an Ensign from Capt Deans Comp^y. for Your Officers. You are to Appoint a Sergeant in your Own Comp^y. Lieu^t Wright has orders from me to Send you a Serg^t & Eight Men from his Comp^y. You will I expect get Volunteers in your Own Comp^y. & Capt Hanleys, without draughting the Comp^{les}. I have wrote to the Capt^{ts} to have their proportion of Men ready. You had better Appoint a day for them to Muster their Comp^{les} and Attend. You are to march as quick as possible I expect you will march next week you will send Your Ensign & fifteen men to Capt Vanbibers fort. Your Lieut^t. & fifteen to Capt Donnalys. & You with the remaining part may continue at Ca[m]p. Union or else where as may be most necessary for the protection or defence of the Inhabitants, in which you will be directed by Capt Stuart. Your Proportion of men will be 20. or more if you can get them from your own Comp^y. The Lieut^t 16. the Ensign ten & with Capt Robinsons 8 will make your Comp^y. 54. You are to use your utmost dilegence in protecting the Inhabi-

PREPARATIONS FOR DEFENSE 193

tants, & repelling an Invasion. let me hear from you, from time to time & You will Oblidge Your Hble Servt

[WILLIAM FLEMING]

To Capt Givens [26]

[Capt. John Stuart to Col. William Fleming. 3ZZ5 — A. L. S.]

GREENBRIER Sept. 3^d. 1776

S^r—I Rec^d an Order p^r Capt. Vanbibber from you for thirty five pounds of the Countrys lead in my care, which I delivered to him, he also say'd you desired to Know how much of the lead was here which I cannot give an Exact account of, for want of an Instrument to weigh it, but I Rec^d. it of the commissary after the Expedition & the weight then was 543^w Capt Arbuckle since had an order for it & I suppose may at different times have carryed away about 200^w I also let Capt. Hamilton on muddy creek [27] have 20^w. as they had not any there which will be delivered back again in case it is not used

---

[26] The Givens were a prominent Augusta County family, James having received a grant of land therein in 1738. This was Capt. George, who had been lieutenant in Dunmore's War, and was promoted to a captaincy on the death of Samuel Wilson.—ED.

[27] Andrew Hamilton was one of the earliest settlers in the Greenbrier region; see *Dunmore's War*, p. 319. Captain Hamilton was chosen by lot to lead troops to re-inforce General Hand in 1777, and upon his return from Point Pleasant led out a party in pursuit of the Indians after the siege of Donnally's fort in 1778.—ED.

against the Enemy. the alarm from Cap\u1d57. Arbuckle has caused a good many people in those parts to move off their familys the Remainder are chiefly gathered in to forts. the Bearer Cap\u1d57 Anderson[26] can Inform you of the Situation of the people at present I have sent Two men to the point to know how Cap\u1d57 Arbuckle is, as soon as they Return I shall inform you you what Inteligance the[y] Bring I have Twenty two men which was Imployed Building the fort I darsay you will not think it Imprudent to Keep them together untill the people is something appeased or we know more of the design of Enimy, the people up the river are Intirely Destitute of ammunition of any Kind. if there is any to come to those parts I Should be glad how soon it Colud [could] be sent out, Cap\u1d57 Anderson will be applying for a small command to stay at mill of his, which will be the only Benifisial one in those parts should the Indians come and should you think proper to allow them might be of great Service. And\u02b7. Wallace & Jn\u1d52. Galloway is now hear with som Recruits of Cap\u1d57 Arbuckles company, they Intend [waiting] untill [MS. torn] returns from the point, when the[y] Design takeing som beafcattle with them, as Cap\u1d57 Arbuckle is in much need of them. I have Supplyed the men, they have with them as well as those I had Raising the fort, with my own salt which is a presious article here & should be Exceeding glad to Know whether I cannot be Repaid in the Salt now in the hands of the

---

[26] Probably one of the family noted in *Dunmore's War*, p. 137, note 95.—ED.

committee should the enimy come & more men be call'd together we shall be very bad off for that article unless som is sent us. I shall be Expedisious in leting you Know of any appearance of the Enimy that may happen and am with Respect

Your Most Humb^l. Servt.

JOHN STEWART

Col^o William Fleming Botetourt   favour of Capt Jno Anderson.

FORTS ON THE OHIO

[Col. Dorsey Pentecost to David Shepherd. 1SS15—A. L. S.]

September 4th, 1776

SIR—It is has been thought Expedient for the Protection and Safety of the frontiers to Station a Number of Men at Different places on the Ohio between Fort Pitt, and the mouth of Grave Creek,[29] and at a Council of war held this day you have been Appointed Commissary for to Victual &c. Such of the Militia as are now or may be Imployed on the present Emergency, and I having also Laid your Appointment before the Committee of the County which they have been pleased to approve, I am therefore to Desire that you immediately proceed to provide Such provisions &c. as shall be wanting on this occassion, taking care to supply them in due Time, & purchase on the best Terms you can on the faith of Government. I need not suggest to you the Great Necessity there is of your Exerting Your self, but am

---

[29] For Grave Creek see *Ibid.*, p. 36, note 64.—ED.

full assured that you will Exert your best Endeavours in facilitating the Business at this Time of alarm and Great Calamity

I am Sir your Most Hm^e Servt

DORSEY PENTECOST C. Liu^t

To David Shepherd Esqr Wheeling [80]

REINFORCEMENTS ORDERED

[Pres. John Page to Col. William Fleming. 1U35 — L. S.]

WILLIAMSBURG in Council Sepr 9th. 1776

SIR—Having received a Letter from the Commissioners appointed to treat with the Northern Indians, representing the Danger which in their opinion threatens Fort Pitt from the hostile Disposition of those Tribes, who under the pretence of treating with the Commissioners are collecting in such numbers, that the present Garrison at that Fort would be unable to baffle their attempts. You are therefore required to pay a particular attention to the orders

---

[80] Col. David Shepherd, eldest son of Thomas, was born in Berkeley County, Virginia, near Shepherdstown, where his father was one of the earliest settlers of the Shenandoah Valley, allied with the Hites and Van Meters. In 1770 he removed to the West and settled at the forks of Wheeling Creek, in what is now Ohio County, W. Va. Having acted as commissary under Pentecost, he was in January, 1777, chosen county-lieutenant for the newly-erected Ohio County, and acted in that capacity until his death in 1795. He commanded Fort Henry during its siege in 1777, and led a regiment on Brodhead's Coshocton expedition (1781). During 1783-85 Shepherd served in the Virginia legislature, and during the Indian wars was efficient in guarding the frontier. For a fuller biography see *West Virginia Historical Magazine*, January, 1903.—ED.

they have sent you, and hold such a body of **Men in**
readiness to march to their assistance, as they may
require.

> We are Sir your h^{le}. Serv^{ts}
> Signed by order of Council
> JOHN PAGE P^t.[81]

P. S. If you can make out another Comp^a you are
also required to send it to Point Pleasant.

> J. P.
> County Lieut. of Botetourt

[Capt. John Stuart to Col. William Fleming. 3ZZ6 — A. L. S.]

GREENBRIER Sep^t. 16th 1776

S^r.—I Rec^d. yours by Express & shall Indeavour
to embody the Number of men you mention with all
expedition. Capt Givens arrived yesterday at camp
union with about thirty men & Expects he will have
as many as will make them thirty seven soon, as a
party is to follow, they will march Immediately to
mudday creek I have not heard anything of Capt
McKee,[82] but his Lieut. Thompson is now at Camp
union & has about seven or Eight of his Recruits

---

[81] John Page (1744-1808), coming of an old Virginia family, was elected first president of the governor's council under the new constitution, June 29, 1776. He was Virginia member of Congress (1789-97), and governor of his state (1802-05).—ED.

[82] For a brief sketch of Capt. William McKee see *Dunmore's War*, p. 348, note 69. He was in command of Fort Randolph during Arbuckle's absence in the spring of 1778, when beseiged by an Indian force.—ED.

gathered there. M^r. Mathews[33] will have the cattle gathered against wedensday night, that they will be ready to start on the next morning, M^r. Wallace & Galloway has now about 20 Recruits at Camp Union & I have Desired Morris to detain with his party of 10 men at muddy creek untill the cattle are ready to Start, however, I apprehend without the addition of som militia to those they are not willing to go, & I understand by Capt Givens his men refuses to go. I shall if no better will do Indeavour to make them 50 Strong as it may be necessary from the presant aperance of danger out of my own Militia, & have them sent off as soon as possible the messengers I sent for the point Returned with a party of Capt. Arbuckles Soldiers who's time was expired & were coming home these brings no further Inteligence than the Indians were all withdrawn from the point and two days before they came away Capt Herrod[34] had arived there from Kentucke, with fourteen men & had met several partys of Indians going down the River who were very sivle, & this I find has made the people at the point less apprehensive of an attack then formerly. but without any other reason than that, & the forbearance of the Indians. I expect more of Capt. Arbuckles men soon & if there is any thing meterial shall let you Know Immediately. one of our scouts from that quarter next the warrior

---

[33] Probably Archer Matthews, brother of George and Sampson, who were captains in Dunmore's War. Archer early removed to the neighborhood of Matthew Arbuckle, in Greenbrier.—ED.

[34] Capt. William Harrod, for whom see *Dunmore's War*, p. 68, note 14.—ED.

fording came in yesterday they have for several days past heared gunns & seen som signs & seems to be much persuaded its Indians but could never discover the certainty. I have nothing more at present to Inform you of & am with Esteem

Your most Ob^d. Humb^l. Servt.

JOHN STEWART.

On Publick Service
To Col. William Fleming Botetourt

DISPOSITION OF THE INDIAN TRIBES

[Summary of a report made by the Commissioners of Indian Affairs at Pittsburgh to Congress, printed in *Amer. Archives*, 5th series, ii, pp. 511-518.]

The report (dated at Pittsburgh, September 25, 1776) is to the effect that news has been received that fifteen hundred Chippewa and Ottawa intend soon to rendezvous at Tuscarawas,[35] with the probable purpose of an attack on Fort Pitt; also that a party of Potawatomi[36] has started to attack the settlements. The Mingo, Wyandot, and Caughnawaga are known to be hostile, and have already taken some prisoners from Kentucky.

---

[35] The Tuscarawas River, branch of the Muskingum, in eastern Ohio, where there were several Delaware Indian towns.

[36] The Potawatomi are an Algonquian tribe who were first encountered by French explorers on the shores of Green Bay, in what is now Wisconsin. Later they had villages in the vicinity of Detroit, St. Josephs (Mich.), and Milwaukee (Wis.). They were early known as "French Indians," being subservient to the whiteman's wishes, and afterwards followed the British directions. Their part in the Revolution was small.—ED.

Fearing an attack of some of these hostiles on Pittsburgh, Colonels Carnahan and Proctor[87] of Westmoreland County, and Col. Dorsey Pentecost of West Augusta, were ordered to call out the militia for the defense of the post. Col. Aenaes Mackay[88] was also ordered to lay in provisions for his battalions at Kittanning.[89] Conferences were held with such

[87] Col. John Carnahan was of Scotch-Irish ancestry and settled first at Carlisle, in Cumberland County, Pa. In 1775 he was appointed high-sheriff of Westmoreland County, holding that office until 1781, being also colonel of the county militia. He was drowned in the Allegheny in 1788. His son James became president of Princeton College.

Col. John Proctor was a neighbor and near friend of Archibald Lochry, for whom he served as executor. He took up land in Westmoreland as early as 1769 and was first sheriff of Bedford, then of Westmoreland upon its erection in 1773. Appointed colonel of the first battalion, he took his men to the Eastern army in 1777. He died some time after 1791.—ED.

[88] Col. Aeneas Mackay's former place of residence does not appear in the records. From 1773-76 he was prominent in Westmoreland County politics, and in July of the latter year became colonel of the 8th Pennsylvania regiment. His regiment was at Kittanning when the commissioners wrote, marching thence to the Eastern army in the following December. The fatigues of the winter expedition were too much for Colonel Mackay, who succumbed to the strain, and died February, 1777, in New Jersey, being buried with military honors at Philadelphia.—ED.

[89] "The Kittanning" was a term applied to a stretch of country along the banks of the Allegheny, about fifty miles above Pittsburgh, where had been several Delaware Indian villages, built soon after 1730. These villages were under the chiefs Captain Jacobs and Shingas, during the French and Indian War, and were a rendezvous for the hostiles who issued thence for attacks upon the frontier. Here also prisoners were detained, and several tortured and burned. In September, 1756, Col. John Armstrong at the head of a punitive party of Pennsylvanians raided the district and burned the villages. No further notice is found of this place until the opening of the land office in 1769 led land speculators thither. However a permanent settlement was not made until 1774, when on the advice of Arthur St. Clair, some Pennsylvania troops were

chiefs as came in to Fort Pitt, and no more outrages being reported from the Mingo party at Kispapoo Town, the minds of the commissioners and inhabitants were somewhat reassured. Friendly chiefs offered to seek Pluggy's Town and the Wyandot in the interests of peace. Finally, four Chippewa came to treat, and were prevailed upon to remain until the arrival of Wasson, their principal chief.[40] All this lessened the necessity for the militia, and led to orders for disbanding most of those that had assembled. Their spirited conduct on the occasion of this alarm, deserves praise. Two spies have been sent to Cuya-

---

stationed here, and a stockade built as a base for the Indian trade. Early in the Revolution there was stationed here a company under Captain Van Swearingen, which remained until the Western battalion, commanded by Colonel Mackay rendezvoused at this place. When marching thence in December, 1776, Mackay left one company under the command of Capt. Samuel Moorhead, who strengthened the fort, and remained as a bulwark against Indian invasions until ordered by General Hand, in the autumn of 1777, to evacuate the blockhouse. In December of the same year a scouting party had a small skirmish at this spot; and again, in 1779, Brady rescued some prisoners here. In June of that year, Col. Stephen Bayard built a fort at Kittanning under the orders of Col. Daniel Brodhead. This he named Fort Armstrong; but under orders it was evacuated in November, 1779, and never again regularly garrisoned. Fort Armstrong was situated about two miles below the present town of Kittanning, and some ruins thereof were visible in the early part of the nineteenth century.—ED.

[40] Wasson was the Chippewa chief who joined Pontiac in the siege of Detroit (1763). One of his nephews having been killed in a sortie, Wasson demanded the death of Capt. Donald Campbell as a matter of revenge, and put him to torture. The following year he humbly sued for peace and forgiveness. This granted, he retired with his band to Saginaw. The chiefs of the Saginaw band of Chippewa continued to use the name of Wasson, which was modified into Owasso, borne by a chieftain living near the present Michigan town of that name. In 1838 the last incumbent of the name was forcibly removed by the government from his village.—ED.

hoga, and the minds of all are somewhat reassured.

Enclosed in this report was one from William Wilson,[41] detailing his experiences during a journey to the Indian tribes in June and July of this same year, in order to invite the tribesmen to a treaty at Fort Pitt. Cornstalk and the Hardman, Shawnee chiefs, accompanied him, and Joseph Nicholson was met en route. While among the Delawares, Wilson determined to go to the Wyandot towns, whereupon Captain White Eyes acted as his escort. At Wingenund's town John Montour joined them, and they all proceeded to the Wyandot town opposite Detroit. There they were present at a council called by the British governor, who threatened Wilson, and tore his message in pieces before the eyes of the Indians.[42] The governor likewise treated White Eyes with contumely, and ordered him to depart from that vicinity.[43]

---

[41] William Wilson was a well-known Indian trader, resident at Pittsburgh, who frequently acted as messenger and interpreter. He had a trading post near Beaver River, and in 1793 gave information that led to the arrest, trial, and acquittal of Capt. Samuel Brady for Indian murders. He was in Detroit the same year, and later went down to Cincinnati, whence he proceeded to Greenville, where he died in 1796.—ED.

[42] See Hamilton's own account of this conference in *Michigan Pion. & Hist. Colls.*, x, pp. 264-267.—ED.

[43] Heckewelder, *Narrative*, p. 146. John Gottlieb Ernestus Heckewelder was born in England, of German parentage, in 1743. In 1754 he emigrated to Bethlehem, Pa. His first visit to the Ohio country was in 1762, when he accompanied the veteran missionary Frederick Post on a tour to the Ohio Indians. During the years 1765-71 he was in temporary service at various missions, in the last-named year becoming first assistant to Zeisberger in the latter's Delaware mission. About 1786, Heckewelder retired to Bethlehem and devoted himself to literary pursuits, writing a *History of Indian Tribes*, philological notes, etc. In 1792, and again the following year, he

Wilson was civilly entertained, however, by the British interpreter, William Tucker,[44] who admitted that he thought it probable that the Indians around Detroit would soon attack the American settlements.

On their return these envoys met Isaac Zane,[45] who brought Half-king, chief of the Wyandot, to see Wilson. The latter secured from this important chieftain a promise of neutrality.

White Eyes has asked the Americans to aid his tribe, the Delawares, to build a strong fort to protect

---

assisted at treaties, and was in the civil service of Ohio 1797–1800. For ten years thereafter, he lived among his former converts at Gnadenhütten, retiring finally to Bethlehem, where he died in 1823.—ED.

[44] William Tucker was born in New Jersey, but early removed with his parents to the frontier of Virginia. In 1754, Tucker's father, while harvesting grain, was killed, and two of his sons captured by a band of Chippewa Indians. Young Tucker was at that time eleven years of age. He was kept a prisoner for seven years, and then entered the Indian trade at Detroit, where he was present during Pontiac's siege. He is said to have given notice of the aboriginal plot to Major Gladwin, and thus saved the garrison. In 1773 he re-visited Virginia, married, and brought to Detroit his bride and several slaves. During the Revolution he was the official Ottawa and Chippewa interpreter, and a captain in the Indian department. At its close, Tucker settled on his farm on the site of the modern Mt. Clemens, and there resided until his death in 1805. His sons were in the American service in the War of 1812-15, and many descendants still live in Michigan.—ED.

[45] Isaac Zane was born on the south branch of the Potomac about 1754, the youngest of several brothers who afterwards became the first settlers at Wheeling. When nine years of age Isaac was captured by Indians and grew up among them, marrying into the Wyandot tribe and living like an aborigine. He often warned the border settlers of their danger from Indian raids, and acted as guide and interpreter. About 1795 he bought a tract of 1800 acres in the present Logan County, and settled near Zanesfield, where he died in 1816.—ED.

them from the Western tribes, whom they fear will attack them because of their friendship for the colonists.

FORT RANDOLPH RE-INFORCED

[Capt. William McKee to Col. William Fleming. 1U38 — A. L. S.]

G. BRIAR Sepr 30th 1776

DEAR SIR—I Rec^d. yours by M^r. Wallace with the Powder and am oblig^d. to you for the Additional ten pounds. I arrived at the Fort Charles in the Sevannah[46] the 27th Inst^t. with only 17 men besides my self. 4 or 5 were almost Ready w^h I Expect here before those are March^d. from this place Lieut^t. Thompson has Enlisted about twenty, fourteen of them will be Ready to go Down I Expect to March between 30 & 40 with M^r. Thompson for Fort Randolph by this Day week. I Rec. a Letter from Maj^r. Nevil Desiring [me] to send Down Men as fast as the cou^d. be Raisd, to supply the Deficiency in the Fort occassioned by the coming away of Capt. Arbucles Men. (And however Desirous I am of Marching my whole Compy together) I think it is absolutely Necessary to Comply with this Measure. The People here are at Present Quite easy a number of men are lately arrived from the point from whom we learn the Shawanese are averse to any Hostility agst us (God Grant that temper may

---

[46] The fort at Camp Union—the site used as a rendezvous for Lewis's division in Dunmore's War.—ED.

long Continue with them). I saw Lieut. Robinson He Inform^d. me he had Recruited Nine. But since I came here have heard he is not sure of any more than one or Two and that he had Nominated a Mullatto to be serg^t. and he had no Right to appoint any if this be the case he is not a good Judge of Propriety Im afraid he will not Raise his Quota, and there are several others wou^d. be willing that Im Confident cou^d. soon Raise their Quota were they Appointed I believe all the other Subalterns will Complete their Number sooner than any that cou^d. be appointed in their Room I shall be Glad to let you know how Matters goes with me and have your advice every oppertunity and am with Respect Sir yours &c

W^m M^{c}KEE

To Col^o. William Fleming Bellmont By favour Capt Jno. Stuart

---

INDIANS RAIDING

[John Cook to Capt. Andrew Hamilton. 3ZZ7 — A. L. S.]

October 2^d. 1776

S^r.—This minet I Rec^d. Express from Clover Lick which is an exact Copy of an Express from fort Pite [Pitt] from Major Nevel at [to] Point Plisent, which gives the folowing acount viz that there is four Companys of Indians Gon out in order for Ware Capt Pluggy and one Compney is Gon for Centuck[47] tow

---

[47] In consequence of the capture of the girls at Boonesborough, and other depredations during the summer, all the stations of Kentucky broke up save three, Boonesborough,

Compnys Crosed the ohigho at y̅e̅ mough of Hockhocken which is alou^d to strick at Greenbrier one Comp^y Cros^d. higher up ye River which is to strick on the head of the west fork[48] or som of those waters. there is sixty Indens in Noumber as Pr Express their is not the Lest apperance of a treaty at Fort Pite for ther is not above forty Indens there and those old Indens and squas and it is the genarel opinon of all the Traders and Interpetars that ther will be a General Ware   the Express Was dated the 25th of Sept and brought up by Capt may and he Desirs the Inhabitantes to have the militia in the Best order they Cane for ther Defence   sent from fort Pite by Stephen Radcaff

    I am s^r your hum^l sar^t

          J^no Cook

N. B. you are by the Express to send an Express to Capt. Stawert so that all the Country my Gate Warning

ther ough[t] to be an Express sent to Co^l. Fleming as this may be Depended on.

Capt. And^w. Hamilton

Harrodsburgh, and McClelland's. It was estimated that fully three hundred settlers left the country, and went back to the settlements. George Rogers Clark and John Gabriel Jones, delegates from the Kentucky settlements to the Virginia legislature, secured an advance of five hundred pounds of powder to protect the new settlements, and conveyed it down the Ohio, landing at Limestone. A party marching in from there with part of the powder, was attacked by Pluggy's gang near the Lower Blue Licks, on Christmas day, two men being killed, including the leader Jones, and two captured. Four days later the Indians attacked McClelland's Station, but were repulsed after losing their leader, Captain Pluggy. See Draper MSS., 4B100-110.—Ed.

[48] The west branch of Monongahela River was then the outward limit of settlement in that region.—Ed.

HOSTILE RAIDS

[Col. Dorsey Pentecost to Capt. William Harrod. 4NN28 —
A. L. S.]

October 16th 1776

Sir—I am from the late Hostilities being committed on the Inhabitants by the Indians, I have thought proper by and with the advice of the Committee of this County & a Council of War held this Day for that Purpose. I have thought Proper to appoint you to the Command of a Company to be Imployed for the Defence and Protection of the Inhabitants, I therefore order that you draft Ten Men of your Company and you will be joined by a Lieut & 10 Men from Capt. Virgins[49] Company, an Ensign & 10 Men from Capt. Owen's Company, a Serjant & 10 Men from Captain Enoch Enoch's[50] Company, and a Sarjt. and 10 Men from Captain Hargess's Company, which you will Take the Command of, and march with all posible Expedition, to the mouth of Fishing Creek on the Ohio,[51]

---

[49] Reazin Virgin was appointed a militia captain of Ohio County in January, 1777. He lived in what is now Fayette County, Pa., and in 1780 removed and located four hundred acres in Franklin Township, Washington County. The Draper MSS. contain several receipts, with his signature, for powder and provisions down to 1780.—Ed.

[50] David Owens was captain of a company of rangers.

Henry Enoch was an early settler in Hampshire County, at the forks of the Great Cacapon River, on the road from Winchester westward. Here a fort was erected in November, 1755, for the protection of the settlers, after Braddock's defeat. Washington stopped here on his return from the Ohio in 1770. A Henry Enoch signed several receipts at Fort Henry, and in 1777 was for a time stationed at Grave Creek fort. His brother Enoch lived in Amwell Township, Washington County, Pa., then considered a part of Virginia.—Ed.

[51] Fishing Creek should not be confused with Fish Creek, only a few miles below Big Grave Creek. The former is

and there make a Camp and that you Scour up the river so as to join the scouts that will be sent down from the Garrison of Grave Creek, & down the Ohio for 10 or 12 Miles, and if you find any Indians on the south side of the Ohio, which have crossed the Ohio with Hostile Intentions you will Treat them as open & avow'd Enemys, and in Case of any Murder being Committed on our Inhabitants that you use your utmost Endeavours to overtake and Chastize them, and I must Strictly injoin you to Cover & Protect the Inhabitants in the best manner the Nature of the Case & your Situation will admit of, and in Case of Any Incursions being made that you Signify it to me by the most Quickes[t] Conveyance, you will take cear to furnish your Company with Sufficient Quantity of Provisions, to march them to grave Creek where you will receive Provisions for your Company, you will use all possible frugality in your Expense. wishing you a good journey, & that you may be able to give a good account of those Rascals that may attempt to Attack our Lives Libertys or property, I am Sir your Humb^e S^t

       DORSEY PENTECOST C. L.

To Capt. W^m. Harrod

---

twenty-six miles below Grave Creek, and comes in from the West Virginia side, with the town of New Martinsville at its mouth.—ED.

PROVISIONS FOR FORT RANDOLPH

[Andrew Donnally and Archer Matthews to Col. William Fleming. 1U41 — L. S.]

Novr. 1st. 1776

we have Purchased a large Drove of Cattle & hoggs for the use of the men at the Point & our Instructions from Co^l. Harison[52] is to ap[p]ly to you for a guard. We shall be Ready to Start from here the twelfth of this Instant & we think their may be men Got here if you think Proper by taking a Small Part out of Each Company with Part of Capt. Givens Company. we shall be glad you would Send Instructions to us as Soon as Posible, as it apears two.Dangerous to go without a guard & may be of a great loss to the Country

S^{ir} We Remain your Hum^e. Servt^s.

AND^w. DONELY &
ARCH^r. MATHEWS

To Col^o. W^m. Fleming, p^r Express

INDIAN DEPREDATIONS

[Col. William Fleming to Donnally and Matthews. 1U42 — A. L. S.]

SIRS—Yours of Novr. 1st. came to hand by the Messenger from Fort Charles. I expect Instructions every day from W^{ms}burg relative to the Continuance of the Men on Our Frontiers till that reaches me I

---

[52] Probably Benjamin Harrison, later of Rockingham, for whom see *Dunmore's War*, p. 272, note 87.—ED.

cannot send you positive Instructions with regard to the Escort. Nor have you mentioned what Number you think might be necessary. It is my Oppinion that those Indians who scalp'd the Men at the Point & fired on the Party near Hockhoking[53] were the same that did the damage at Wheeling[54] & were on their Return   if so they are gon home, & the dainger in going to the Point may not be great. However as You do not design to Start before the 12th. I shall have it in my power to write you particularly before then.   I am Sir &c

Wm FLEMING
Novr 3. 1776

Donaly & Mathews

---

[53] Pentecost gives a full description of this event in his letter of Nov. 5 to Patrick Henry, *post*. The party was under the charge of Robert Patterson, afterwards of Lexington, Ky. Patterson went to Kentucky in 1775, and in 1776 was in command of a party of seven, returning up the Ohio, carrying despatches to the commander at Wheeling. They passed Point Pleasant in safety, but during the night of the 11th or 12th of October were fired upon near the mouth of Hockhocking River. Patterson was one of those severely wounded, and lay in the woods eight days until rescued by a party from the Grave Creek fort. See his pension statement, Draper MSS., 1M1. The names of his men were David Perry, Isaac Green, James Templeton, James Wernock, and Joseph McNutt, of whom the last two were killed.—ED.

[54] The *Pennsylvania Gazette* of Nov. 6, 1776, contains the following: "WILLIAMSBURG, VA., Oct. 25.—By a gentleman from Fort Pitt we learn, that eleven settlers at the mouth of Wheeling, about fifty miles below that post, were killed by the Tawahs, Wyandots, Mingoes, and other disaffected Indians, on the 9th of this instant." This is doubtless an exaggerated report of the killing of two women and capture of a boy, mentioned by Pentecost, *post*.—ED.

[Capt. Matthew Arbuckle to Capt. John Stuart. 1U40 —
A. L. S.]

FORT RANDOLPH Novr. 2^d 1776

SIR—I think it my Duty to acquaint you with every Particular relative to Indian affairs as they occur to me here in hopes what information I can give you may be a great means of giving you Satisfaction Besides securing you from Danger. Since I wrote you last I immediately after that accident Sent two Spies cross the Ohio with orders not to return for ten Days without making some Discovery —— Nine of which elapsed without any. But Yesterday (which was the tenth) as they were returning about a Mile from the Ohio Bank just opposite this fort they saw some Indian Signs & was immediately fired on by an Indian not above eight yards Distance. Just at the very moment the foremost of the Spies was jerking his Gun off his shoulder in order to Shoot & the Indian Bullet took the Box of his Gun (just Opposite his Breast) & lodged there the Spy received very little Damage only grazed on the Arm in two or three Places either by Part of the Bullet or of the Box lid—— Such as Buck Shot might have done The Spies Shot at him as soon as Possible Both, & he fell But recovered immediately & he & his Partners Cleared them selves as quick as Possible, with the loss of his Shot Pouch Powder horn & many other little articles the Damn^d. Savages had the assurance to Camp there within a Mile of this Fort but on their own Side of the River. they were so Provident as to Bring a String for a Prisoner but unluckily lost it in the fray along with the other Articles. I intend keeping out Spies both up, Down, & over the Ohio Constantly & shall always endeavour to Protect the Inhabitants on the Frontiers to the utmost of my power I hope you will inform me Particularly what Success we have had against the Cherokees as soon as Convenient. we are not Certain what Nation of Indians they are of; whom our Spies Defeated but they Suppose them to be either Shawnies or Mingoes.

I am Sir your very Hb^{le}. Servt

MATTHEW ARBUCKLE

P. S. you will much Oblige me by giving M^{rs}. Arbuckle an acc^t. from me at this Place as soon as Convenient.

[To Capt. John Stewart. Green brier.]

[Col. Dorsey Pentecost to Gov. Patrick Henry. Draper's combined summary and transcript from Virginia *State Records*, in Draper MSS., 13S190, 191.]

WEST AUGUSTA, Nov. 5, 1776.

He is exerting himself to defend & protect the people, has one company at mouth of Fishing creek & another on the heads of Dunkerd & Middle Island Creeks;[55] speaks of the cruel depredations "of the infernal, relentless band of Mingoes.

---

[55] Dunkard Creek is a Western affluent of the Monongahela, embouching in Greene County, Pa. A famous Indian war-road led up Fish Creek and along Dunkard, hence the

HOSTILE RAIDS

"On the 9th of October two women were killed at the mouth of Fish Creek, & a little boy taken prisoner. The husbands of the women were in canoes moving home from the fort at Grave Creek; one of the men upon hearing the women fired on, ran ashore & discharged his gun at one of the Indians, & it is thought wounded him, as the party that went to bury the dead the next day, found near where he stood three bags of paint, a hoppus, a pair of moccasons, a looking glass & a head dress.

"On the 11th of the same month, seven men on their return from Caintuck were fired on in their camp nearly opposite the mouth of Hockhocking; one was killed on the spot & scalped; one shot through with two bullets, of which he died the next day; two of the men had an arm broken each, one slightly wounded, the other two not hurt. When the men awaked, the Indians were amongst them with their tomahawks and war clubs; a scuffle ensued, but the Indians being prepared & having the advantage the men were obliged to run, one was cut with a tomahawk by the side of his back bone to the hollow of his body, another cut under the shoulder to the ribs. After plundering the camp, they crossed the river. One of the well men ran back to Fort Randolph, the other (Edward Mitchell) a near neighbor of mine, sent the person who was slightly wounded up to Grave Creek, & hid the wounded in

---

white settlers in that district were especially exposed to depredations.

Middle Island Creek rises in Doddridge County, W. Va., and enters the Ohio in Pleasants, about twenty-five miles below Fishing Creek.—ED.

an obscure place & sustained them nine days upon
paw paws. The Captain of the militia stationed at
Grave Creek, with 33 men of his own company,
joined with an Ensign & 12 men of the Regulars at
Wheeling, went down, & four days ago came up
with the wounded, who are likely to do well."
Speaks of Indian sign being seen all over the upper
Ohio region, & the people forted, scouts & spies out,
&c., houses & corn fields destroyed where deserted.

NEWS FROM WILLIAMSBURGH

[Capt. William McKee to Col. William Fleming. 1U39—
A. L. S.]

Honour^d. Sir—Yours by Capt. Stuart only came
to hand last Night on my Return from Will^{ms}burg
at w^c place I have been to Receive the advance for
my Compy and some Necessary Disbursement^s. I
have Just Rec^d an acc^t. of the safe arrival of the Detachment I sent to Fort Randolph I Intend Marching another Detachment of between 40 & 50 Monday
n[oon] (God Willing) Under two Subalterns (viz)
[MS. torn] and Gilmore. And shall now make an
application to you for about an Equal [quanti]ty of
Powder you sent before (viz) 20^{lb} [Ms. torn] to
Each Man near ½^{lb} w^c I think is little [enough] w^c
I hope youll Be kind Enough to Send by the bearer
John Moor from the Same Cask you sent the other.
Dear Sir after Informing you of my being at the
Metropolis you think strange if I had no News to

Impart Indeed Sir News are not so plenty there as they Rather Expect some Important News from our Quarter Relative to our Expedition Southwesterly God Grant they may be Good and I hope thay will From New York nothing of Importance has Transpir^d, some Private Letters say Howe has sent or Gone up the North River ten thousand Men above General Washingtons lines and from that movement some Decissive Stroke is Expected. The affair of Ticonderoga w^c I Suppose you have heard of had not arriv^d. there last Saturday If that is true it^s. an Important Blow. But I cou^d. wish it were better Confirm^d. Some French Vessels have lately arrived and a Prize of Considerable Value. Some Private Intelligence have been Rec^d. by the Assembly with w^c they appear well pleased but they keep it a profound secret. Col^o. Bland Died Suddenly of an appoplexy last Saturday Morning having the Day before Declared himself warmly in favour of Establishment[56] That Affair is to be Decided the 11th Instant the Majority both in & out of Doors Seem [to] be for breaking it. I heard a long Debate in the House about a Bill for Docking Entails. But it Carried by

---

[56] Col. Richard Bland (1710–76), a prominent patriot, had opposed the stamp act. A representative of Virginia in Congress, he had been a leader during the stirring days of the early Revolution. Like most of the older statesmen he was a conservative on the subject of religious liberty. The major portion of the legislative session of the autumn of 1776 was occupied with discussion of the question of an established church. An act was passed November 19 exempting dissenters from paying tithes for the established church. Complete religious liberty, however, was not secured until the passage in 1785 of Jefferson's bill for religious liberty.—ED.

a great Majority. The most Important thing the House was about when I left the City was a Bill for Raising five new Battalions in this Commonwealth agreeable to a Resolve of Congress and fixing the Regular advancement of officers in the old Battalions and the appointment of Field officers. our Troops on the Ohio are Regimented Col°. Crawford to have the Command and to be compleated to a full Battalion During the war if the Men are willing.[57] The Compys of one Hundred Men are to be Reduced to 68 Rank & file & those of 50 Raised to that Quota. But I am to Continue to Recruit Under the former ordinance till further orders I have now above 68. Many other things of a Political Nature 'begin to Crowd themselves into my Imagination not worth communicating I am Dear Sir your Friend & Hble serv^t.

W^m McKee

Nov 2^d. 1776

TREATY OF 1776

[Summary of a letter from Col. George Morgan to the President of Congress, dated Nov. 8, 1776, in *Amer. Archives*, 5th series, iii, pp. 599, 600.]

The cloud which has threatened to break over this part of the country has now dispersed.[58] The Six Na-

---

[57] This is the well-known 13th (or West Augusta) regiment of the Virginia continental forces.—ED.

[58] Morgan appears to have been too sanguine, or too politic, to admit the continued dangers. In a letter to Dorsey Pentecost, written Nov. 17, 1776, he takes the latter to task for ex-

tions, Delawares, Shawnee, Munsee, and Mahican envoys have assembled here to the number of six hundred and forty-four, and promised inviolable peace with the United States, and neutrality during the war with Great Britain. The perpetrators of all the recent mischief are a band formerly situated near Cross Creeks, on the Ohio, but now removed to the heads of the Scioto.

Recent murders reported are of two women at Fish Creek, where a boy is missing, one man killed and four wounded opposite Hockhocking River, and two soldiers killed and scalped not far from Fort Randolph.

Several chiefs have accepted the invitation to visit Congress, which is a further proof of their peaceable disposition.[59]

---

citing alarm; see Bausman, *History of Beaver County*, i, p. 71. It will be noted that the Western tribes were absent from the treaty—the Wyandot, Chippewa, Miami, and Ottawa. Murders continued to be committeed; see Hildreth, *Pioneer History*, pp. 111, 113, and Pentecost's letters, *post*. In December two scouts were overtaken near Bridgeport, Ohio, opposite Wheeling, one being killed and the other captured; see J. H. Newton, *History of the Panhandle of West Virginia* (Wheeling, 1879), p. 97.—ED.

[59] Twelve chiefs were taken to Philadelphia at an expense of nearly twelve hundred dollars. They were introduced on Dec. 7, when a pacificatory speech was made, to which, two days later, they made an unimportant response. See *Journals of Congress* (new ed.), v, pp. 1010, 1011, 1013.—ED.

HOSTILITIES IMMINENT

[Col. Dorsey Pentecost to Capt. William Harrod. 4NN34 — transcript, probably in Harrod's handwriting.]

Nov 12th 1776

SIR—I am now at Cap. Wells upper station[60] and did Intend as Low as yours but the Comissarry is so Low that I Expect that he will Not Live and I have a grate deal of Business to Settel with him which will purvent my Coming Down I am tharefore to advise you that Detroyt and niagara are Reinforced and a Runner from S^t duskay arived Last Friday with A letter which I Saw Informing that they Expect that that place will be fortified and garrisoned[61] this Win-

---

[60] Richard and Alexander Wells emigrated from Baltimore County, Md., to the waters of Cross Creek, W. Va., about 1772.—ED.

[61] As a locality Sandusky was known from the earliest occupation of the country, a portage being made from the river of that name to the upper waters of the Scioto. The first recorded settlement of Indians was that following the secession of the Huron (Wyandot) chief Nicolas, who went thither from the neighborhood of Detroit about 1745, with the purpose of trading with the English. Gradually a considerable number of the Wyandot settled upon the bay and river of Sandusky. A trading house was established (1750) on the south shore of the bay, which is sometimes alluded to as the "old French fort." It did not, however, appear to have been a settled post, and apparently was abandoned before 1759. In 1761 the English had a blockhouse built on the south shore of the bay, which was garrisoned by thirty men. These were massacred in May, 1763, and their commander, Ensign Paully, taken captive. The following July, Captain Dalzell took vengeance by burning the Wyandot lower town. These Wyandot towns assumed much importance during the Revolution, but there seems to be no evidence that the proposed British fort and garrison was ever established. During the War of 1812–15 Lower Sandusky was fortified, and the gallant defense of Fort Stephenson is an heroic incident in the annals of the Western border.—ED.

ter and in the Spring as the Winedots Cockinwaugau Mingows &c are now Concluding thare to Attack us in three Different placess: Viz Fort Pitt Fort Randulph and Som place betwixt and that thare is now A party Out which Intend Strikeing us About now in Order to Lay it on the Deleways and Shawneways as the[y] Return from the P[itt] treaty and Brake the Peace between us and them I am tharefore to advise you to keep up Strick gard and if aney Indians Appears on our side you are to Chastise them in the Best manner you Can and Look on them as Open and Avowed enemise. fore the deliways and Shanaways are not so mutch as to put ashore on our Side Except thare Intended to Come to Your Camp then tha are to Hollow over and you are to go and fetch them and then you are to treat them Civelly 9 of the Chiefs are gon to set in the Congress 3 of the Senekays also are gone the Latter I think Nothing of. tha desire to go to War with us and have declared an Independency from the Six Nations. I have sent down an Acount of the Melitia with the Comisoners to the Congress who Intend we shall be paid by the Contenent. The Governor has Aprouved of my Conduct in regard of the Melitia and has left it to me how many Men Should be kept to Cover the Settlements and the Comisiners have Left the time of dischargeing them to me Likewise if no A'codents happens Ile keep up the Stations till About the 10th of the Next Month.

I was Informed a Numbers of peopel has Combined to Cross the Ohio and kill some of 'the Indians on thire Return from the treaty An action of this kind would forever Distroy the faith the Indians harbour of us and as a war is Sartin from the Norrad [Northward] Indians in the spring I think we Should keep the Nabouring Indians as mutch in our favour as possable I tharefore desire and Require you if you should find that aney Should Attempt the Like you Exert your Power to frustrate it.

DORSEY PENTECOST

on the Publick Sarvis
To Capt William Harrod Fishing Creek

PRECAUTIONARY ORDERS

[Dorsey Pentecost to Capt. William Harrod. 4NN36— A. L. S.]

November 21st 1776

SIR—I am glad to hear you are safely arrived and fixed at your Station, but am Sorry to hear your drafts did not fully appear, but I have now taken cear [care] to furnish them & they will Soon be with you. I am Exceeding sorry to hear of the misfortune of Row's boys,[62] I am to beg that you do evrything in your Power to Serve your Country in whose abilities I place the greatest confidence in your abilities, all the fear I have for you is that you will be too rash, I am strictly to recommend to you that you are cearful and use good Oeconomy and dont be too Venturesome, but Keep a good look out for I am really

---

[62] Not far from the garrison at Grave Creek, about the middle of September, two sons of Adam Rowe were set upon by Indians, the elder being killed, and the younger captured; see letter of Pentecost in Bausman, *Beaver County*, i, p. 72.—ED.

apprehensive you are in great danger, and if you find any Indians on our side the river Treat them as Open and avowed Enemies & do Every thing in your power to Protect the Inhabitants and your selves, & I recommend that you build some Snug close Little garrison for your Own Defence, and you will be Supplied with Provision by Mr Shepherd. Colo Cannon will be with you in a few days.[68] I have ordered another Company to the mouth of fish Creek your duty will then be much easier. I rest assured of your best Endeavours and am Dr Bill

Your Very H{le} Servt
DORSEY PENTECOST

P. S. no man is to be suffered to leave the Post untill they are releved by others under the Severest Penalty and it is my Positive orders that you do not suffer your men to Cross the river to hunt under no pertence whatsoever

---

[Col. John Canon's orders to Capt. William Harrod. 4NN38 — A. D. S.]

December 7th 1776

1. you are to keep up a Recular Sargents Gard Except where it makes the Dutey Too hard by sending

---

[68] Col. John Canon removed to the Western country early in 1774. He was justice of the peace for Augusta County, and colonel of militia for its western district, being thus next in rank to Pentecost. Upon the erection of Yohogania County, he held the same position. In 1787 he laid out the town of Canonsburg, where he became concerned in the Whiskey Rebellion. Colonel Canon founded the academy that became Jefferson College, and died at his Canonsburg residence in 1799.—ED.

out men to Gard the Inhabitants in that Case you must keep as good a Gard as you Can.

2. you are not to suffer any man to Exempt himself from his Dute or Leave his Post with out your Leave or the Leave of the oficer first in Command in your Absence and that furlows be only given in Rale Case of Necesaty,

3 you are not to sufer any of your men to make it Practice of s[h]uteing About the Garrison without your knoladge or Acquanting t.ie Garison As Evry such Brach of orders will be Looked ypon as an Alarm.

4 you are to Assist the Inhabitants with what Guard you Can Spare with Prudence for the Safety of the Garrison to Anable them to Save their Crops,

5 you are to Send Such Scouts as you Can Spare from the garison to Recuniter the River up and Down as far as the[y] Can Return the Same Day, and not to sufer them to neglect their Dutey in Hunting or other wise.

6 If any Discoverys Should be mad[e] or mischief Done you are to Signify it to the next field oficer with all Possible Despatch,

As the Dutey we ow to our Creator Should never be neglected I hope Sir you will not Sufer men to Practice of prefain Swareing or Brackng the Sabat Day by hunting or other wise

8 and as I hope Evry man here Come for the Security and protection of their Cuntry and as it is the gratest honour a Solder can have to obay the Commands of their oficers, I hope there will be no Complaints on that Account,

TAKING PRECAUTIONS

9 you are to proseed to Inclouse your self with some Kind of a fort as Soon as you Can get Horse and the Assistance of the Inhabitants,

10 you are to see that the men Perade Dayley and Endeavour to Larn their Exe[r]cises.

JOHN CANON

General orders to Capt. William Herod

PREPARATIONS FOR DEFENSE

[Summary of a letter from Gov. Patrick Henry to Col. Dorsey Pentecost, in Crumrine, *History of Washington County, Pennsylvania*, p. 185.]

This letter, dated Williamsburgh, Dec. 13, 1776, states that the danger of hostilities in the spring should cause measures to be taken to prepare the militia to act in the most efficient manner. Magazines are to be erected in Yohogania, Monongalia, and Ohio counties,[64] lead has been ordered sent to the frontier, and Captain Gibson's cargo of powder is expected. Spies should be kept out, and arms and accoutrements put in the best possible order.

---

[64] In October, 1776, the Virginia assembly defined the limits of West Augusta district, at the same time dividing it into three counties, Ohio, Yohogania, and Monongalia. For their militia officers see *post*.—ED.

SITUATION AT GRAVE CREEK

[The inhabitants of Grave Creek to Capt. William Harrod.
4NN44 — A. D. S.]

SIR—we the Subscribers finding it impossible to Defend ourselves against the Common Enemy of this Country by the Militia's being drawn away from this Garrison & if we do not Get Some Assistance Immediately we will be obliged to Quit this place it being the frontier fort & so near to the savage that we hope you will be so Kind as to Get as many of Your men as you Can to Stay to our Assistance as we understand you have a very great Influence over your men and as there is not any particular Orders for men to be Stationed at this place David Shephard Esqr. will find you & your men provisions while you stay here & we flatter ourselves At the same time that the Commissioners for paying the former Militia will in no ways refuse to pay you & your men for this Service done the Country as well as those done by the former Cap^{ts} at this Place S^r. your Complyance in this request will very much oblige y^r. very Humble Servants

Grave Creek fort
2^d January 1777

YATES CONWELL	ZEPHANIAH BLACKFORD
JAMES WILLIAMS	MORGAN JONES
MATTHEW KARR	CHARLES M^{c}CLEAN
JOSEPH TOMLINSON	JAMES CALDWELL
STEPHEN PARR	JOHN WILLIAMS
DAVID M^{c}CLURE	WILLIAM M^{c}MECHEN
SAMUEL HARRIS Sen	

To Capt Wm Harrod at Grave Creek

[Agreement to serve in the militia. 4NN45 — A. D. S.]

We whose Names are hereunto Subscribed do agree to Join Capt Wm Herrods Comp^y and Serve under him as Militia Soldiers to Assist the Inhabitants of Grave Creek fort to Defend themselves against the Savages for a Term of Time Not Exceeding fifteen days & as the same is done without proper orders we do agree to run the risk of the Colony's paying us for the same he the s^d Capt Herrod is to make 'proper Application if the s^d Colony does not pay the s^d Capt Herrod In behalf of us we agree to Loose the same provided that David Shepherd Esqr. finds us provisions during the time at his proper risk as witness our hands this 2^d day of January 1777

JOSEPH M^{c}CLAIN	PAUL ARMSTRONG
JOHN M^{c}CLAIN	MATTHEW KERR
JAMES HARRIS	SAMUEL STILWELL
STEPHEN HARRIS	JOHN BOYD
THOMAS KNOX	MICHAEL FLOOD
GEORGE KNOX	JOSEPH GLEN
JAMES M^{c}MECHEN	ADAM ROW Jun.
JOSEPH ALEXANDER	JAMES DAVIS
ADAM ROW	JOHN HARKNESS
FRANCIS PURCELL	PHILLIP O FINN

SUPPLIES FROM NEW ORLEANS

[Col. Dorsey Pentecost to Capt William Harrod. 4NN46—
A. L. S.]

YOUGHIOGHENY COUNTY January 28th 1777

CAPTAIN WILLIAM HARROD

SIR—I have received his Excellency the Governor's directions to endeavour to find out where Captain Gibsons Cargo of Powder is.[65] In consequence of which I am to order that you do with all possible expedition raise a Company of Fifty privates in Conjunction and with the assistance of Lieutenant Nathan Hammond and Ensign Andrew Steel,[66] with whom, and under

---

[65] Capt. George Gibson and Lieut. William Linn left Fort Pitt July 19, 1776, and reached New Orleans some time in August. There, aided by Oliver Pollock, they succeeded in purchasing ten thousand pounds of gunpowder for $1800. Gibson was at one time thrown into prison by a concerted arrangement with the Spanish governor, to mislead the British spies in the town. He got off by ship in October, and safely conveyed to Virginia a large portion of the powder.

Meanwhile, Lieutenant Linn, set out Sept. 22, 1776, to return to Fort Pitt by way of the Mississippi and Ohio rivers. He reached the Spanish post on the Arkansas Nov. 26, and was cordially received by its commandant. Owing to the illness of his men and the lack of provisions, he determined to winter at this post, hunting and drying meat for the return voyage in the spring; see his letter to Pollock from Arkansas Post, transcribed in Draper MSS., 60J277. After leaving the Arkansas, Linn sent an express to St. Louis for aid; but fearing the consequences, he hastened to pass the mouth of Ohio before the appointed date, and later learned that he thus escaped capture by a party of Indians, engaged, no doubt, by the Spanish authorities, to intercept him. The powder and boats were portaged by hand around the Falls of the Ohio (Louisville). The British obtained information of this exploit after his passage. See *Wis. Hist. Colls.*, vii, p. 407.—ED.

[66] Both these officers had been concerned in the first settlement of Kentucky. Nathan Hammond first visited that country in 1773. In 1775 he was one of the founders of Boiling

your Command, you are Immediately to proceed down the Ohio, taking all possible Care to examine Stricktly the mouth of all Creeks and Rivers which you pass, & when you arrive at the Mouth of Kentucke or at the Falls of Ohio, I think it would be advisable to send to Harrod's-Burgh,[67] and make inquiry after Captain Linn & the said Cargoe, whom you are to conduct with the utmost Safety agreeable to these Instructions. If you should not fall in with Captain Linn (who superintends and Conducts the said Cargo) before you arrive at the Mouth of Ohio, I think it will be necessary that you pass up the Mississippi to the Kaskaskias Village,[68] where you will make in-

---

Springs settlement, and a delegate thence to the Transylvania legislature at Boonesborough. He probably returned up the Ohio during the alarm of 1776. He was later in Kentucky, being killed by the Indians before 1780, probably on Hammond's Creek in Anderson County.

Andrew Steel was one of the party with Joseph Lindsay, who re-inforced Harrodsburgh in 1775, and camped on the site of Lexington. He was recorded as a lot-holder in Louisville in 1779.—ED.

[67] Linn sent overland to Harrodsburgh an express, who arrived there March 9, bringing needful succor. Clark, in his manuscript diary, gives the name of this messenger as Ebenezer Corn.—ED.

[68] It seems curious that the American authorities should expect to find their cargo of supplies at a village guarded by a British post; but doubtless they already counted on the sympathy of the French habitants with the American cause, which later was of great assistance to George Rogers Clark. Moreover, there were a number of American traders at the village, some of whom did supply Linn on his return voyage. See C. W. Alvord, "Cahokia Records," in *Illinois Historical Collections* (Springfield, 1907), ii, p. xxxiii.

Kaskaskia was probably the oldest French settlement in the West, being begun about 1700, and having a continuous history since that time. In 1719 it was erected into a parish, and in 1765 transferred from French to British authority, under which latter it remained until its capture by George Rogers

quiry & probably meet with Captain Linn with his Cargo, & if you don't meet him before you get there, when you meet him, you will conduct him with the utmost Safety and the said Cargo up to the House of James Austurgass on the Monongahela River, & immediately advise me thereof. I desire that all possible care may be observed, as I have great reason to apprehend Danger from the Savages. If you hear nothing of Captain Linn at the aforesaid places, you will proceed on untill you meet him. If you find it conducive to the good of the Service you are ordered upon, you will engage the necessary Interpreter or Interpreters, who should be worthy, Trusty persons. Colonel David Shepherd will furnish you with Beef, Pork, and Craft, at the mouth of Grave Creek; and your Lieutenant will apply to Joseph Parkison[69] for flour & Salt, & send him to my house for the necessary Ammunition. You will not fail to leave proper Spies on the River Ohio, in case you move up to Harrod's-Burgh, & at the mouth of Ohio, in case you

---

Clark in 1778. Organized by the Americans as the Illinois County of Virginia, it so remained until 1789, when it became part of the Northwest territory. Kaskaskia was the capital until the organization of the state, when the records of the commonwealth were transferred to Vandalia (1819). The early French, British, and American records have lately been recovered, largely through the personal efforts of Professor Alvord. The site of old Kaskaskia is now almost entirely covered by the Mississippi River.—ED.

[69] Joseph Parkison was of English descent and came from Conococheague settlement in 1770. He bought land on what is now the site of Monongahela City, Washington County, Pa., where he established a ferry (well-known in the annals of the Whiskey Rebellion), and kept a tavern as well as a store for general merchandize. He laid out Williamsport on his land in 1796—a name changed in 1835 to Monongahela City.—ED.

go up to the Kaskaskias Village, lest Captain Linn should Slip your Notice in the Interim. Depending on your Strict adherence to these Instructions, I have the pleasure of being

Sir Your mo: obed^t. Servt.
DORSEY PENTECOST
County Leu^t. of Yohogania

P. S. If you run out of Provisions ammunition or any other article necessary for your Subsistance, or by any wise to Facilitate the Expedition, you will purchase it, & draw on Government or me for the Pay, which Shall Punctually be paid but I must once more recommend the utmost Frugality, Prudence and Good Conduct

I am &c.
DORSEY PENTECOST
C. L. Y. C.

On the Public Service
  Captⁿ. William Herrod
    on his Way to the Mississippi

MILITIA ARRANGEMENTS

[Col. Zackwell Morgan to Capt. William Harrod. 4NN53 — A. L. S.]

You are hearby Required to Draught one Liu^t [Lieutenant] and one Sar^t and fifteen men of your Company to Randevouse at the hous of John Swaringans[70] under the command of Capt Abner Howel up-

---

[70] John Swearingen, originally of Dutch ancestry, removed from Maryland as early as 1770, and settled in what is now Springhill township, on the cross-road between Cheat River

on the first notis which by his Excelencis Express Desire is to be appinted the Place of Randevouse for this County and as a General Dra[u]ght is now making Which you will Strictly observe Gaven under my hand this 31 Day of January 1777

          Zack[ll] Morgan [71]

To Capt William Harrod

[Orders of the Executive Council of Virginia. 13S112 — transcript by L. C. D.]

Feb. 12th, 1777. Colonel Pentecost to cause 100 militia under proper officers of Yohogania County to garrison Fort Pitt until relieved by regulars.

That two companies of men be raised to garrison Forts Pitt and Randolph, under Capts. Robert Campbell and John Robinson.[72] Thady Kelley and Andrew

---

and Redstone. His son Van was a famous captain in the Revolution, and father-in-law of Capt. Samuel Brady. John was still, in 1785, a resident of what is now Fayette County, Pa.—Ed.

[71] Zackwell Morgan was of Welsh descent, and with his brother David emigrated from Berkeley County, Va., about 1768, to the present site of Morgantown. Here Zackwell settled and laid out the town about 1785. A family tradition relates that he served under Forbes in the French and Indian War. During the Revolution he was lieutenant for Monongalia County. In 1755 he married Drusilla Springer, and had several sons, two of whom, Levi and James, were noted scouts, and served in St. Clair's army in 1791. Morgan gave these orders to Harrod as a result of resolutions adopted at a council of war held at Catfish Creek, Jan. 28; see Crumrine, *Washington County, Pa.*, p. 186.—Ed.

[72] Robert Campbell was a half-brother of Col. John Campbell. He made his home in Pittsburgh, but later removed to

McClure 1st lieutenants, William Anderson and James Brenton [73] 2nd lieutenants, John Ward and George Willis ensigns—all to serve during the war; Captain Campbell, Lieuts. Kelley and Anderson and Ensign Ward with their company to command the garrison at Fort Pitt; Captain Robinson, Lieuts. McClure and Brenton and Ensign Willis at Fort Randolph. John Campbell of Pittsburgh [74] to provision the 200 men at Fort Pitt.

Jefferson County, Kentucky, where he died without heirs sometime before 1806.

John Robinson was a captain of the Washington County (Pa.) militia in 1784. He probably lived on Robinson's Run in that county.—ED.

[73] Thady Kelley was a noted spy and ranger, one of those who led McDonald's expedition in 1774.

The McClures lived on Ten Mile Creek, and were prominent in that region.

William Anderson had a farm near Raccoon Creek, Washington County, Pa. In 1779 he was wounded by Indians, escaped to Dillow's blockhouse, and was saved. One of his name acted as deputy muster-master at Fort McIntosh in 1779, and afterwards resided in Mercer County, Pa., until 1806.

James Brenton (or Brinton) had been out with McDonald in 1774, and after ranging throughout 1777, and serving with Hand in the spring of 1778, commanded a company on McIntosh's expedition. Later he was a major on Crawford's Sandusky expedition (1782), and although slightly wounded, returned to his home in Washington County. After the Revolution he removed to Kentucky, and lived in Mercer County, where he was killed by the Indians about 1788.—ED.

[74] Col. John Campbell was an Irishman by birth, who came to America while young, and going West entered the Indian trade. In 1764 he laid off a town on the present site of Pittsburgh. In 1774 he was at the Falls of Ohio (Louisville), where he purchased a large tract of land adjoining Connolly's. During the early Revolution he acted as commissary at Fort Pitt. In the summer of 1779, he was on a visit to the Falls of Ohio, where he took passage with Col. David Rogers's party from New Orleans on their return journey up the river. Near Cincinnati, Rogers was defeated by a large force of Indians, who captured Campbell. The latter was taken to Detroit, and

[Gov. Patrick Henry to Maj. David Rogers.[75] 1SS39 —
A. L. S.]

WILLIAMSBURGH Feb. 13th. 1777

SIR—You are to cause fifty men of your Militia most proper for the purpose to be stationed at the Mouth of the little Kanhawa, & also fifty others at the Mouth of Wheeling, under the proper officers for

---

ultimately to Quebec, where because of his open defiance the British refused to have him exchanged until the very close of the Revolution. In 1784 he took up his residence near Louisville, where he was for a time chairman of the trustees for Clark's Grant in Indiana. He was sent to the Virginia legislature from Kentucky, was member of the constitutional convention of 1792, and speaker of the Kentucky senate in 1798. He died the following year, leaving a large estate to collateral heirs.—ED.

[75] David Rogers was a native of Ireland who early emigrated to America, and settled as a merchant at Oldtown, Md. In 1775 he made a settlement five miles above Wheeling, on the Ohio, and marched a company to Pittsburgh. The following year, he represented West Augusta district in the Virginia legislature, and was appointed captain in the continental service. For some reason he did not qualify, and being the best-known resident was appointed March 4, 1777, as county-lieutenant for the new Ohio County. In April he was re-elected to the Virginia senate. The Indian forays, however, made his settlement unsafe, and he removed back to Mount Braddock, in the present Fayette County, Pa., where he resigned his county-lieutenantship, whereupon David Shepherd was (June, 1777) appointed in his stead. Later he married the widow of Capt. Michael Cresap, and located on the Potomac in Hampshire County. Early in 1778, he was chosen a special envoy to New Orleans to convey goods thence to the Western states. Leaving Pittsburgh in June, he reached New Orleans in September, and found that his goods were awaiting him at St. Louis. These secured, he obtained an additional guard at the Falls of Ohio from George Rogers Clark. While ascending the river he and his convoy were waylaid (Oct. 4, 1779) by a large party of Indians, just above the mouth of the Licking, all being captured save thirteen. Rogers was himself killed by Simon Girty, who later boasted of the deed.—ED.

Gov. Patrick Henry

After the painting by Sully

the Defence of those posts & the neighbouring Inhabitants until further orders.

I address my self to you on this occasion not knowing who is the superior officer in the county where [you] reside.

I should be glad to hear what is become of the powder Capt. Gibson purchased at Orleans & what you have done in the Business of buying provisions. I am Sir y^r. mo. hble serv^t.

P. HENRY J^r.

To Major Rogers of Ohio by Mr Kelly

[Orders of the Virginia Council. 13S109 — transcript by L. C. D.]

March 4, 1777. John Campbell appointed and commissioned County Lieutenant, John Cannon Colonel, Thomas Brown Lt. Colonel, and Henry Taylor, Major, of the county of Yohogania.[76]

David Rogers county Lieutenant, David Shepherd

---

[76] Col. Thomas Brown was an early settler (1768) on the Monongahela. In 1776 he bought Cresap's property on the site of Redstone Old Fort, and in 1785 laid out the town called from his name, Brownsville. He died in 1797, aged fifty-nine years, leaving two sons and three daughters.

Maj. Henry Taylor came from Maryland in 1770, and settled just north of the present town of Washington. In December, 1777, he resigned his position as major, being succeeded by Gabriel Cox. Taylor was the first presiding judge of Washington County, and in 1793 brigadier-general of militia. In the latter capacity he aided Wayne in his campaign (1794). Major Taylor died in 1801 in the sixty-third year of his age.—ED.

Colonel, David McClure Lt. Colonel, and Samuel Mc-
Colloch Major of Ohio County.[77]

[Officers of Monongalia County. 3NN128-130 — transcript
by L. C. D.]

MONONGALIA CO: Vª. April, 1777

Zackquill Morgan, County Lt., Col. Danl. McFarland, Lt. Col., Thos. Gaddis, Maj. John Evans.[78]

---

[77] David McClure was a prominent resident of the Grave Creek locality. He continued as lieutenant-colonel of the county until his death, which occurred about 1788.

Maj. Samuel McColloch was a noted borderer, born in 1750, who came about 1770 from the South Branch of the Potomac to the waters of Short Creek. In the autumn of 1777, while bringing relief to the besieged at Fort Henry, he was set upon by Indians, and escaped by leaping his horse over a precipice two hundred feet high. In 1779 he was elected to represent Ohio County in the Virginia legislature, and was out with Brodhead on the latter's campaign. He was in charge of Van Metre's fort on Short Creek during the Revolution, being shot and mortally wounded by Indians not far from that fort (July 30, 1782).—ED.

[78] Col. Thomas Gaddis settled (1769) in what is now Fayette County, near the site of Uniontown. He was later a militia officer for Westmoreland County, Pa., and having volunteered for Crawford's expedition (1782) was elected by the troop as field-major (third in command). He conducted a distillery upon his premises and was active in the Whiskey Rebellion. About 1816 he sold his farm and removed to the Miami region of Ohio, where he died.

John Evans was of Welsh descent, and born in Loudoun County, Virginia. He was an early settler on Decker's Creek, near the Morgans' settlement on the Monongahela, his estate being known as "Walnut Hills." He was out with McIntosh in 1778, colonel under Brodhead in 1779, and prominent in militia affairs throughout the Revolution. He died at his home in Monongalia County in 1834, aged ninety-six years. His son Capt. Jack Evans was a prominent scout in the Indian wars, and his descendants still live in the vicinity of his West Virginia home.—ED.

ORGANIZING MILITIA

Capt. Harrod & company then at Grave Creek from Monongalia County.

Capt[s]., Jesse Pigman, John Minor, W[m]. M[c]Cleery, Charles Craycraft, Henry Enoch, Abraham Teegardin, Thomas Crooke, Jacob Prickett, John Hord, & Jacob Rich:[79] That Capts. Pigman & Henry Enoch raise two companies to go under Col. Shepherd against Pluggy's Town.

---

[79] The early records of Monongalia County were burned, so that it is not possible to identify all of these captains.

Jesse Pigman, who made a settlement in Monongalia County in 1773, was a member of the grand jury for Augusta County in 1775.

John Minor commanded at Statler Fort, having come to the Monongahela region as early as 1764. He had a large estate near the forks of Cheat River and built there the first flourmill of the region. Upon his land coming within Pennsylvania he became (1791) a member of the legislature of that state, and secured the erection of Greene County. He aided in building the boats for Clark's expedition (1778), and traded to New Orleans. He died in 1833 in his ninetieth year.

William McCleary was a prominent lawyer of what is now Monongalia County, W. Va. He acted at one time as commissary for the forts, and was colonel of the militia in 1784. He also served as attorney-general for the county court until his decease some time after 1810.

Charles Cracroft was born near Frederick, Maryland, but lived near Harper's Ferry until his removal to the West in 1774, when he settled near Van Buren, Washington County, Pa. In 1779 he was out as major, with Brodhead, and two years later volunteered under Clark, being captured with Lochry's detachment, and imprisoned at Quebec until the close of the Revolution. He died on his farm in 1824.

Abram Teagarden and his brother William settled first at Redstone, and later moved into Greene County, Pa., on the upper waters of Wheeling Creek. Two of the second generation served in Wayne's campaign.

Jacob Prickett belonged to the family who forted on the Monongahela in what is now Marion County, W. Va. The fort was attacked in 1774, and Josiah Prickett killed.—Ed.

[Gov. Patrick Henry to Col. David Rogers. 1SS41 — A. L. S.]

Wᴹˢʙᴜʀɢʜ, Mᴀʀᴄʜ 4ᵗʰ. 1777.

Sɪʀ—I have to desire that the field officers of your county will fill up the commissions herewith sent for the proper Captains & subaltern officers of your militia.

I am Sir Yʳ. mo. hbˡ. servᵗ.
P. Hᴇɴʀʏ. Jʳ.

In Council.
Cotʸ. Lieutenᵗ. of Ohio Cotʸ.

PLUGGY'S TOWN EXPEDITION ORDERED

[Orders of the Virginia Council. 1SS43 — A. D. S.]

Iɴ Cᴏᴜɴᴄɪʟ Wᴍsʙᴜʀɢ march 12 1777

This Board having from time to time recivᵈ. undoubted Inteligence of Repeated hostilities Commited on the Subjects of this Commonwealth by the Indians of Pluggys Town and not Withstanding the Just Remonstrances made to them by our Agents for Indian Affairs they have not been Brought to a Sense of Duty, but from their repeated Injurys there is the greatest Reason to Expect increased Insolence in Stead of that good Neighbourhood we wish to Cultivate with all the Indian Tribes. and whearas the obstinate and wicked Disposition of the Said Indians of Pluggy's Town have been Represented to Congress, and they Seem to have no prospects of Conciliation but have referd to this Board the Propriety of making war on them if it can be done without exciting the jealousy & discord with the other Neighbouring Nations.[80]

Resolved. that George morgan Esqr. Superintendent of Indian Affairs and Colonel John Nevill (or in case of his absence Robert Campbell Esqr.) do Confer with Such Chief or Chiefs of the Delewares and Shawnese Indians as may be Rely'd on for Secrecy and fidelity and Represent to them the Necessity of Chastising the S^d. Indians and in Case the S^d. gentlemen Shall find that the said Shawneeses and Delewares do not give Reason to apprehend Discord with them by Reason of Such a Proceeding Resolved

That 300 militia men commanded by a Col^r Major six Captains six Lieutenants six Ensigns and a Proper number of noncommissioned officers be Ordered to make an Expedition to said Pluggys Town in order to Punish that People for their unprovoked Crueltys Commited on the Inhabitants of Virginia

That the officers commanding this Expedition have it in Charge at their peril and that all those Concernd that no Injurys provocation or ill treatment of Any kind Be done or Suffered to the Delewares and Shawnees Indians through Whose Country they Pass, But on the other hand that the said officers be Strictly charged and commanded to conduct them Selves towards them, as our faithful Friends and Brethren Government being Detirmined to revenge the Least Injury done them

That the officers commanding the Expedition apply

---

[80] February 27, 1777, Congress resolved to request Virginia to consider the propriety of an expedition against Pluggy's Town, and these orders were issued in consequence of that request; see *Journals of Congress* (new ed.), vii, p. 166.—ED.

to George Morgan Esqr. for amunition Provisions and Stores necesary for the Party who is Requested to give any assistance in his Power [to] forward the undertaking

That the Commanding officer ought to be directed to Shew mercy to the Women and Children and to such of the men as Surrender them Selves and to Send all Prisoners taken by his Party belonging to S^d. Pluggys Town to this City and as the Success of this Expedition will Depend upon the Dispatch with which it is conducted Resolved That if a majority of the field officers and Captains who are to be engaged in it shall judge it best, that the men Shall be Directed to march on horse Back finding their own horses and carrying their own Provisions and that they ought to receive a Reasonable allowance for so Doing

That Col^r. David Shepherd of Ohio Coty be Commander in Chief of the Expedition that Major hinry Taylor of Yoghyogania Coty be the major and that they nominate the Captains and Subaltirn officers out of those Commissioned in the Cotys of monnongahale Yoghyagane & ohio Counties or Either of them[81]

ARCH BLAIR[82] *Clerk*

A Copy

---

[81] These orders are likewise printed in *Penna. Archives*, v. pp. 258-260, accompanied by a personal letter from Patrick Henry to Morgan and Neville, emphasizing the delicacy and secrecy needed to be observed. See also Bausman, *Beaver County*, p. 73.—ED.

[82] Archibald Blair (1753-1824) was a native of Williamsburgh, and a relative of Rev. James Blair, first president of William and Mary College. He was clerk of the committee

[Gov. Patrick Henry to Col. David Rogers. 1SS45 — A. L. S.]

WMS.BURGH March 13th. 1777

SIR—You will please give to Col⁰. Shepherd & Major Taylor all the assistance which is requisite in raising & preparing three hundred men for an Expedition ag^t. Pluggys Town. I do not mean to restrict these gent^n. to any par[ticu]lar Coty in getting the proper Number of Militia, but hope every one on y^r. side of the Mountains will exert himself to give success to this measure. I am Sir Y^r. hbl serv^t.

P. HENRY J^r.

The Coty Lieuten^t. of Ohio

REINFORCEMENTS FOR FORT RANDOLPH

[Capt. John Stuart to Col. William Fleming. 3ZZ9 — A. L. S.]

GREENBRIER March ye 21st 1777

D^r SIR—As I informed you by Wilson of the apointment for assembling the draughts on this quarter ye 20th Inst. they meet accordingly, & altho I had made the strictest enquirey for bacon &c. for the march it was out of my power to procure one pound. I therefore ordered those who were willing to go to provide each man 10 days provision (which I thing is little anugh to march the distance at this season) and to be ready to march on monday ye 21st Inst. but as a number has refused upon their draughts I

---

of safety, and then of the Virginia council from the outbreak of the Revolution until 1800. In 1789 he married Mary Whiting, by whom he left three children.—ED.

am convinced there will not be a company of 50 men, I therefore thought it would be proper to aquaint you & would be glad to know whether it will be worth my while to go with what is willing which I believe will not be more than 30 or thereabouts or send them with Lieut. Ward,[88] & have another draught made and march after them myself, if the company can be made up, but as Capt Arbuckle is Just come from Williamsburg & informes me that the governor & Council has petitioned the congress for continueing the regulars on the Ohio I am in hopes there will be no occasion for going at this time, as it will be attended with much inconvenience to many of the people, but of this I make no doubt you have Rec^d notice by now, but if the case is that we must go I think it would be highly necessary to prosecute the delinquents who has refused their draughts, & it will be the more effectually done if each particular Capt. Receive your orders for that purpose, as well as for draughting the proportion of the next division for compleating the company otherwise it appears to me they will in a short time pay but little respect to authority. I did every thing in my power to assemble such as engaged volunteers w^t Capt Byrnside before I Rec^d your last by Mr Madison but to no purpose

---

[88] Lieutenant Ward was without doubt a nephew of Capt. Matthew Arbuckle, and son of Capt. James Ward who was slain at Point Pleasant (see *Dunmore's War*, p. 276, note 93). There were several sons in the Ward family, of whom the eldest at home was William. He afterwards removed to Mason County, Ky., where he served in the state legislature (1792-95). About 1800 he removed to Ohio, where in 1804 he laid out the town of Urbana, in Champaign County. He died in this neighborhood in 1822.—ED.

for there was never more than a dozen appeared [at]
once I shall be glad how soon the messenger can return that I may know how to proceed

I am your most Humb^l Servt

JOHN STEWART

N. B. please to send me some each [itch] ointment by the bearer J. S.

Since I wrote a soldier of Capt Arbuckles arived from for[t] Randolph who Informs that they had but 3 or four days provision when he Left that and that the soldiers were determined to abandon the garrison in a few days unless a supply came from for[t] pitt, which was expected, the same person Informs he was sent by Lieut. Thompson who had been up the new river for corn, to the inhabitants there about Kelleys[84] to let them know there was a party of Indians coming up the river which was discovered shooting Turkeys the particulars of this I cannot inform you as I did not see the man but had it from Capt Arbuckle

J. S.

On publick service to
Col^o. William Fleming Botetourt pr express

---

[84] For the location of Kelly's place see *Dunmore's War*, p. 112, note 62.—ED.

SITUATION AT WHEELING

[Col. David Shepherd to Gov. Patrick Henry (?). 1SS47 — A. L., draft in Shepherd's handwriting.]

WEELIN OR OHIO COUNTY March 24th 1777

SIR—By a Letter Directed to Maj^r David Rogers and Likewise the Order in Council of the 12 of February it was ordered that this County Should Send fifty men to the Little Kanawa and fifty men to the Mouth of Whelin, application being made to me I Called a council for that purpose of the field officers and Captins of the County and after Considering the State of the County and Our Militia not Consisting of more than 350 Affective men and having a frontier of Eighty Miles and that Laying the Nearest and most Exposed to the Indians and the Late alarming accounts from the Indian towns[85] I Receiv^d Inteliganc by way of the Kanaway that they have Burnt one white prisoner at the Shawnee towns Lately which alarms the people very much suposed to be a Soldier Named Elijah Matthews taken at Grave Creek, under those and many other Surcomstances of the Like Nature, and no garison being Built at the Little Kanaway and there Never been any men at that Station I hope Sir under those Sircomstances

---

[85] See *post* for O'Hara's account of a war-party leaving the Shawnee towns. Early in March also, a band of Shawnee under Blackfish began to harry the few Kentucky settlements, hovering around Harrodsburgh, killing William Ray and capturing Thomas Shores, and attacking the fort itself on the morning of the 7th. The defenders sallied forth, and drove them away, with losses on each side. The same day a detached party of Indians appeared before Boonesborough, and before refuge was found in the fort killed and wounded two persons. See Draper MSS., 4B115-117.—ED.

you will not Consider our Disobaying of orders a breach of trust or Disafected to the Commonwelth ass our pressing Necessity forced it to we therefore thought it proper to order fifty of our militia to Whelin and fifty more to grave Creek and twenty five to the Beach Bottom[86] which places appeared to us to be the most fiting to Defend us against the Indians and protect the Inhabitants of this and part of the other Countys. according to your former order we have sent spies towards the Indian Country one part[y] of which Come across a party of Indians in Camp and fired on them wounded one which got of[f] by the assistance of the Rest a deep creek being betwen them they got clear they Lef their Kittle a Number of Bows and arrows and had all the apperance of woryers [warriors].

[Col. David Shepherd to (?). 1SS48 — A. L., draft in Shepherd's handwriting.]

WEELIN March 24th 1777

SIR—Please to Send by the Barer Daniel McClane the Barril of Powder which I chose and Likewise 163lb of Lead and 300 flints I should take it ass a great favour if you could Supply me with a Bar off Steel to Repair gunlocks and other things for the use of the militia that is Stationed on the River I hope

---

[86] Beech Bottom Fort stood about three miles below Wellsburgh, and twelve above Wheeling, in what is now Buffalo District, Brooke County. It protected the settlement of the Hedges family. Occupied only in 1777; its history is related in subsequent documents.—ED.

you will give Some Direction for the Victualing the
Militia that will be Stationed at grave Creek Whelin
an the Beach Bottom ass in our Council it was not
thought proper to Send men to the Little Conway
and Leave our frontiers Defenceless and ass there
was No garison built there Neither had we Directions for that purpose if we had the men to Spare
it was thought proper

ALLIES TO BE PROTECTED

[Gov. Patrick Henry to the County Lieutenant of Ohio.
1SS49—A. L. S.]

WMS.BURGH March 27th. 1777

SIR—I have rec[d]. Information that the Delaware
Indians apprehend a dangerous War with our
Enemys, on account of their Fidelity to us. You are
to use every means in your power to protect them.
If they demand it, you are to send a party of Men
to their Towns if in Virginia to assist them in build[g].
Forts, & in such a Number as the Exigency of Affairs makes necessary. While there they are to defend our faithfull allys to the last Extremity. If the
Indians chuse to come into our settlements for Shelter, make them Welcome, & share with them all your
provisions ammunition warlike stores as long as any
lasts to divide. Any Injury done them, is done to
us while they are faithfull. In one Word, support
protect defend & cherish them in every Respect to
the utmost. Act in concert with the Neighbouring

IROQUOIS HOSTILE

counties & communicate these orders to M^r. Morgan the Agent & the commanders of the Regulars.

I am Sir Y^r. hble serv^t.

P. HENRY J^r.

The County Lieutenant of Ohio

THE SIX NATIONS HOSTILE

[Col. Zackwell Morgan to Capt. William Harrod. 4NN56—
A. L. S.]

April 2^d. 1777

I received your Letter by Mr McLaughlin, and have sent you 17½ Pounds Powder. I have not one Single Pound of Lead, here but shall Endeavour to supply you with some, on Monday, pray, try to have your whole Company together as soon as Possible, at Grave Creek & keep a sharp Lookout, for fear of the Indians I am informed Col^o. Shepherd has Employed a man to refit the Battoe, but if you want Pitch or Oakum, for it you must Send to M^r. Robert Campbell, at fort Pitt, who will Supply you those articles. be very active as much Depends on your Good Conduct, at Grave Creek. The Six nations have killd one man & taken another at the Kittaning and have Ordered us all to Quite [quit] this Country, directly in Writting, besides their Leaving the Implements of Warr, Common to them, when they Declare War[87] This is Confirmed by the Delawares,

---

[87] Early in 1777 the British officers at Niagara had, in obedience to instructions from headquarters, sent out the Indians against the frontiers. February 14, they captured Andrew McFarlane near the Kittanning fort. A month later, as Capt.

and I think there is no Dispute of a War, with the Villians.

M^r. Chew[88] will bring Provisions, Amunition & Sufficient for your Journey Down the River Which I hope will be Prosperious, about the first of **May** [have] all things in readiness, when I hope no more Delays [will] Stop this Necessary Journey

I am your Friend & H̱ble Ser^t

ZACK^{ll} MORGAN

William Harrod, Esqr

Samuel Moorhead was returning from the fort to recruit, he found (March 18) one by the name of Simpson killed, and his own brother, who had been with him, captured. By the corpse was a war-belt, a tomahawk, and a pouch containing a letter addressed to the inhabitants; for this letter, see Hildreth, *Pioneer History of the Ohio Valley*, p. 117. It was to this incident that Morgan refers; see *Pennsylvania Historical Register*, 2nd series, ii, p. 235. That the Six Nations were sent out by British orders is proven by the letters of Guy Johnson in *N. Y. Colon. Docs.*, viii, pp. 711–713.—ED.

[88] Maj. James Chew belonged to the Virginia branch of that family, and was the youngest son of Thomas, for many years magistrate of Orange, then of Spottsylvania County. James's elder brother, Colby Chew, was an early explorer in Kentucky with Dr. Thomas Walker. James was for a time surveyor of Monongalia County, and appears to have acted as special agent and commissary for the Ohio forts. He married (1765) Mary Caldwell, and died before January 27, 1783. See Draper MSS., 5ZZ76.—ED.

OPERATIONS SUSPENDED

PLUGGY'S TOWN EXPEDITION ABANDONED

[Gov. Patrick Henry to Col. David Shepherd. 1SS51 — A. L. S.]

WMS.BURGH April 12th. 1777.

SIR—The Expedition against Pluggys Town is to be laid aside by a Resolution of Congress.[89]

I am Sir Yr. hble servt.

P. HENRY

Colo. David Shepherd, Ohio
public Service   by Express

[John Page to Col. George Morgan and Col. John Nevill. 1SS53 — transcript by Morgan.]

WMS.BURGH in Council April 15th. 1777

GENTLEMEN—As an Express was sent off to you last week in consequence of a vote of Congress to suspend the operations which were meditated against Pluggy's Town; and as Congress have under their consideration many of the important articles mention'd in your Letter now before us,[90] & the ensuing

---

[89] This resolution of Congress was adopted March 25, upon the receipt of a letter from Col. George Morgan, dated the fifteenth of the same month; see *Journals of Congress*, new ed., vii, p. 201. The letter of Morgan is printed by Bausman, *Beaver County*, p. 69. In it he deprecates any expeditions into the Indian country "which may involve us in a general & unequal Quarrel with all the Nations who are at present quiet but extremely jealous of the least encroachment on their Lands." This letter determined the authorities to pursue a pacific policy, and act only upon the defensive.—ED.

[90] Referring to their letter of April, 1, 1777, printed in *Penna, Archives*, v. p. 288; *Beaver County*, p. 74; and Hildreth, *Pioneer History of the Ohio Valley*, pp. 119-122.—ED.

Assembly should be consulted on some of them—we can only at present recommend it to you to prevent an Indian War as far as lies in your power, & to be prepared against any attack in the best manner your situation will admit of

I am Gentⁿ. Your most obed^t. serv^t.

JOHN PAGE

P. S. We are as much at a loss to know where St. Louis is, as you can be, but suppose it to be where you mention.[91]

To Col^o. George Morgan &
    Col^o. John Nevill at Fort Pitt.
To Colonel David Shepherd [92] Ohio County
On the public Service By Express

Rec^d. Fort Pitt April 27th
GEO. MORGAN

[Gov. Patrick Henry to Col. John Nevill. 1SS55 — A. L. S.]

W^{MS}.BURGH April 21, 1777.

SIR—Your Despatches by Express arrived here last Saturday; in answer to which I can only refer you to my former Letters respecting the Expedition against Pluggy's Town and as that Business is, by order of Congress laid aside, You must on that ac-

---

[91] This was in reply to the following postscript to the letter mentioned in the foregoing note: "The County Lieutenant who is ordered to send 100 men to meet Cap. Lynn with the Powder, is at a loss to know how far to proceed, or where S^t. Louis, on the Mississippi is—there being one place of that name 160 miles above the mouth of Ohio & no settlement or Fort less than 400 miles below the Ohio—the nearest is at the River Arkansa."—ED.

[92] This letter, copied by Morgan, was forwarded to Col. David Shepherd for his perusal.—ED.

count incur no further Expence, indeed, as the Letter alluded to must have got to your Hands soon after the present Express set off I am in hopes it will give you full satisfaction with regard to all your Inquiries.

We are just informed by Congress that they for some time past, have had the critical situation at Fort Pitt, under their consideration and have formed a Resolution of sending one thousand Rifles for the use of the garrison, and for supplying such of the militia, as may be hereafter called upon to defend that Post.[98] I am Sir

Your mo. ob^t. Servt.

P. HENRY

To Col^o. John Nevill at Fort Pitt
On public Service P. Express

DEPREDATIONS ON THE FRONTIER

[Col. William Crawford to President of Congress. 14S121 — transcript by L. C. D.]

FORT PITT, 22nd April, 1777.

HONORABLE SIR—Having received orders to join his Excellency General Washington in the Jerseys with the battalion now under my command, which orders I would willingly have obeyed, had not a council of war held at this place (proceedings of which were transmitted to Congress by express) resolved

---

[98] See resolution of Congress April 9, 1777, in *Journals*, vii, p. 247.—ED.

that I should remain here until further orders.[94] I am sorry to find the accounts therein contained are likely to prove but too true, and from the late depredations and murders which were committed by the Indians at different places in this neighbourhood, makes it appear to me as if a general irruption was threatened. On the 6th & 7th instant, they killed and scalped one man at Raccoon Creek, about twenty five miles from this place; at Muchmore's plantation, about forty five miles down the Ohio, they killed and scalped one man, and burnt a woman and her four children; at Wheeling they killed and scalped one man, the body of whom was much mangled with tomahawks and other instruments suitable for their barbarity;[95]

---

[94] For a brief sketch of Col. William Crawford see *Dunmore's War*, p. 103, note 48. Crawford, at first appointed lieutenant-colonel of the 5th Virginia, next took command of the 7th regiment. He was sent to West Augusta in the autumn of 1776 to raise a new contingent, later known as the 13th (or West Augusta) regiment, enlisted on condition that if an Indian war should occur in the spring this command was to be retained in the West. The council of war to which Crawford refers was held at Fort Pitt, March 24, when it was determined that in view of the threatened dangers Crawford and his men should be retained on the frontier; see Butterfield, *Washington-Crawford Letters*, p. 65, note. This letter is also printed in that collection. In August, Crawford's regiment joined Washington near Philadelphia.—ED.

[95] For further particulars of these murders, see extract from *Maryland Journal, post*. Shadrach Muchmore died in 1775, when his will was proven in West Augusta district. His widow appears to have married again, probably to a man named Arnot. A son, Jonathan Muchmore, was captive among the Indians; see his affidavit in *Beaver County*, p. 151.

The man killed at Raccoon Creek was a late emigrant from New Jersey, named Ogden. The one slain near Wheeling was Roger McBride.

The Delawares had warned the settlements that a party of

PROTECTING THE FRONTIERS

at Dunkard's Creek, one of the west Branches of the Monongahela river, they killed and scalped one man and a woman and took three children;[96] and at each of the above places they burned houses, killed cattle, hogs &c.

I have taken all possible means for the protection of this country, as the nature of my circumstances would afford. I am at a great loss for arms; two thirds of the battalion have none. Had I been at this post when the accounts of the above cruelties came here, I would have transmitted them immediately to you; but being busily employed in putting the battalion to proper stations for the frontiers,[97] this together with my bad state of health prevented my getting here sooner than the 18th instant, and finding that no authentic accounts had been transmitted to Congress, think it my duty to inform you of the above facts, and that I only wait further directions, as I have received no marching orders dated since the council held at this place resolved that I should wait till further orders.

I am with the greatest respect y^r. honours most obe^t. and very humble serv^t.

W. CRAWFORD

Hon. J. Hancock, Pres^t. Congress

---

eighteen Mingo were out with murderous intent; but the warning was not in time. See Hildreth, *Pioneer History*, p. 123.—ED.

[96] This was probably the attack on the family of William Morgan, assigned to the year 1778. See Thwaites, *Withers's Chronicles of Border Warfare*, p. 240.—ED.

[97] The council of war of March 24 had determined that Crawford should send a hundred men to Kittanning, and station twenty-five each at Logstown, Holliday's Cove, and Cox's, upon the Ohio.—ED.

[Col. George Morgan to Col. David Shepherd. 1SS56—
A. L. S.]

FORT PITT May 3ᵈ. 1777

SIR—The within letter Colˡ Nevill forwarded to me supposing it was intended for me & directed to him by mistake. Mʳ. Macaster arrived yesterday & as you had sent him & I did not write to the Govʳ. at all by him, & he tells me he has no Letter directed for you I suppose this was designed for you. I therefore embrace this first opportunity of sending it to you.[98] I desire you will store the Bacon you have bought in a very safe place under your own particular Care till further Orders & shall be glad to sug[gest that] we may settle & that I may take your Receipt for the Quantity

I am Dʳ. Sir Your most obᵗ Servant

GEO: MORGAN

To Colˡ Shepherd.

[Col. Zackwell Morgan to Capt. William Harrod. 4NN54—
A. L. S.]

May 7 1777

DEAR SIR—As Captᵗ Lin is Got up with his Powder[99] and no call for the men Down the River you will Pleast to Continue your Company at Grave

---

[98] This refers to Gov. Patrick Henry's letter to Col. John Neville, dated April 21, *ante*. The letter of Morgan is written on the reverse of that sheet.—ED.

[99] Linn arrived at Wheeling May 2, 1777. He brought with him ten thousand pounds of gunpowder, according to an affidavit filed by Col. David Shepherd, 1SS13, as follows: "Ohio

Creek untill the Express Returns from the Govenor for your being there is Looked on as a Grate safe Gard to us at this time Pleast send scouts Down about fish Creek and if you Should make any Discovery of any of the Dam theeves cuming in Pleast send in word Imediately from your friend and
Hum^b Sar^t
Zack^{ll} Morgan

To Capt William Harrod, at Grave Creek

[Transcribed by Draper from the *Maryland Journal* of Tuesday, May 20th, 1777.]

Philadelphia, May 15.

By a gentleman lately arrived from the Ohio, we have the following intelligence. About the beginning of last month Mr. James O'Hara[1] was trading at the

---

County June the 8th 1789 Sir—Agreable to an order of Council 29th of Decem^r 1788 I have made Every Serch in my power and find Nothing worth Making Return of Except that in the Blank &c of Blank year a Certain Lieu^t William Lin and others from Orleans Delivered at the Mouth of Weelin within this County 10000 Weight or thereabout of gunpowder for the use of the State of Virginia the same was kept there some time and then ordred to the Station of fort pitt by a Continental officer Col^o Wm Crawford." The powder was issued both by David Shepherd and Zephaniah Blackford, commissary of stores, as is proven by receipts found in Draper MSS, 1SS 24-28.—Ed.

[1] James O'Hara was an Irishman who before 1773 entered the Indian trade near Fort Pitt. He enlisted in the 9th Virginia regiment, being employed as quartermaster. During the Whiskey Rebellion he was quartermaster-general of the army, and served in a similar capacity under Wayne (1794). O'Hara's business capacity aided in the building up of Pittsburgh, where in 1797 he established the first glass manufactory west of the Alleghenies. In 1804 he was director of the Pitts-

Shawanese towns on the Scioto where he was informed that there was a gang of young Indian fellows ready to go to war, consisting of fifteen Shawanese, two Wiandots, and one Mingo; Mr. O'Hara was also informed that they intended to waylay him on his return to Pittsburgh; upon which he happily changed his course, and arrived safe at the above place with his people and effects.[2] Two or three days after his arrival an express came to Fort Pitt, with an account that the widow Muchmore and her three children, were found almost burned to cinders, and her late husband killed and scalped near where the house stood, opposite the mouth of Yellow Creek on the Ohio. The same day another express arrived who brought an account of a man being found murdered near Wheeling; also one Ogden, a Jersey man, was found killed and scalped near the mouth of Raccoon Creek. All the above murders were perpetrated on or near the Ohio. Two days after the above expresses, another arrived from Dunkard Creek, near the mouth of Cheat River, with an account of three men being killed and scalped there, and three others missing. Lieut. Mason,[3] at the head of ten militia,

---

burgh branch of the Philadelphia bank; and died in 1819 leaving a large estate, mainly in landed property, part of which is still held by his heirs. His daughter married William Croghan Jr., nephew of George Rogers Clark.—ED.

[2] See Heckewelder's report of this incident in his *Narrative*, pp. 155, 156. The Wyandot attempted to waylay O'Hara near the Delaware towns, but by the interposition of the Christian Indians, and the Moravian missionary, he escaped.—ED.

[3] Samuel Mason (he spells the name Meason) commanded a company at Fort Henry during its first siege (Sept. 1, 1777), and was severely wounded in a sally against ambushed Indians. In 1778 he commanded the same fort. He appears to

gallantly followed the murderers of the Muchmore family, and after a pursuit of twenty-five miles, came up with the savages, who fought for some time and then gave way. Mr. Mason and his little party followed them some miles further, but having no provisions, and being in danger of falling into an ambuscade, returned to the field of battle, where they found one dead Indian, whom they scalped, some horses and other booty which the savages had taken from some white people. Mr. Mason thinks that they either killed or desperately wounded more of the Indians, as much blood was seen on the ground. This brave young man was born near Winchester in Virginia, and will no doubt meet a reward adequate to his merit. Another party followed the gang who committed the murder near Cheat, and it is hoped can give a good account of them. It was the general opinion, that the Indians had divided themselves into three parties, and committed the murders much about the same time.

The inhabitants of the above mentioned places were in the utmost consternation; some flying one way and some another, and a few set about building forts;

---

have lived first on Buffalo Creek, afterwards on Wheeling, a mile or so above the town, where he kept an ordinary. At the close of the Revolution he removed southward, settling about 1790 at Red Banks, now Henderson, Tenn., and later on the Mississippi. Here he became leader of a band of highway robbers, and committed many crimes between 1795 and 1803. At one time he was captured by the Spanish authorities, but succeeded in escaping. In the latter year, a reward of $500 was offered by the governor of Mississippi for his head. Thereupon he was shot and beheaded by two of his own gang of desperados. These men were afterwards apprehended and hung.—ED.

but it is hoped that the arrival of Brigadier General
Hand will dissipate all their fears, and add life and
vigour to their undertakings.[4] As Brigadier Hand
is universally loved on the Ohio,[5] the people will no
doubt flock to his standard and cheerfully go forth
to chastise the savage foe.

---

[4] Upon the receipt of accounts of the hostile intent of the Western Indians and of the exposed condition of the frontiers, Congress resolved that an experienced officer should be sent to Pittsburgh to take command, embody the militia, and plan the defense. On April 9, 1777, the board of war reported in favor of Edward Hand, recently appointed brigadier-general. Congress voted a thousand rifles and five tons of lead to be sent to Fort Pitt. Hand was (April 10) ordered to this garrison, and the next day given discretionary power, being voted $4000 for works or supplies, while three tons of gunpowder were arranged for.—*Journals of Congress*, new ed., vii, pp. 247, 252, 256, 270. Hand arrived at Fort Pitt, June 1.—ED.

[5] Edward Hand, M. D., was born in Clyduff, County Leinster, Ireland, Dec. 31, 1744. Educated as a physician, he was in 1767 appointed surgeon's mate of the 18th Royal Irish infantry, and sailing from Cork reached America in July of the same year. The regiment was at once ordered to Fort Pitt, where Hand made himself popular with all classes. In 1772 he purchased an ensign's commission; but when his regiment was ordered East in 1774, he resigned and received his discharge, settling in Lancaster, Pa., where in 1775 he married Catharine Ewing. On the outbreak of the Revolution he at once enlisted, being appointed lieutenant-colonel of the 1st battalion of Pennsylvania riflemen. Joining Washington before Boston, he was with the continental army at Long Island, and in the Jersey campaign. In April, 1777, he was appointed brigadier-general and sent to the West as commander-in-chief. Recalled at his own request early in 1778, he served throughout the war, being adjutant-general at the siege of Yorktown. After peace was declared, he retired to his estate near Lancaster and practiced medicine. He was a member of the old Congress in 1784-85 and of the Pennsylvania constitutional convention of 1790, and served several terms in the state legislature. In 1798 he was chosen one of the major-generals of the army in anticipation of a war with France. General Hand was of a genial disposition, popular with his superiors

[Col. Zackwell Morgan to Capt. William Harrod. 4NN54—
A. L. S.]

May 27 1777

DEAR CAP^t.—I was favoured with your Letter of the 22 of this instant by Mr M'Laughlin am glad you have Provaled on your men to Continue Longer as we are Like to have trubelsum times I shall set out to morrow for Fort Pitt to meet the General when I shall be Better abel to Informe you of what is to be dun and in what Manner we are to act I expect there will be several Companies to be rased and hope you will Still Continue I Pay but Littel Regard to Cornplantes untill Both Stor[i]es is heard I have not any nues worth menti[o]ning At this time to you.

I am Sir your Rail frind and Hum^b. Sar^t

ZACK^{ll}. MORGAN

To Capt William Harrod

---

and subordinates in the army; his work on the frontier was hampered by causes beyond his control. He died at his home, "Rockford," Sept. 3, 1802.—ED.

RETURN OF MILITARY STORES AT FORT PITT
[1U52.—D. S.]

Date	Lbs of good Powder	Lbs of bad Powder	Lbs of Lead	Flints	Lbs of Bar Iron	Lb? of Steel very bad	Axes	Spades & Shovels	Pick Axes	Carpenter's Tools	Smith's Tools part of	Whip Saws	Cross Cut Saws	Broad Axes	Files for Saws	Horn Lanthorns for Magazine	Scales & Weights	Steel Yards	Writing paper	Quills	Ink powder	Coopers Tools	Spare Locks
1777.																							
April 12th Remained &ret. of this date Issued since 12th Apl	3534½ 62¾	1825	4603 161	10,042 359	1180 494½	176¾ 20½					1												
May 1st Remains	3472¾	1825	4442	9 683	685½	156¾					1												

FORT PITT May 1st. 1777
JOSEPH SKELTON Comy. Stores.

To Col. Geo: Morgan.   Examined   GEO. MORGAN

FORT PITT May 1st, 1777
Return of Military Stores remaining in the Magazine.

INDEX

Albany (N. Y.), 160.
Albemarle County (Va.), 25, 153.
Alexander, Capt. —, 149.
Alexander, Joseph, 225.
Alexandria (Va.), 138-140, 142.
Algonquian stock, 199.
Allanawissica, Shawnee chief, 26, 103, 126.
Allen, Ethan, 129.
Almon, J., *Remembrancer*, 55, 92.
Alvord, C. W., discovers documents, 225; *Cahokia Records*, 143, 227.
Amherst, Gen. Jeffrey, 135.
Amwell Township (Pa.), 207.
Anderson, Capt. John, 194, 195.
Anderson, William, 231.
Anderson County (Ky.), 227.
Andrews, James, 149.
"Angelica," British vessel, 150.
Anipassicowa, Shawnee, 115.
Arbuckle, Capt. Matthew, 194, 196, 240; commandant, 175, 176, 178, 182, 193, 194, 197, 198, 204, 241; expedition, 182; letters, 185-187, 211, 212; sketch, 158.
Arbuckle, Mrs. Matthew, 212.
Arkansas Post. See Fort Arkansas.
Armstrong, Capt. —, 168, 170.
Armstrong, Col. John, 200.
Armstrong, Paul, 225.
Arnold, Benedict, expedition, 137.
Arnot, —, 250.
Aughunta, Wyandot, 52.

Augusta Academy, 10.
Augusta County (Va.), 140, 158, 175, 183, 221, 235.
Austergass, James, 228.
Avon (N. Y.), 161.
Avone. See Canawaugus.

Baby, Duperon, 44, 54, 62.
Baby, James, 44.
Baltimore County (Md.), 218.
Battles: Big Island, 170. Blue Licks, 154, 175. Chemung, 161. Concord, 10-15. Fallen Timbers, 75. Germantown, 139. Lake Erie, 151. Lake George, 159. Lexington, 10-15. Oriskany, 152, 159-161. Point Pleasant, 240. Yorktown, 256.
Bausman, Joseph H., *History of Beaver County, Pa.*, 158, 217, 220, 238, 247, 250.
Bavard, James, 63.
Bawbee, —, educated in Virginia, 126.
Bayard, Col. Stephen, 201.
Baynton, Wharton & Co., 31.
Beard, Lieut. —, 192.
Beaver, Delaware chief, 46.
Bedford County (Pa.), 74, 200.
Bedford County (Va.), 7, 173, 174.
Belmont, Virginia estate, 153.
Belvidere, Virginia estate, 153.
Berkeley County (Va.), 196, 230.
Bethlehem (Pa.), 45, 202, 203.

INDEX

Big Appletree, Mingo chief, 48.
Big Bone Lick (Ky.), 189.
Big Knife, Indian appellation for whites, 15, 77.
Big Lick (Va.), 169.
Blackfish, Shawnee chief, 242.
Blackford, Zephaniah, 224, 254.
Blacksburg (Va.), 11.
Blacksnake, Seneca chief, 159-167; portrait, 160.
Black Wolf, Mingo chief, 102.
Blair, Archibald, 238, 239.
Blair, Rev. James, 238.
Bland, Col. Richard, 23, 35, 215.
Bluejacket, Shawnee chief, 41, 44.
Blue Licks, lower, 206. See also Battles.
Boiling Springs (Ky.), 227.
Bolton, David, 127, 132, 149.
Bondy, Joseph Douaire de, 148.
Boone, Daniel, 16, 177, 186, 187; cuts road, 2, 9; captured, 4, 144.
Boone, Jemima, 187, 189, 205.
Boonesborough (Ky.), 2, 102, 187, 205, 227, 242.
Botetourt County (Va.), 8, 17, 155-157, 168, 169, 174, 175, 177, 183, 184, 197.
Bowman, George, 170.
Bowman, Capt. John, 154, 170.
Bowyer, Henry, 17.
Boyd, John, 225.
Braddock, Gen. Edward, expedition, 22, 36, 136, 207; battlefield, 191.
Bradstreet, Col. John, 133, 134, 150, 151.
Brady, Samuel, 201, 202, 230.
Brady's Bend, 160.
Braxton, Carter, 23, 146.
Brenton (Brinton), James, 231.
Bridgeport (O.), 217.
Brinton. See Brenton.
Brodhead, Daniel, 46, 196, 201, 234, 235.
Brothertown Indians, 62.
Brown, Rev. John, 10-12.

Brown, Capt. Samuel, 179, 181, 182.
Brown, Col. Thomas, 233.
Brownsville (Pa.), 233.
Bryant's Station (Ky.), 154.
Buffalo Historical Society, 161.
Bullitt County (Ky.), 180.
Burgoyne, Gen. John, 96, 153.
Burr, Aaron, 32.
Butler, Col. John, 152, 172.
Butler, Richard, 55, 63, 64, 158; sketch, 151.
Butler, William, 151.
Butterfield, C. W., *Washington-Crawford Letters*, 250.
Byrnside, Capt. —, 240.

Cabell, William, 23.
Caldwell, James, 224.
Caldwell, Col. John, 67, 69, 135.
Caldwell, Mary, 246.
Caldwell, Col. William, 44.
Callaway, Elizabeth, 187, 189, 205.
Callaway, Frances, 187, 189, 205.
Callaway, Col. James, 173.
Callaway, Col. Richard, 186.
Callaway, William, 173.
Cameron, Allen, 138.
Campbell, Col. Arthur, 102.
Campbell, Capt. Donald, 201.
Campbell, Col. John, 230-233.
Campbell, Robert, 230, 231, 237, 245.
Campeau, Jacques, 148.
Campeau, Jean B., 148.
Campeau family, 148.
Camp Union (Fort Charles, Levels, Savannah), 178, 181, 184, 192, 197, 198, 204, 209.
Canajoharie (N. Y.), raid, 159-161.
Canawaugus (Avone), Indian village, 160-162, 167.
Canon, Col. John, 221-223, 233.
Canonsburg (Pa.), 221.

INDEX

Captain Jacobs, Delaware chief, 200.
Captain Pipe, Delaware chief, 80, 88, 126, 127.
Carleton, Gen. Guy, 23, 24, 127–135, 141; sketch, 96, 97.
Carlisle (Pa.), 191, 200.
Carnahan, James, 200.
Carnahan, Col. John, 200.
Carrington, Paul, 23, 146.
Castle Hill (Va.), 25.
Catfish, Delaware chief, 61.
Cattaraugus County (N. Y.), 159.
Caughnawaga (N. Y.), 171, 172.
Caughnawaga (Que.), 65.
Caughnawaga (Cochawawagas) Indians, 81, 82, 199, 219.
Céloron, Pierre Joseph, 26, 158.
Champaign County (O.), 240.
Chapoton, Jean Baptiste, 148.
Charleston (W. Va.), 184.
Chau Chau Chau sadea. See Flying Crow.
Chautauqua portage, 158.
Chenussaw, Shawnee hostage, 34, 39, 42, 57–60.
Cherokee Indians, sell lands, 1–4, 53; hostile, 15, 156, 170, 173, 175, 176, 186, 187; robberies, 15, 104; towns, 179.
Cherry Valley (N. Y.), raid, 159, 160.
Chew, Colby, 246.
Chew, Maj. James, 246.
Chew, Thomas, 246.
Chillicothe (O.), 57.
Chiningué. See Logstown.
Chippewa (Saulteur) Indians, 217; at Fort Pitt, 201; neutral, 70, 71; hostile, 190, 199; captive, 203; sketch, 131.
Chiswell lead mines, 155, 173.
Christian, Col. William, 16; letters to, 7, 8, 17; militia colonel, 8, 21; sketch, 5.
Cincinnati (O.), 202, 231.

Circleville (O.), 57.
Clark, George Rogers, expeditions, 15, 130, 136, 141, 144, 145, 149, 154, 179, 227, 228, 232, 235; delegate, 206; nephew, 254; diary, 227.
Clark's Grant (Ind.), 232.
Claus, Capt. Daniel, 131.
Cleveland (O.), 68.
Clover Lick (Va.), 205.
Cold Spring (N. Y.), 159.
Connolly, Maj. John, 18–20, 40, 43, 152; letter, 71–73; letter to, 16; treats with Indians, 35–38, 68; buys land, 231; plot, 136–142; Narrative, 19, 139.
Continental Congress, Journals of, 145, 217, 247, 249, 256.
Conococheague (Pa.), 228.
Conwell, Yates, 224.
Cook, John, letter, 205, 206.
Cooper, James, 186, 189.
Corn, Ebenezer, 227.
Cornplanter (John O'Bail), Seneca chief, 39, 160–165; portrait, 162.
Cornstalk, Shawnee chief, 26; letter for, 7; at Fort Blair, 14, 15, 103, 104; message to, 70, 74; at Fort Pitt, 36, 41, 71, 76; speeches, 42, 74, 75, 92, 98, 100–105, 111, 113–116; with Wilson, 202; treats with English, 187; sketch, 7.
Coronyatta, Wyandot, 52.
Coshocton (Goshachgunk), 45, 46, 124, 196.
Cox, Maj. Gabriel, 233.
Cox's Station, 251.
Coyashota. See Guyashusta.
Cracroft, Capt. Charles, 235.
Crawford, Col. William, surveys, 5, 153; in Dunmore's War, 56; continental officer, 216, 234, 253; letter, 249–251; Sandusky expedition, 91, 234; death, 46, 80; sketch, 250.

Creek Indians, 45.
Creeks: Beaver, 86. Big Beaver, 43. Big Sandy, 163. Buffalo, 162, 255. Catfish, 230. Chartier, 22. Corcosan (Caucussing), 48. Cross (W. Va.), 217, 218. Dunkard, 212, 251, 254. Elk (W. Va.), 184. Fish (W. Va.), 207, 208, 212, 213; garrison, 221; scouting, 253; raid, 217. Fishing (W. Va.), 207, 208, 212, 220. French (Pa.), 158, 162, 163. Grave (W. Va.), 228, 234—see also Fort Grave Creek. Hammond (Ky.), 227. Indian (Va.), 178, 181. Killbuck (O.), 48. Loramie (O.), 15, 144. Meadow (Va.), 182. Middle Island (W. Va.), 212, 213. Muddy (Va.), 178, 181, 182, 198—see also Fort Muddy. Paint (Ky.), 14. Paint (Va.), 183. Pine (Pa.), 27. Raccoon (Va.), 231, 250, 254. Robinson (Pa.), 231. Sandy (W. Va.), 6, 13, 14. Short (W. Va.), 234. Ten Mile (W. Va.), 231. Walhonding—see White Woman's. Walkers (Va.), 179. Wheeling (W. Va.), 196, 232, 235, 242, 255—see also Fort Henry, Wheeling. White Woman's (O.), 48. Wolf (Va.), 177. Yellow (O.), 254.
Cresap, Capt. Michael, 232, 233.
Crèvecœur, Hector St. John de, map, *frontispiece*, 48, 63.
Crockett, Capt. Walter, 168, 169.
Croghan, George, 15, 26, 28, 171.
Croghan, William, 254.
Crooke, Capt. Thomas, 235.
Crumrine, Boyd, *Washington County, Pa.*, 223, 230.
Cumberland (Pa.), 151.
Cumberland County (Pa.), 144, 171, 191, 200.
Cumberland Gap (Ky.), 2.

Cumberland settlement (Tenn.), 3.
Custaloga, Delaware chief, 80.
Cuttena (Cuttemwha), Shawnee hostage, 39, 42, 43, 57-59.
Cuyahoga (Kacayuga), 62. See also Cuyahoga River.

Dalzell, Capt. James, 218.
Dandridge, Dorothea, 7.
Danville (Ky.), 154.
Darlington, W. P., *Gist's Journals*, 48.
Dartmouth, Lord, letter to, 65.
Davidson, George, 182.
Davis, James, 225.
Dean, Capt. —, 192.
De Jean, Philip, 148, 149.
Delaware (O.), 56.
Delaware Indians, 19, 28, 29, 39, 45, 52, 54, 62, 66, 116, 129, 130, 158, 171, 174; lands, 40, 62, 86, 87; towns, 37, 43, 45, 46, 125, 127, 199, 200, 244; clans, 88; language, 64; missions, 45, 202—see also Moravians; hostile, 61, 124; pacific, 156, 188; warn settlements, 44, 245, 250; consulted, 237; treat with Connolly, 35, 37; at treaty of 1775, 76, 80, 82, 86, 92, 94, 108, 113, 114, 120-122; speech, 46, 47; speech to, 46, 47, 98; message to, 80, 152, 202; at treaty of 1776, 217, 219; ask protection, 203, 244.
De Peyster, Arent Schuyler, 128, 130.
Desnoyers, Pierre, 131.
Desnoyers family, 131.
Detroit, 44, 68, 74, 101, 128, 130, 137, 141, 150, 199, 202, 203, 218; founded, 131; in Pontiac's War, 134, 201, 203; Indians at, 36, 155, 187; commandant, 136, 158; garrison, 147, 148, 218;

INDEX

militia, 132, 148, 149; expedition against, 145, 147, 172, 189; merchants, 149, 150; captive at, 231; taken by English, 134; Americans, 95. See also Fort Detroit.
Devil's Hole Massacre, 159, 160.
Dickenson College (Pa.), 191.
Digges, Dudley, 23, 146.
Dinwiddie, Gov. Robert, 4, 66.
Dobie, —, 134.
Doctor, Mohawk Indian, 67.
Dodge, John, 55, 92, 148.
Donelson, Col. John, 3.
Donelson, Rachel, 3.
Donnally, Andrew, 183, 184; letters, 209, 210.
Dorchester, Lord. See Carleton.
Dragging Canoe, Cherokee Indian, 2.
Draper, Lyman C., 2, 25; visits Blacksnake, 159; *Life of Boone*, 187.
Draper's Meadows (Va.), 11.
Drouillard, George, 128.
Drouillard, Pierre, 128.
Duncan, David, 61.
Dunmore, Earl of, governor of Virginia, 1, 17, 19–21, 34, 36–40, 56, 59, 74, 98, 99, 106, 116, 118, 119, 121; disputes with Virginia, 11, 41, 57; orders forts evacuated, 13; messages to Indians, 7, 71–74; Connolly with, 137–140, 142; War of 1774, 15, 28, 39–41, 49, 61, 81, 93, 124, 143, 147, 177, 179, 182, 204; sketch, 1.
"Dunmore," British vessel, 149.

East Florida, governor, 138.
Economy (Pa.), 27.
Elliot, Matthew, 74.
Enoch, Capt. Enoch, 207.
Enoch, Henry, 207, 235.
Eppes, Francis, 22.
Erie (Pa.), 151, 158, 162.

Evans, Capt. Jack, 234.
Evans, Maj. John, 234.
Ewing, Catharine, 256.

Falls of Ohio, 46, 226, 227, 231, 232. See also Louisville.
Fauquier County (Va.), 154.
Fayette County (Ky.), 154.
Fayette County (Pa.), 207, 230, 232, 234.
Ferguson (Farquharson), —, 134.
Field, Ezekiel, 51, 98.
Filson Club, *Publications*, 2.
Fincastle County (Va.), 5, 8, 16, 21, 23, 167–169, 172, 173.
Finley, Dr. Samuel, 12.
Fleming, Mrs. Anne, 17.
Fleming, Col. William, county lieutenant, 184, 197, 200; letters, 168, 169, 174–176, 179, 180, 184, 192, 193, 209, 210; letters to, 12–17, 156, 157, 167–169, 177, 178, 181–183, 185–187, 193, 196–199, 204, 205, 209, 214–216, 239–241; sketch, 12.
Flood, Michael, 225.
Floyd, Capt. John, 5, 6, 153, 154.
Flying Crow (Chau chau chau sadea), Seneca chief, 90, 91, 99, 107, 108.
Fonda (N. Y.), 171.
Forbes. Gen. John, expedition (1758), 145, 171, 191, 230.
Force, Peter, *American Archives*, 8, 13, 18, 19, 21, 65, 67, 90, 95, 126, 136, 137, 139, 143–145, 151, 158, 170, 171, 186, 216.
Foreman, Capt. William, 91, 145.
Forts: Arbuckle's, 181. Arkansas, 226. Armstrong, 201. Beech Bottom, 243, 244. Blair, location, 7; commandant, 7, 12, 103, 106, 111, 112; provisioned, 5, 6; garrison, 4, 7; evacuated, 13–17; burned, 93, 111, 117, 185—see also Fort Randolph, Point

Forts—Continued.
Pleasant. Charles—see Camp Union. Chartres (Ill.), 137, 141. Clark, 141. Crown Point, 54. Culbertson's, 180. Detroit, 54, 55, 62, 97, 126, 137, 150, 151—see also Detroit. Dillow, 231. Donnally, 182, 184, 192, 193. Dunmore, 6, 13, 142—see also Fort Pitt. Duquesne, 27, 163. Enoch, 207. Erie, 150, 151. Fincastle, 13, 138, 142—see also Fort Henry, Wheeling. Franklin, 163. Freelands, 160. Frontenac, 134. Gage, 137, 141. Grave Creek, 195, 207, 208, 210, 213, 214, 220-225, 235, 242-245, 252, 253. Henry, 145, 196, 207, 234, 254—see also Wheeling. Laurens, 41. Le Bœuf, 158. Machault, 162. McIntosh, 231. Muddy Creek, 197, 198. Niagara, 24, 131, 135, 162; commandant, 152; captured, 151, 159; Indians at, 65, 67-70, 171, 172; reinforced, 218; raids from, 158, 245. Oswegatchie, 131, 132. Oswego, 134. Ouiatanon, 158. Pitt, 19, 20, 64, 135, 136, 139, 144, 151, 158, 159, 226, 241, 254; garrison disbanded, 20, 66; American garrison, 21, 112, 125, 145, 230, 231; reinforced, 166, 167, 256; contractor, 61; commissary, 231, 245; trade at, 151, 253; endangered, 188, 196, 200, 219, 249; Indian agent, 152, 158; private claims, 143; treaty called for, 50, 53, 55, 56, 59, 66-68, 78, 79; Wood at, 35, 42, 43, 65; stores, 253, 258; council of war, 249-151; conference, 159-167, 171, 200, 201; Indian prisoners, 49; news from, 189, 205, 206, 210—see also Pittsburgh, and Treaties. Presqu'Isle, 151, 158, 162. Prickett, 235. Randolph, attacked, 91, 197; endangered, 219; reinforced, 204, 205, 209, 214, 230, 231, 239-241; news from, 185, 211, 212, 241; depredations near, 26, 210, 213, 217; sketch, 185—see also Point Pleasant. Sandusky, 218. Schuyler, 159. Shepherd, 145. Statler, 235. Stephenson, 218. Ticonderoga, 54, 215. Vanbibber, 192. Van Metre, 284. Venango, 163. Wells, 218.
Frankfort (Ky.), 154.
Franklin, Benjamin, 28.
Franklin (Pa.), 162, 163.
Franklin Township (Pa.), 207.
Frazer, John, 162.
Frederick (Md.), 186, 139, 235.
Frederick County (Va.), 20, 22, 43, 170.

Gaddis, Col. Thomas, 234.
Gage, Gen. Thomas, 135-137, 139, 140.
"Gage," British vessel, 127, 149.
Galloway, John, 194, 198.
Gambel, Thomas, 135, 136.
Gates, Gen. Horatio, 143.
Geneva (N. Y.), 160.
George III (England), proclamation of 1763, 4, 5.
Georgetown (Md.), 186.
Gibson, Capt. George, 73, 144, 145, 223, 226, 233; sketch, 144.
Gibson, Col. John, 26, 126, 144, 152; at Williamsburgh, 155, 156; letters to, 71-73, 137; trading post, 27, 65.
Gilmore, —, 214.
Girty, Simon, interpreter, 28, 43, 67; escapes to British, 74; kills Rogers, 232; sketch, 28.
Gist, Christopher, 15.
Givens, Anne, 188.
Givens, Capt. George, 192, 196, 197, 198, 209.
Givens family, 198.

INDEX

Gladwin, Maj. Henry, 208.
Glen, Joseph, 225.
Gnadenhütten (O.), 45, 68, 208.
Goshen (O.), 38, 45.
Grant, Capt. Alexander, 132.
Granville County (N. C.), 2.
Great Lakes, shipping, 127, 132, 149, 150.
Green, Isaac, 210, 213.
Green Bay (Wis.), 199.
Greenbrier (Va.), 113, 197, 239; settlements, 100, 192, 193, 198; alarmed, 156, 177-181, 204.
Greenbrier County (Va.), 183.
Greenbrier levels. See Camp Union.
Greene County (Pa.), 235.
Greenville (O.), 202.
Gregory, Capt. Daniel, 183.
Grosse Pointe (Mich.), 132.
Guyashusta (Coyashota, Kiasola, Kyashota), Seneca Indian, 31, 126; speech, 108, 110, 111, 118-120, 122, 123; visits Niagara, 151, 152, 171, 172.
Guy Park (N. Y.), estate, 65.

Hagerstown (Md.), 136.
Haldimand, Sir Frederick, 96, 128, 136, 148.
Half King, Wyandot chief, 91, 92, 203.
Hamilton, Capt. Andrew, 193, 205, 206.
Hamilton, Henry, Detroit commandant, 147, 149; letter, 127-135; captured, 128, 130, 149; council with Indians, 202; sketch, 135; portrait, 128.
Hamilton, S. M., *Letters to Washington*, 19.
Hammond, Nathan, 226, 227.
Hampshire County (Va.), 207, 232.
Hancock, John, letter to, 249, 251.

Hand, Gen. Edward, 193, 200, 231, 256, 257.
Hands Meadows, 169.
Hanley, Capt. —, 192.
Hannastown (Pa.), 18.
Hanover County (Va.), 7.
Hardman, Shawnee chief, 57-61, 202.
Hargess, Capt. —, 207.
Harkness, John, 225.
Harmar, Josiah, 41.
Harper's Ferry (Md.), 235.
Harris, James, 225.
Harris, Mary, 43.
Harris, Samuel, 224.
Harris, Stephen, 225.
Harrison, Col. Benjamin, 23, 209.
Harrod, Capt. James, 43.
Harrod, Capt. William, commission, 145, 146; returns from Kentucky, 198; letters to, 206, 207, 218-221, 245, 246, 252, 253, 257; station, 235; petitions to, 224, 225; orders, 221-223, 226-230.
Harrodsburgh (Ky.), 43, 170, 206, 227, 228, 242.
Harvie, John, 153, 191.
Hastings, Marquis of. See Rawdon.
Hay, Jehu, 130, 131, 133, 149.
Hazard, Samuel, *Register of Pennsylvania*, 191, 246.
Heart, Capt. Jonathan, 163.
Heckewelder, John, *Narrative*, 87, 95, 126, 202; sketch, 202.
Henderson, James, 183.
Henderson, John, 183.
Henderson, Col. Richard, 1-4, 16.
Henderson (Tenn.), 255.
Hendrick, Mohawk chief, 131.
Henry, Patrick, 7, 11, 21, 23; governor of Virginia, 146, 210; letters, 223, 232, 233, 236, 238, 239, 244, 245, 247-249, 252; orders, 226; letters to, 212-214, 242, 243; portrait, 232.

INDEX

Herbert, Capt. —, 183.
Heron, James, 55.
Hickman, Molly, 29.
Hildreth, Samuel P., *Pioneer History*, 32, 217, 246, 247, 251.
Hite, Joist, 170.
Hite family, 196.
Holliday's Cove, 251.
Hord, Capt. John, 235.
Howard, Capt. John, 134.
Howe, Gen. William, 189, 215.
Howell, Abner, 229.
Huggins, William, 179, 181.
Huron Indians. See Wyandot.

Illinois country, 31, 143, 149; garrison, 137, 141.
Illinois County (Va.), 228.
Illinois Historical Collections, 227.
Indiana Company, 31.
Ingles, Col. William, 14, 17.
Iroquois Indians, 36; sell lands, 53, 61, 65; disposition, 70, 245; headship, 123; missions, 45, 131; agent, 152; language, 131; neutrality, 162-167, 172; at treaty of 1775, 80, 82, 85, 87, 89-92, 99, 107, 108, 113-119, 121, 122; of 1776, 216; speech to, 109, 121, 124. See also Mingo and Seneca.
Islands: Big, 175. Montour's (Neville's), 23, 28, 153.

Jackson, Andrew, 3.
Jacobs, John J., *Michael Cresap*, 25.
January, Mrs. Ezekiel, 176.
Jefferson, Thomas, 23, 143, 153, 215.
Jefferson College, 221.
Jesuit missionaries, 141, 147.
Jogues, Isaac, Jesuit missionary, 171, 172.
Johnson, Guy, 65, 67, 246.
Johnson, Sir John, 152.
Johnson, Sir William, 65, 74, 80, 91, 99, 124, 131, 152, 159, 171.
Jonnston, J. Stoddard, *First Explorations of Kentucky*, 2.
Johnston, William, 182.
Jones, Rev. David, *Visits*, 57.
Jones, Gabriel, 153.
Jones, John Gabriel, 206.
Jones, Joseph, 146.
Jones, Morgan, 224.

Kalalamint, Delaware chief, 88.
Kanawha County (W. Va.), 184.
Karr, Matthew, 224.
Kataawa, Shawnee, 103.
Kaskaskia (Ill.), 137, 141, 143, 145, 154, 227, 229; sketch, 227, 228.
Kelley, Thady, 230, 231, 233.
Kelly's settlement, 241.
Kenightie, Iroquois, 126.
Kenton, Simon, 48, 128.
Kents, —, 169.
Kentucky, 128, 213; lands purchased, 1-4; explored, 2, 117, 246; road to, 2, 8; early settlers, 2, 7, 9, 61, 111, 112, 226; surveys, 4, 5; boundary, 6; removal to, 10, 16; raids, 9, 15, 16, 56, 104, 105, 175, 176, 179, 186, 187, 199, 206, 242; forts, 53; alarm, 153, 154; abandoned, 198, 205, 206; militia, 170; legislature, 2, 232.
Kentucky County (Va.), 8, 154.
Kerr, Matthew, 225.
Kiasola. See Guyashusta.
Kickapoo Indians, 3, 158.
Kightor, Iroquois, 126.
Killbuck, Delaware chief, 38, 46, 124; sketch, 38.
King George County (Va.), 146.
Kiscapoo (Kiskapookee, Kispapo), town, 68, 201.
Kishanosity. See Hardman.
Kisquaquawha, Shawnee chief, 102, 103.

INDEX

Kittanning, 200, 201, 245, 251.
Knox, George, 225.
Knox, Thomas, 225.

Labadie, Angeline, 128.
La Demoiselle, Miami chief, 15.
Lakes: Erie, 36, 53, 86, 150, 162. Ontario, 149. Superior, 131. See also Great Lakes.
Langlade, Charles, 15, 150.
Lancaster (Pa.), 171, 191, 256.
Lancaster County (Pa.), 144.
Lancaster County (Va.), 12.
La Presentation. See Fort Oswegatchie.
La Richardie, Père de, 147.
Lead mines, Chiswell, 155, 173.
Lee, Gen. Charles, 145.
Lee, Francis Lightfoot, 23.
Lee, Hancock, 153, 154.
Lee, Richard Henry, 23.
Lee, Robert E., 10.
Lee, Thomas Ludwell, 146.
Lee, Willis, 153, 154.
Lee's Station (Ky.), 175, 188.
Leestown (Ky.), laid out, 154.
Lernoult, Capt. Richard B., 128, 130, 147.
Lewis, Andrew, 39; in Dunmore's War, 182, 204; Indian commissioner, 20, 30, 34, 42, 81, 82, 90, 100, 105, 112, 127; speech, 75, 76, 102.
Lewis, Mrs. Andrew, 183.
Lewis, Thomas, 21, 24.
Lewis and Clark expedition, 128.
Lewisburg (Va.), 183, 184.
Lexington (Ky.), 154, 210, 227.
Lexington (Va.), 10.
Liberty Hall. See Augusta Academy.
Limestone (Ky.), 206.
Lincoln, Mrs. Abraham, 154.
Lincoln County (Ky.), 170.
Lindsay, Joseph, 227.
Linn, Capt. William, expedition, 226–229, 248; arrives with powder, 252, 253; sketch, 144, 145.
Little Carpenter, Cherokee Indian, 2.
Livingston County (N. Y.), 161.
Lochry, Col. Archibald, 200, 235.
Lockhart, Capt. —, 168, 170.
Lockhart, Jacob, 182.
Lockhart, Patrick, 155, 156.
Logan, Indian chief, 48, 49.
Logan County (O.), 203.
Logstown (Pa.), 26, 65, 251.
Lord, Capt. Hugh, 137, 141.
Lorimier (Laramie, Lorimie), Peter, 144.
Loudoun County (Va.), 234.
Louisa County (Va.), 12.
Louisburg, siege, 184, 185.
Louisville (Ky.), 227, 232; settled, 145. See also Falls of Ohio.
Loup Indians. See Mahican.
Lynch, Charles, 174.

Macaster, —, 252.
McBeath, George, 150.
McBride, Roger, 250.
McClain, Daniel, 243.
McClain, John, 225.
McClain, Joseph, 225.
McClean, Charles, 224.
McCleary, Capt. William, 235.
McClelland's Station (Ky.), 56, 206.
McClenechan (McClanahan), Capt. William, 169, 170.
McClure, Andrew, 230, 231.
McClure, David, 224, 234.
McClure family, 231.
McConnell, Adam Baxter, 175, 176, 188.
McConnell, Andrew, 175, 188.
McConnell, William, 176, 189.
McConnell, William Barber, 175, 176, 188.

McCulloch, Maj. Samuel, 234.
McDonald, Maj. Angus, expedition, 145, 154, 231.
McDowell, Josiah, 182.
McFarland, Col. Daniel, 234.
McFarlane, Andrew, 245.
McIntosh, Gen. Lachlan, expedition, 231, 234.
McKee, Alexander, 74, 76, 152.
McKee, Capt. William, 197; letters, 204, 205, 214-216.
McLaughlin, —, 245, 257.
McMechen, James, 225.
McMechen, William, 224.
McNutt, Joseph, 210, 213.
McQuinney, —, 102.
McTavish, Simon, 150.
Mackay, Col. Aeneas, 200, 201.
Mackinac (Michilimakinac, Missilimalkinak), 130, 134, 135, 150, 151.
Madison, John, 25.
Madison, Capt. Thomas, 169, 240.
"Magdalen," British ship, 11.
Mahican (Loup, Mohegan) Indians, 62, 217; town, 48.
Mahican John, Delaware, 127-129.
Malden (Ont.), 75, 128.
Mangagata, Ottawa, 53.
Marin, Pierre Joseph, sieur, 151.
Marion County (W. Va.), 235.
Martin, Capt. Joseph, 154.
Maryland, 3, 144; *Journal,* 250, 253.
Mascoutin Indians, 3, 158.
Mason, George, 23, 146.
Mason, Samuel, 254, 255.
Mason County (Ky.), 240.
Massachusetts, Revolution in, 8, 11-13. See also Battles, Concord and Lexington.
Matthews, Archer, 198, 209, 210.
Matthews, Elijah, 242.
Matthews, George, 198.
Matthews, Sampson, 198.
May, John, 174, 206.

Meadville (Pa.), 162.
Ménard, Catharine, 148.
Mercer, James, 23.
Mercer County (Ky.), 231.
Mercer County (Pa.), 163, 231.
Miami (Tawixatwee, Twigtwee) Indians, 3, 15, 56, 58, 115, 158, 170, 171, 217.
Michigan Pioneer and Historical Collections, 127, 202.
Milkman, Shawnee chief, 58.
Milwaukee, Indian site, 199.
Mingo (Iroquois, Seneca) Indians, 29, 39, 52, 66; prisoners, 18, 19; towns, 37, 48, 56, 217; message to, 74, 78, 79; treat with Connolly, 35, 37; at treaty of 1775, 76, 80, 82, 85-87, 94; speech to, 97; pacific, 156, 188; hostile, 15, 49, 175, 176, 188, 199, 201, 210, 212, 219, 251, 254; sketch, 15. See also Iroquois, Pluggy and Seneca.
Minor, Capt. John, 235.
Mississippi, governor, 254.
Mitchell, Edward, 213, 214.
Moccasin Gap, 2.
Mohawk Indians, 81, 171, 172.
Mohegan Indians. See Mahican.
Monongahela City (Pa.), 228.
Monongalia County (Va.), 234, 235; erected, 223; officers, 230, 234, 235, 238; records, 235; surveyor, 246.
Montgomery, John, 191.
Montgomery, Gen. Richard, 132.
Montgomery County (N. Y.), 171.
Montgomery County (Va.), 8, 11.
Montour, Andrew, 28.
Montour, John, interpreter, 28, 158, 202.
Montreal, 24, 129, 132, 134, 137.
Montressor, Capt. John, 150.
Moor, John, 214.
Moorhead, —, captured, 246.
Moorhead, Capt. Samuel, 201, 246.

Moravian Missions, 38, 64, 202; towns, 44, 45. See also Delaware Indians.
Morgan, Gen. Daniel, 183.
Morgan, David, 230.
Morgan, Evan, 31.
Morgan, George, 258; at treaty, 31; investigates charges, 28; Indian agent, 152, 159, 176, 237, 238, 245; letters, 158, 216, 217, 252; letters to, 238, 247, 248; information, 188, 189, 246, 247; Indian name, 32; sketch, 31; portrait, 30.
Morgan, James, 230.
Morgan, Levi, 230.
Morgan, William, 251.
Morgan, Zackwell, county lieutenant, 235; letters, 229, 230, 245, 246, 252, 253, 257; sketch, 230.
Morgan settlement, 234.
Morgantown (Va.), 230.
Morganza (Pa.), estate, 32.
Morris, —, 198.
Morris, Lewis, commissioner, 23, 24, 28, 30, 33, 82, 90; speeches, 76, 77, 82-84, 89, 93, 94; letter to, 158; sketch, 33; portrait, 76.
Morrisania (N. Y.), estate, 33.
Mount Braddock (Pa.), 232.
Mount Clemens (Mich.), 203.
Mountains: Alleghanies, 252. Blue Ridge, 11. Flattop, 183. Laurel Hill, 18.
Muchmore, Jonathan, 250.
Muchmore, Shadrach, 250, 254.
Muchmore family, 254, 255.
Munsee Indians, 48, 88, 217.
Munseeka. See Nimwha.

Nashville (Tenn.), settled, 3.
Nelson, Thomas, 23.
Neville, Capt. John, 22, 112, 113, 125, 145, 237; letters to, 238, 247-249, 252; message from, 204,
205; conference with, 171, 172; sketch, 22.
New London (Ct.), 149.
New Madrid colony, 32.
New Martinsville (W. Va.), 208.
New Orleans, 177, 231-233, 235, 253; expedition, 144, 145, 226-229.
New Philadelphia (O.), 45.
New Schöenbrunn (O.), 45.
New York Indians, 62; news from, 215.
Newau, Shawnee hostage, 39, 42, 43, 57-59.
Newcomer (Netawatwes), Delaware chief, 38, 46.
Newcomerstown, 45, 63.
Newton, J. H., *Panhandle of West Virginia*, 217.
Niagara, portage, 132, 133, 147. See also Fort Niagara.
Nicholas, Indian, 48.
Nicholson, Joseph, 176, 202.
Nicholson, Thomas, 80.
Nicolas, Wyandot chief, 36, 218.
Nimwha (Munseeka), Shawnee chief, 41; speech, 121-123.
Ninnis, Ottawa, 53.
Norfolk (Va.), 139.
North Carolina, 1, 2, 176, 179.
Northwest Territory, 228.
North West Company, 150.

O'Ball, John. See Cornplanter.
O'Callaghan, E. B., *New York Colonial Documents*, 65, 246.
Occam, Samson, 62.
Oconastota, Cherokee Indian, 2.
O'Finn, Philip, 25.
Ogden, —, 250, 254.
Ogdensburgh (N. Y.), 132.
Oguhaenjes. See Caldwell, Col. John.
O'Hara, James, 242, 253.
Ohio Company, 154.

INDEX

Ohio County (Va.), 196, 253;
  erected, 223; officers, 232-234,
  236, 238, 239, 242, 244, 245.
Old Britain. See La Demoiselle.
Old Callotte, Wyandot, 128, 129.
Oldtown (Md.), 232.
Olumpias, Delaware chief, 28.
Onas, Indian appellation, 77.
Orange County (Va.), 246.
Oswego. See Fort Oswego.
"Ottawa," British vessel, 127.
Ottawa (Taway) Indians, 71, 217;
  towns, 68; treat with British,
  155; speech from, 53; at treaty
  of 1775, 80, 82, 85, 89, 92-94, 96,
  108, 110, 114, 116, 119; speech to,
  98; with Wyandot, 50-52; message, 56, 70, 101, 102; interpreter,
  203; hostile, 156, 190, 199, 210.
Owasso (Mich.), 201.
Owen, Capt. David, 207.
Oxen, George, 17.

Page, John, 23, 146; letters, 196,
  197, 247, 248.
Paintsville (Ky.), 14.
Parkison, Joseph, 228.
Parr, Stephen, 224.
Patterson, Robert, 210, 213.
Patton, Col. James, estate, 12.
Pauling, Henry, 174, 175.
Paully, Ensign —, 218.
Pendergrass, Garret, 43.
Pendleton, Edmund, 23, 167, 168.
Penn, William, 77.
Pennsylvania, governor, 13; officers, 18, 22; traders, 41; boundary, 18, 141; *Archives*, 19, 238,
  247; *Colonial Records*, 145;
  Gazette, 210; *Magazine of History*, 19; *Packet*, 136, 176, 188,
  189.
Pentecost, Col. Dorsey, 210, 217,
  230; letters, 195, 196, 207,
  212-214, 218-221, 226-229; county

lieutenant, 200; letter to, 216;
  sketch, 27.
Perry, David, 210, 213.
Perry, Oliver H., fleet, 151.
Pheasant, Delaware, 115.
Pick (Pict) Indians, branch of
  Shawnee, 14-16, 56, 58.
Pickaway County (O.), 63.
Pickawillany, captured, 15.
Picquet, Abbé, 181.
Pigman, Capt. Jesse, 235.
Piqua (O.), 15.
Pipe. See Captain Pipe.
Pittsburgh, 18, 20-23, 26-28, 32, 33,
  41, 45, 46, 74, 127, 129, 158, 175,
  189, 190, 198, 200, 202, 232, 254;
  powder brought to, 145; expedition against, 158; town laid out,
  231, 253. See also Fort Pitt.
Pittsylvania County (Va.), 3.
Pluggy, Mohawk, 56, 205, 206;
  son, 102, 106.
Pluggy's Town, 48, 56, 102, 201;
  expedition, 235-239, 247, 248.
Pointe de Montreal, 147.
Point Pleasant (W. Va.), garrison, 4, 158, 176, 193, 194; re-inforced, 197; Indians leave, 198;
  settlers, 177, 184; soldier killed,
  210; message, 205. See also
  Forts Blair and Randolph.
Pollock, Oliver, 226.
Pontiac's conspiracy, 27, 36, 38,
  41, 44, 80, 130, 131, 134, 147, 148,
  151, 162, 171, 201, 203, 218.
Post, Christian Frederick, 27, 29,
  202.
Potawatomi Indians, 199.
Potier, Pierre, 147.
Powell's Valley, 2, 153.
Prairie du Chien (Wis.), 150.
Prescott, Gen. Richard, 132, 135.
Preston, Col. William, 21, 24;
  surveyor, 4, 5; county lieutenant, 8, 14; home, 11; letters, 1-6, 8, 9, 156, 157, 172-174; letters

INDEX

to, 7, 10-12, 153, 154, 174-176; sketch, 1.
Prickett, Capt. Jacob, 235.
Prickett, Josiah, 235.
Princeton (N. J.), 82.
Princeton College, president, 200.
Proctor, Col. John, 200.
Purcell, Francis, 225.

Radcaff, Stephen, 206.
Ramsay, J. G. M., *Annals of Tennessee*, 179.
Randolph, Peyton, 23, 35-88; letter to, 66, 67; fort named for, 185; sketch, 66; portrait, 66.
Rawdon, Lord Francis, 135, 136.
Ray, William, 242.
Reaume, Hyacinthe, 148.
Reaume, Pierre, 148.
Reaume, Susanne, 44.
Recollect missionaries, 147, 148.
Red Banks (Miss.), 255.
Red Jacket, Seneca chief, 160, 161, 163; speech, 165, 166; portrait, 164.
Redstone (Pa.), 229, 233.
Rich, Capt. Jacob, 235.
Richmond (Va.), 66, 143, 153; convention at, 8, 13.
Rinhen, William, 150.
Rivers: Allegheny, 27, 38, 39, 65, 160, 162, 163, 200. Arkansas, 248. Beaver, 202. Bluestone, 183. Cheat, 229, 235, 254. Cherokee —see Tennessee. Clinch, 5, 6. Cumberland, 1, 3, 144. Cuyahoga, 46, 68, 86, 201, 202. Detroit, 62. Floyd's Fork, 180. Gauley, 182. Genessee, 161, 167. Great Cacapon, 207. Great Kanawha, 6, 7, 17, 61, 68, 93, 101, 103, 104, 106, 111, 158, 177, 182-184, 242—see also New. Great Miami—see Miami. Green (Ky.), 2. Greenbrier, 182. Hockhocking, 101, 105, 116, 206, 210, 213, 217. Holston, 153, 157, 168, 170, 173, 175. Hudson, 62, 215. Kaskaskia, 141. Kentucky, 1-4, 61, 63, 101, 102, 154, 175, 188, 227. James, 11, 156. Levisa, 14. Licking (Ky.), 186, 187, 323. Little Kanawha, 232, 242-244. Mahican—see Corcosan Creek. Maumee, 56, 75. Miami, 15, 60, 144, 234. Mississippi, 31, 82, 144, 145, 177, 226-228, 248. Mohawk, 152, 172. Monongahela, 167, 206, 212, 228, 233-235, 251. Muskingum, 46, 87, 101, 199. New, 169, 179, 180, 241—see also Great Kanawha. Niagara, 150. Ohio, 38, 50, 53, 59, 67, 74, 111, 117, 202, 206, 207, 253; lands, 1, 5; forks, 18, 171; affluents, 6, 11; Indians, 140; as boundary, 61, 87, 107, 112, 130, 156, 206, 219; guarded, 195, 246; scouting, 203, 211, 213, 231; troops, 215, 240; expedition, 144, 145, 226, 228. Potomac, 203, 232, 234. Roanoke, 169. St. Lawrence, 81. Salt (Ky.), 180. Sandusky, 36, 46, 80, 86, 143. Sandy—see Sandy Creek. Scioto, 57, 63, 81, 188, 217, 218, 254. Sorel, 134. Susquehanna, 46. Tennessee, 3, 6, 63, 99, 109. Tuscarawas, 45, 46, 199. Wabash, 3, 56, 80, 141, 158. Watauga, 1, 2, 173.
Rives, William C., 25.
Rives, Mrs. William C., *Tale of our Ancestors*, 25.
Roads, Wilderness, 2, 9.
Robertson, James, 3.
Robinson, Lieut. —, 205.
Robinson (Robertson), Capt. James, 168, 169, 192.
Robinson, Capt. John, 230, 231.
Rocheblave, Philippe de, 141.
Rockford, Pennsylvania estate, 257.
Rockingham County (Va.), 209.

INDEX

Rogers, Col. David, 231-233, 236, 239, 242.
Rogers, James, 70.
Roosevelt, Theodore, *Winning of the West*, 170.
Ross, Alexander, 143.
Rotunda. See War Post.
Row, Adam, 220, 225.
Row, Adam Jr., 225.
Russell, Col. William, 167, 168, 173, 175; commandant, 5-7, 12, 104; letters, 12-17; letter to, 7; sketch, 1.

St. Clair, Gen. Arthur, letters, 19, 200; expedition of 1791, 41, 144, 152, 230.
Ste. Genevieve (Mo.), 143.
St. Joseph (Mich.), 199.
St. Leger, Barry, expedition, 131.
St. Louis (Mo.), 226, 232, 248.
Saginaw (Mich.), 201.
Salem, Moravian town, 45.
Salt Licks, Indian town, 56.
Sanders, —, 102.
Sandusky, towns, 55; Indians, 91, 92; lower, 36; upper, 50, 91; expedition, 231; news from, 218; sketch, 218. See also Fort and River Sandusky.
Sandwich (Ont.), 41, 128, 147.
Sault Ste. Marie (Mich. and Ont.), 131.
Savannah. See Camp Union.
Schoharie (N. Y.), raid, 159.
Schönbrunn (O.), 45.
Schuyler, Gen. Philip, 24.
Scott, Charles, 22.
Seneca Indians, treat with English, 65, 67; at Fort Pitt, 158-157, 172, 219; villages, 161; chiefs, 160; hostile, 158, 162. See also Iroquois and Mingo.
Shade, Shawnee chief, 58, 60.
Shaganaba, Ottawa chief, 89, 90.
Sharpsburg (Pa.), 27.
Shawanese Ben, 59.

Shawnee Indians, 35, 36, 39, 41, 51, 52, 66, 111, 112, 128, 129, 174; towns, 15, 26, 36, 40, 42, 56, 57, 63, 101, 128, 176, 188, 190, 254; hostages, 11, 18, 120, 122, 129—see also Chenusaw, Cuttena, Newau; apprehensive, 15, 16, 29; message to, 70, 71; at treaty of 1775, 74, 80, 82, 85-87, 92, 94, 99, 100, 108, 114, 116, 119-123; speeches to, 41-43, 58-60, 62, 96, 101; agree to terms, 125; return prisoners, 152, 175; at treaty of 1776, 158, 171, 217, 219; pacific, 156, 188, 204; hostile, 190, 212, 254; join raids, 63, 186, 189, 242; burn prisoner, 252; consulted, 237; removal, 144. See also Cornstalk, and Nimwha.
Shelby, Capt. Evan, 179.
Shenandoah Valley, 11, 196.
Shenango. See Logstown.
Shepherd, Col. David, commissary, 221, 224, 225, 228, 245, 253; county lieutenant, 232-235, 252; commands expedition, 238, 239; letters, 242-244; letters to, 195, 196, 247, 248, 252; sketch, 196.
Shepherd, Thomas, 196.
Shepherdstown (Va.), 196.
Shingas, Delaware chief, 200.
Shippensburgh (Pa.), 61.
Shores, Thomas, 242.
Silverheels, Shawnee chief, 41.
Simms, Col. Charles, 153.
Simple (Simplicus Bocquet), Père, 147, 148.
Simpson, —, 246.
Six Nations. See Iroquois.
Skelton, Joseph, 258.
Smyth, John F. D., 188, 189.
Snake, Mingo chief, 48.
Snake, Shawnee chief, 58.
South Carolina, governor, 132;
Speed, Thomas, *Wilderness Road*, 2.
Spotswood, Alexander, 22.

INDEX

Spottsylvania County (Va.), 246.
Springer, Drusilla, 230.
Springhill, Virginia estate, 10, 12.
Springhill Township (Pa.), 229.
Stedman, —, 133.
Steel, Andrew, 226, 227.
Stephen, Col. Adam, 6, 20; letter, 65; Indian commissioner, 80, 84; at treaty of Fort Pitt, 81, 82, 90, 100, 105, 112, 127; among Shawnee, 103; sketch, 6.
Sterling, James, 148, 149.
Stilwell, Samuel, 225.
Stone, Mingo chief, 102.
Stuart, John, British Indian agent, 138.
Stuart (Stewart), Capt. John, 205, 214; militia officer, 181, 192, 206; letters, 177, 178, 181–183, 193, 194, 197–199, 239–241; letters to, 179, 180, 184, 211, 212.
Sullivan, Gen. John, 161.
Sulpician missionaries, 131.
Surrahawa, Wyandot, 52.
Swearingen, John, 229, 230.
Swearingen, Van, 201, 230.

Tabb, John, 23.
Taimenend, Morgan's Indian name, 32.
Tate, Samuel, Kentucky pioneer, 9.
Taway Indians. See Ottawa.
Tawixatwee Indians. See Miami.
Taylor, Hancock, 154.
Taylor, Maj. Henry, 233, 238, 239.
Tays, Thomas, messenger, 12.
Teagarden, Abram, 235.
Teagarden, William, 235.
Tecumseh, birthplace, 63.
Templeton, James, 210, 218.
Tennessee, settlement, 3.
Tetepuska, Delaware, 126.
Thompson, Lieut. —, 197, 204, 241.
Thompson, William, 148.
Thwaites, R. G., *Daniel Boone*, 2, 77; *Early Western Travels*, 29; *Jesuit Relations*, 148; *Withers's Chronicles*, 251.
Tinkling Spring, church, 12.
Todd, John, 154.
Todd, Levi, 154.
Tomlinson, Joseph, 224.
Touraighwaghti. See Jehu Hay.
Tracy, Alexander de Prouville, Marquis de, 172.
Transylvania Company, 1–4; legislature, 227.
Treaties: Bouquet's (1764), 27, 38, 41, 80, 118, 124. Camp Charlotte (1774), 18, 84, 49, 106, 121, 122. Conestoga (1718), 46. Fort Harmar (1789), 80, 159. Fort McIntosh (1785), 80. Fort Niagara (1775), 65, 67–70. Fort Oswego (1777), 65, 159, 160. Fort Stanwix (1768), 5, 31, 53, 61, 99, 171; (1784), 159, 160. Greenville (1795), 41, 80, 91. Jay's (1794), 132. Lancaster (1748), 124. Logstown (1754), 171. Paris (1783), 150. Pittsburgh (1775), 25–127, 152. British report, 127–130, 135; (1776), 46, 189, 191, 196, 202, 206, 216–219. Watauga (Sycamore Shoals, 1775), 1–3.
Trent, Maj. William, 171.
Tucker, William, 203.
Tuscarawas County (O.), 45.
Twigtwee Indians. See Miami.
Twitty, Capt. William, 9.

Uniontown (Pa.), 234.
Urbana (O.), founded, 240.

Van Bibber, Isaac, 177.
Van Bibber, Jacob, 177.
Van Bibber, John, 177.
Van Bibber, Matthias, 177.
Van Bibber, Peter, 177, 180, 182, 193.

INDEX

Van Buren (Pa.), 235.
Van Meter family, 196.
Vandalia (Ill.), 228.
Venango County (Pa.), 163.
Vincennes (Ind.), 128, 130, 136, 149.
Virgin, Capt. Reasin, 207.
Virginia, 2, 33, 34; boundary, 2, 18, 141; militia, 8, 9; education in, 10; religious liberty, 215; convention, 21, 66, 67, 143, 153, 155, 167, 168, 174; assembly, 3, 8, 13, 16, 18, 196, 206, 232, 234; council, 190, 230, 233, 236, 239, 240; endangered, 180; buys lands, 53; Kentucky part of, 4, 8; *Gazette*, 11; *House Journal*, 3; *Magazine*, 43; *State Records*, 212.

Waddell, Rev. James, 10, 12.
Walapachakin, Delaware chief, 88.
Walker, Felix, 9.
Walker, John, commissioner, 20, 28-31, 34; at treaty, 81, 82, 90, 100, 105; speech, 94-100; sketch, 20.
Walker, Dr. Thomas, explores Kentucky, 2, 246; home, 43; descendants, 25; Indian commissioner, 20, 23, 24, 27, 30, 34, 39, 42, 81, 82, 90, 100, 105, 112, 126, 127; speeches, 105-107, 110, 116-119, 122, 125, 135; committee of safety, 146; commissioner (1776), 191.
Wallace, Andrew, 194, 198, 204.
Walnut Hills, Virginia estate, 234.
War Post (Rotunda), Wyandot chief, 51-55.
Wars: French and Indian (1754-63), 4, 15, 20, 28, 36, 38, 56, 65, 131, 134, 136, 148, 152, 173, 188, 191, 200, 230. King George's (1744-48), 171; 1812-15, 150, 151, 159, 161. See also Pontiac's Conspiracy.

Ward, Edward, 171.
Ward, Capt. James, 240.
Ward, John, 231.
Ward, Lieut. William, 240.
Warren (Pa.), 160.
Warren County (N. J.), 144.
Warrior Ford, 180, 182, 198, 199.
Washington, George, 34; in French and Indian War, 22; visits West, 5, 26-28, 162, 207; commander of Revolutionary Army, 143-145, 215, 249, 256; appointment, 78; receives chiefs, 159, 161; letter to, 19; donation, 10.
Washington, Col. William, 17.
Washington Academy. See Augusta Academy.
Washington and Lee University, 10.
Washington (Pa.), 233.
Washington County (Pa.), 32, 207, 228, 231, 233, 235.
Washington County (Va.), 8.
Wasson (Owasso), Chippewa chief, 201.
Watauga, settlement, 179.
Wayne, Gen. Anthony, campaign (1794), 41, 44, 75, 151, 233, 235, 258.
Weiser, Conrad, 26, 28, 131.
Wells, Alexander, 218.
Wells, Richard, 218.
Wernock, James, 210, 218.
West Augusta (Va.), 18, 22, 37, 153, 200, 212, 232, 250; committee, 171; captain, 146; regiment, 215, 250; divided into counties, 223.
West Virginia, boundary, 6; *Historical Magazine*, 133, 134, 196.
Westmoreland County (Pa.), 18, 61, 74, 175, 176, 189, 200, 234.
Wewelatimiha, Shawnee, 126.
Wheeling (W. Va.), 196; garrison, 13, 22, 214, 232, 242-244; stores, 252; early settlers, 206,

232; depredations near, 210, 217, 250, 254. See also Forts Fincastle and Henry.
Whiskey Rebellion (1794), 22, 191, 221, 228, 234, 253.
White Eyes, Delaware chief, 19, 38, 61; town, 45, 46, 63; message to, 71-74, 79, 80, 137; at treaty, 82; speeches, 40, 41, 84, 85-89, 99, 100, 120, 121, 123-125; with Wilson, 202-204.
White Mingo, Seneca chief, 27-33, 39; house, 67; speeches, 40, 77; speeches to, 77, 79; sketch, 27.
Whitefish, Shawnee chief, 103.
Whiting, Mary, 239.
Wilkins, Col. John, 137.
William and Mary College, 238.
Williams, Benjamin, 159.
Williams, James, 224.
Williams, Jarret, 179.
Williams, John, 224.
Williamsburgh (Va.), 8, 11, 18, 35, 40, 41, 126, 143, 146, 155, 180, 189, 196, 209, 210, 214-216, 223, 232, 236, 238, 239, 247.
Williamsport. See Monongahela City.
Willis, George, 231.
Wilson, —, 239.
Wilson, James, Indian commissioner, 23, 24, 82, 90; speech, 77-79; sketch, 77; portrait, 90.
Wilson, William, 202, 203.
Winchester (Va.), 20, 22, 42, 43, 65, 207, 255.
Windsor (Ont.), 44.
Wingenund, Delaware chief, 46, 126; town, 202.
Winston, Alice, 7.
Winston, Dorothea D., 7.
Winston, Edmund, letter, 7.
Winston, William, 7.
Wirt, William, *Letters of a British Spy*, 12.

Wisconsin, Indians, 15, 62; fur-trade, 150; *Historical Collections*, 127, 226.
Wolf. See Cuttena.
Wood, James, commissioner, 20, 34, 81, 82, 90, 100, 105, 112, 127; visits Indians, 34-66; in danger, 49, 50; investigates charges, 28-31, 33; rewarded, 67; brings message, 27, 39; *diary*, 25, 34-66; sketch, 20.
Woodford, William, 21.
Wright, Lieut. —, 192.
Wryneck, Shawnee chief, 41.
Wyandot (Huron, Petun, Tobacco) Indians, towns, 36, 44, 50, 53, 55, 56, 66, 143, 202, 203, 218; whites among, 203; language, 130, 147; divisions, 36, 218; interpreter, 128; treat with English, 44, 47, 52, 54, 55, 155; message to, 39; firm, 70, 101, 102; at treaty of 1775, 76, 80, 82, 85-87, 92, 94, 108, 110, 113, 114, 116, 119, 126; speeches to, 50, 51, 81, 82, 97, 109; respected, 130; neutral, 203; hostile, 102, 106, 156, 199, 201, 210, 219, 254; not at treaty of 1776, 217; sketch, 36.
Wyoming (Pa.), raided, 152, 159-161.
Wythe, George, 23.

Yeates, Jasper, 191.
Yohogania County (Va.), 171, 221; erected, 223, 226; officers, 229, 233, 238; militia, 230.
York (Va.), 20.
Yorktown (Va.), 137.

Zane, Isaac, 203.
Zanesville (O.), 203.
Zeisberger, David, 45, 64, 202.

www.ingramcontent.com/pod-product-compliance
Lightning Source LLC
Chambersburg PA
CBHW021833220426
43663CB00005B/231